SPORTS IN AMERICA

RECREATION, BUSINESS, EDUCATION, AND CONTROVERSY

ISSN 1557-5535

SPORTS IN AMERICA

RECREATION, BUSINESS, EDUCATION, AND CONTROVERSY

Stephen Meyer

INFORMATION PLUS® REFERENCE SERIES
Formerly Published by Information Plus, Wylie, Texas

 GALE
A Cengage Company

Farmington Hills, Mich • San Francisco • New York • Waterville, Maine
Meriden, Conn • Mason, Ohio • Chicago

Sports in America: Recreation, Business, Education, and Controversy

Stephen Meyer

Kepos Media, Inc.: Steven Long and Janice Jorgensen, Series Editors

Project Editor: Laura Avery

Rights Acquisition and Management: Ashley Maynard, Carissa Poweleit

Composition: Evi Abou-El-Seoud, Jeff Sumner, Mary Beth Trimper

Manufacturing: Rita Wimberley

Product Design: Kristin Julien

For product information and technology assistance, contact us at
Gale Customer Support, 1-800-877-4253.
For permission to use material from this text or product,
submit all requests online at **www.cengage.com/permissions.**
Further permissions questions can be emailed to
permissionrequest@cengage.com

Cover photograph: © Steve Pepple/Shutterstock.com.

Gale
27500 Drake Rd.
Farmington Hills, MI 48331-3535

ISBN-13: 978-0-7876-5103-9 (set)
ISBN-13: 978-1-4103-2560-0

ISSN 1557-5535

This title is also available as an e-book.
ISBN-13: 978-1-4103-2592-1
Contact your Gale sales representative for ordering information.

Printed in the United States of America
1 2 3 4 5   22 21 20 19 18

TABLE OF CONTENTS

Why do people care so much about sports? This chapter defines sports and profiles the depth of Americans' passion for them. It summarizes sports participation, attendance, and viewership statistics. The chapter also briefly outlines the major team and individual sports in the United States, as well as the Olympics, and examines the relationship between these sports and the media. Finally, it touches on the connection between sports and health, the phenomenon of sports gambling, and the ways that sports and politics occasionally intersect.

CHAPTER 2

What sports do people like to play and what sports do they like to watch? Using data from a variety of sources, this chapter looks at the numbers for sports participation and attendance at sporting events, covering all the major team sports as well as newer and emerging sports, such as snowboarding. It also studies the money Americans spend on sports equipment and which sports they spend it on.

CHAPTER 3

Given that business, sports, and the media are so intimately connected, it is sometimes difficult to determine where one ends and the other begins. This chapter delves into the financial relationship between big-time sports and television, from its roots during the early days of television to the present. It also reports on viewership numbers, advertising issues, and public image concerns.

CHAPTER 4

This chapter focuses on the major professional sports in the United States: baseball, football, basketball, and hockey, as well as soccer, which is on its way to joining the list. How did these sports rise to their current status, and where are they headed? The structure of the leagues and the often combative relationship between players and team owners are analyzed. The chapter also addresses the building of new stadiums and the controversy of using public funds to finance these stadiums.

Not every sports enthusiast is interested primarily in the major team sports. Many prefer, for example, the head-to-head competition of golf, tennis, auto racing, and/or boxing, which are all covered in this chapter. The chapter also discusses the leagues or structures of these sports, how they operate, and how much money the top professionals earn.

College and high school athletics are both an element of a well-rounded education and a training ground for hard-core professional competition. These dual roles often come into conflict. College sports have become big business, and as a result high schools have not escaped the influence of money. This chapter assesses participation in school sports, the influence of money on the academic institutions that sponsor them, and other issues such as gender equity and the benefits of participation.

CHAPTER 7

The Olympic Games are an idealistic attempt to bring the world together to celebrate friendly athletic competition. Although the movement falls short of this goal in numerous ways, the Olympics remain wildly popular across the globe. This chapter reviews the history, and the business, of the Olympic Games, covering both the Summer and Winter Olympics and the associated games for people with disabilities.

CHAPTER 8

It is no secret that physical activity is an important part of a healthy lifestyle. This chapter looks at some of the specific health benefits of sports participation, both physical and mental. It also evaluates the risks that are involved in athletic pursuits, from physical ailments such as bruises, broken bones, and concussions to the emotional trauma that affects children who are thrown into overly competitive environments.

What are steroids? What are dietary supplements, and why are many of them banned in most sports? How are the governing bodies of sports fighting back? This chapter describes the variety of substances athletes use in the belief that they will make them stronger and faster. It provides the history of performance-enhancing substances, from herbal concoctions used during the ancient Olympics through the more recent BALCO and Biogenesis scandals, while investigating how banned substances have affected Major League Baseball, professional cycling, and other major sports.

CHAPTER 10

Sports gambling is a huge business in the United States, and most of it is underground. From pari-mutuel betting on horse and greyhound races, to legal sports bookmaking in Nevada, to the office Super Bowl pool, to offshore internet betting operations, this chapter surveys the scope of sports gambling in the United States. It also considers the problems sports gambling sometimes creates.

PREFACE

Sports in America: Recreation, Business, Education, and Controversy is part of the *Information Plus Reference Series*. The purpose of each volume of the series is to present the latest facts on a topic of pressing concern in modern American life. These topics include the most controversial and studied social issues of the 21st century: abortion, capital punishment, care for senior citizens, crime, the environment, health care, immigration, national security, social welfare, women, youth, and many more. Although this series is written especially for high school and undergraduate students, it is an excellent resource for anyone in need of factual information on current affairs.

By presenting the facts, it is the intention of Gale, a Cengage Company, to provide its readers with everything they need to reach an informed opinion on current issues. To that end, there is a particular emphasis in this series on the presentation of scientific studies, surveys, and statistics. These data are generally presented in the form of tables, charts, and other graphics placed within the text of each book. Every graphic is directly referred to and carefully explained in the text. The source of each graphic is presented within the graphic itself. The data used in these graphics are drawn from the most reputable and reliable sources, such as the various branches of the US government and private organizations and associations. Every effort has been made to secure the most recent information available. Readers should bear in mind that many major studies take years to conduct and that additional years often pass before the data from these studies are made available to the public. Therefore, in many cases the most recent information available in 2018 is dated from 2015 or 2016. Older statistics are sometimes presented as well, if they are landmark studies or of particular interest and no more-recent information exists.

Although statistics are a major focus of the *Information Plus Reference Series*, they are by no means its only content. Each book also presents the widely held positions and important ideas that shape how the book's subject is discussed in the United States. These positions are explained in detail and, where possible, in the words of their proponents. Some of the other material to be found in these books includes historical background, descriptions of major events related to the subject, relevant laws and court cases, and examples of how these issues play out in American life. Some books also feature primary documents or have pro and con debate sections that provide the words and opinions of prominent Americans on both sides of a controversial topic. All material is presented in an evenhanded and unbiased manner; readers will never be encouraged to accept one view of an issue over another.

HOW TO USE THIS BOOK

Sports have an enormous presence in American life. Many Americans engage in sporting activities of one type or another and enjoy watching sports in person or on television. The American passion for sports has made it a major industry worth billions of dollars. It has also brought with it a host of problems. Illegal sports gambling is commonplace. Athletes at all levels have been caught using performance-enhancing drugs. Professional athletes and their teams squabble over their shares of the profits to the dismay of fans. The lure of money has also had a corrupting influence on major college sports and encouraged student-athletes to quit school and turn professional at an increasingly young age. Meanwhile, less popular sports, including many women's sports, struggle for attention and funds.

Sports in America: Recreation, Business, Education, and Controversy consists of 10 chapters and 3 appendixes. Each chapter examines a particular aspect of sports and American society. For a summary of the information that is covered in each chapter, please see the synopses that are provided in the Table of Contents. Chapters generally begin with an overview of the basic facts and background information on the chapter's topic, then proceed to examine subtopics of particular interest. For example, Chapter 2: Sports Participation and Attendance begins with an overview of participation trends in competitive athletics, examining which team and individual sports enjoy the greatest popularity among Americans. In addition, it assesses participation rates in a range of other athletic activities, such as hiking, cycling, and fishing, as well as extreme sports such as skateboarding and snowboarding. The chapter provides information about sporting goods purchases in the United States, before proceeding with an analysis of attendance figures at major sporting events. It concludes with a summary of new security measures that have been implemented in the aftermath of the terrorist attacks at the 2013 Boston Marathon and the November 2015 bombings outside of the Stade de France in Paris. Readers can find their way through a chapter by looking for the section and subsection headings, which are clearly set off from the text. They can also refer to the book's extensive Index if they already know what they are looking for.

Statistical Information

The tables and figures featured throughout *Sports in America: Recreation, Business, Education, and Controversy* will be of particular use to readers in learning about this issue. These tables and figures represent an extensive collection of the most recent and important statistics on sports and their role in American society—for example, graphics cover the number of Americans who participate in various sports, the amounts spent by parents for their children to participate in school sports, the amounts wagered and won on sports betting in Nevada, and the values and revenues of particular sports teams. Gale, a Cengage Company, believes that making this information available to readers is the most important way to fulfill the goal of this book: to help readers understand the issues and controversies surrounding sports in the United States and to reach their own conclusions.

Each table or figure has a unique identifier appearing above it for ease of identification and reference. Titles for the tables and figures explain their purpose. At the end of each table or figure, the original source of the data is provided.

To help readers understand these often complicated statistics, all tables and figures are explained in the text. References in the text direct readers to the relevant statistics. Furthermore, the contents of all tables and figures are fully indexed. Please see the opening section of the Index at the back of this volume for a description of how to find tables and figures within it.

Appendixes

Besides the main body text and images, *Sports in America: Recreation, Business, Education, and Controversy* has three appendixes. The first is the Important Names and Addresses directory. Here, readers will find contact information for a number of government and private organizations that can provide further information on sports and related issues. The second appendix is the Resources section, which can also assist readers in conducting their own research. In this section the author and editors of *Sports in America: Recreation, Business, Education, and Controversy* describe some of the sources that were most useful during the compilation of this book. The final appendix is the detailed Index. It has been greatly expanded from previous editions and should make it even easier to find specific topics in this book.

COMMENTS AND SUGGESTIONS

The editors of the *Information Plus Reference Series* welcome your feedback on *Sports in America: Recreation, Business, Education, and Controversy*. Please direct all correspondence to:

Editors
Information Plus Reference Series
27500 Drake Rd.
Farmington Hills, MI 48331-3535

CHAPTER 1
SPORTS IN AMERICAN SOCIETY: AN OVERVIEW

WHAT ARE SPORTS?

A sport is a physical activity that people engage in for recreation, usually according to a set of rules, and often in competition with each other. Such a simple definition, however, does not capture the passion many Americans feel for their favorite sports. Sports are the recreational activity of choice for a huge portion of the US population, both as spectators and as participants in sporting competitions. When enthusiasts are not participating in sports, they are flocking to the nation's arenas and stadiums to watch their favorite athletes play, tuning in to see games and matches broadcast on television, listening to sports broadcasts on the radio, or following games and score updates on their computers, cell phones, and other electronic devices.

There are two broad categories of sports: professional and amateur. A professional athlete is paid to participate; an amateur athlete is one who participates without receiving compensation. The word *amateur* comes from the Latin word for "love," suggesting that an amateur athlete plays simply because he or she loves the game.

SPORTS PARTICIPATION

Sports participation is difficult to measure because there are many different levels of participation, from backyard games to organized leagues, but analysts continue to refine research methods. The most direct approach is through surveys. Each year the Sports & Fitness Industry Association (SFIA; formerly the Sporting Goods Manufacturers Association) conducts an extensive nationwide survey about Americans' participation in sports. The SFIA notes in *2017 Sports, Fitness, and Leisure Activities Topline Participation Report* (2017) that more Americans played basketball than any other team sport in 2016. It estimates that 22.3 million people aged six years and older played basketball at least once that year. Other popular team sports included indoor and outdoor soccer

(17 million combined participants), grass, court, and beach volleyball (16 million combined), baseball (14.8 million), fast-pitch and slow-pitch softball (10.2 million combined), and flag football (6.2 million).

Many Americans participate in individual sports as well. The SFIA identifies bowling as the most popular individual competitive sport, and it estimates the number of participants at 45.9 million in 2016. According to SFIA estimates, this number represents a decline of 14.8% since 2011, when 53.9 million Americans went bowling at least once. The SFIA indicates that 23.8 million Americans aged six years and older went golfing at least once in 2016. Tennis was also popular in 2016, with 18.1 million Americans getting out on the courts at least once.

Figure 1.1 illustrates shifts in sports participation trends between 2011 and 2016. During this period participation rates in individual sports dropped steadily, whereas a greater percentage of respondents were involved in fitness sports in 2016 compared with 2011. Participation in racquet sports, team sports, water sports, and winter sports also saw modest growth between 2011 and 2016, whereas participation in outdoor sports decreased slightly. Figure 1.2 presents a breakdown of athletic participation rates by age group and type of activity.

Another way to gauge interest in sports is by examining how much money people spend on equipment. Figure 1.3 presents trends in consumer spending on sporting goods between 2014 and 2016, by category. More than two-fifths (44.9%) of Americans aged six years and older spent money on athletic footwear in 2016, which was a slight decline from the previous two years. In 2016 high proportions of Americans aged six years and older also spent money on athletic apparel (42.8%) and outdoor recreation activities (40.1%). During these years it also became increasingly common for school districts to charge students to participate in school sports. This system is typically referred to as "pay to play." As Figure 1.4

FIGURE 1.1

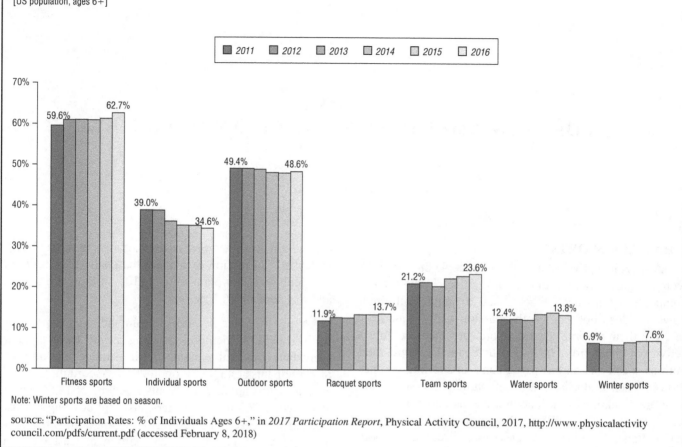

Sports participation trends, 2011–16

[US population, ages 6+]

Note: Winter sports are based on season.

SOURCE: "Participation Rates: % of Individuals Ages 6+," in *2017 Participation Report*, Physical Activity Council, 2017, http://www.physicalactivity council.com/pdfs/current.pdf (accessed February 8, 2018)

shows, more than a quarter (28.5%) of parents of middle and high school students reported paying $200 or more for their child to participate in school athletics in 2016.

SPORTS ATTENDANCE

Besides participation, another measure of interest in sports is the number of people who attend athletic events in person. Sports attendance in the United States is dominated by the four major team sports: baseball, football, basketball, and hockey. In professional team sports, attendance is affected by two main factors: the size of the market in which the team plays and the team's current success. Big-city teams and winning teams typically draw bigger crowds than small-town teams and losing teams.

According to Ballparks of Baseball, in "2000–2009 Ballpark Attendance" (2018, http://www.ballparksofbase ball.com/2000-2009-mlb-attendance/), overall attendance at Major League Baseball (MLB) games peaked in 2007, when it topped 79.4 million spectators. By 2009, following the effects of the Great Recession that began in December 2007, this figure had fallen to 73.4 million. In "2010–2017 Ballpark Attendance" (2017, http://www

.ballparksofbaseball.com/2010s-ballpark-attendance/), Ballparks of Basebal reveals that MLB attendance dipped slightly to 73.2 million in 2010. Thereafter, it began to gradually rise again to 74 million in 2013, before dipping to 72.7 million in 2017.

The National Basketball Association (NBA) experienced a similar trend during this period. After setting an overall attendance record of 21.8 million spectators during the 2006–07 season, NBA attendance fell to 21 million in 2009–10, according to ESPN (formerly known as the Entertainment and Sports Programming Network) in "NBA Attendance Report—2010" (2018, http://www.espn .com/nba/attendance/_/year/2010). Following the lockout-shortened 2011–12 season, total attendance at NBA games hovered around 21.3 million in 2012–13. In the press release "NBA Breaks Attendance Record for Third Straight Season" (April 13, 2017, http://www.nba.com/article/ 2017/04/13/nba-breaks-all-time-attendance-record-third-straight-season#/), the NBA reports that, beginning in 2014–15, the league enjoyed record-breaking attendance figures over three consecutive years, culminating in a total regular-season attendance of just under 22 million in 2016–17.

FIGURE 1.2

Sports participation by generation, 2016

[US population, ages 6+]

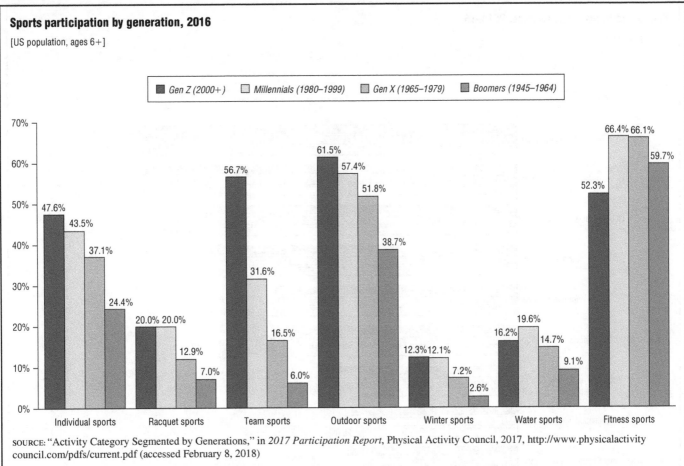

SOURCE: "Activity Category Segmented by Generations," in *2017 Participation Report*, Physical Activity Council, 2017, http://www.physicalactivity council.com/pdfs/current.pdf (accessed February 8, 2018)

According to the National Football League (NFL), in *2017 Official National Football League Record and Fact Book* (August 4, 2017, https://operations.nfl.com/media/ 2696/2017-record-and-fact-book.pdf), 17.3 million spectators attended regular-season NFL games in 2007. This figure steadily declined over the next four years, eventually falling to 16.6 million in 2011. NFL regular-season attendance proceeded to climb again during the next six seasons, except for a slight dip in 2015, and in 2016 it reached 17.1 million. In "2017 NFL Attendance Data" (2018, https://www.pro-football-reference.com/years/2017/ attendance.htm), Pro Football Reference indicates that regular-season NFL attendance rose to nearly 17.3 million in 2017.

Hockey Attendance notes in "NHL Yearly Attendance" (2018, http://www.hockeyattendance.com/league/nhl/) that total regular-season attendance at National Hockey League (NHL) games approached 21.5 million during the 2011–12 season. Attendance dropped sharply during the lockout-shortened season of 2012–13, when only 12.8 million spectators attended regular-season games, before rising to a record 22.3 million in 2013–14. ESPN shows in "NHL Attendance Report—2016–17" (2018, http://www.espn .com/nhl/attendance/_/year/2017) that by the 2016–17 season, attendance had fallen slightly, to 21.5 million.

Amateur athletic events also attract large numbers of spectators in the United States. In *2017 Football Attendance* (February 15, 2018, http://fs.ncaa.org/Docs/stats/ football_records/Attendance/2017.pdf), the National Collegiate Athletic Association (NCAA) reports that 36.6 million fans attended NCAA Division I–Football Bowl Subdivision games in 2017. Men's college basketball also enjoyed widespread popularity in 2016–17. According to the NCAA, in *2017 NCAA Men's Basketball Attendance* (August 8, 2017, http://fs.ncaa.org/Docs/stats/m_basket ball_RB/Reports/attend/2017.pdf), attendance at Division I men's basketball games reached nearly 27 million during the 2016–17 season.

Youth sports also have the capacity to draw large crowds. One of the most popular youth sporting events in the United States is the Little League World Series, an annual baseball tournament that features teams from all over the world. In "Lack of Pennsylvania Team Blamed for Decrease in Little League World Series Attendance" (PennLive.com, August 27, 2017), John Beauge reports that a record 467,964 spectators attended 32 Little League World Series tournament games in 2015. This figure fell sharply over the next two years, to 314,520 in 2016 and 292,208 in 2017.

FIGURE 1.3

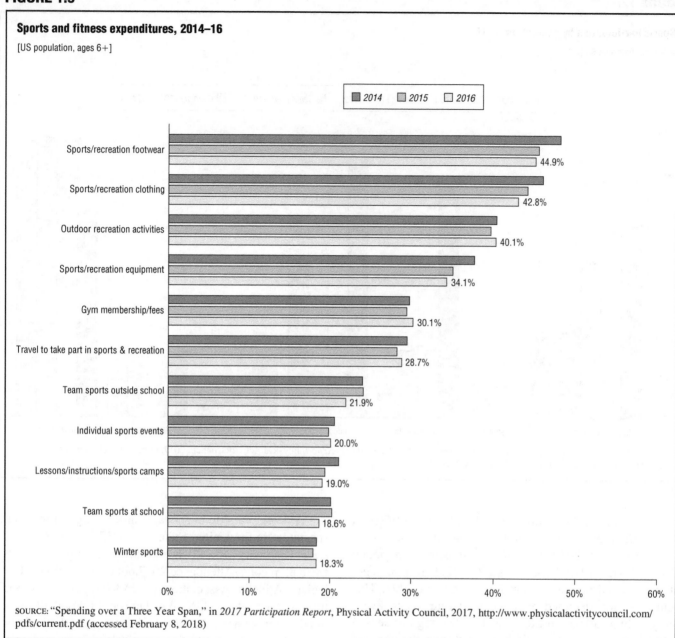

Sports and fitness expenditures, 2014–16

[US population, ages 6+]

Legend: ■ 2014 ▨ 2015 ☐ 2016

- Sports/recreation footwear — 44.9%
- Sports/recreation clothing — 42.8%
- Outdoor recreation activities — 40.1%
- Sports/recreation equipment — 34.1%
- Gym membership/fees — 30.1%
- Travel to take part in sports & recreation — 28.7%
- Team sports outside school — 21.9%
- Individual sports events — 20.0%
- Lessons/instructions/sports camps — 19.0%
- Team sports at school — 18.6%
- Winter sports — 18.3%

(X-axis: 0% 10% 20% 30% 40% 50% 60%)

SOURCE: "Spending over a Three Year Span," in *2017 Participation Report*, Physical Activity Council, 2017, http://www.physicalactivitycouncil.com/pdfs/current.pdf (accessed February 8, 2018)

PROFESSIONAL SPORTS

Professional sports is a multibillion-dollar industry in the United States. Indeed, US athletes, led by football player Andrew Luck (1989–) and basketball stars LeBron James (1984–), Kevin Durant (1988–), Stephen Curry (1988–), and James Harden (1989–), are among the highest-paid athletes in the world. As Figure 1.5 shows, five of the 10 highest-earning athletes in 2017 were from the United States.

Team Sports

The four biggest professional sports leagues in North America are MLB, the NFL, the NBA, and the NHL. Maury Brown notes in "Exclusive Infographics Show NFL, MLB, NBA and NHL Sponsorship Growth over Last Decade" (Forbes.com, August 25, 2017) that these four leagues generated $32.3 billion in revenues in 2016–17.

Baseball has long been considered "America's national pastime." MLB (2018, http://m.mlb.com/teams/) consists of 30 teams that are divided into the 15-team American League and the 15-team National League. Each league is in turn divided into three divisions (East, Central, and West). The MLB season consists of 162 games, running roughly from early April through late September, followed by playoffs and the World Series.

Since 2006 the United States has also played host to an international baseball tournament known as the World Baseball Classic (WBC). The WBC first emerged following the 2005 decision of the International Olympic

FIGURE 1.4

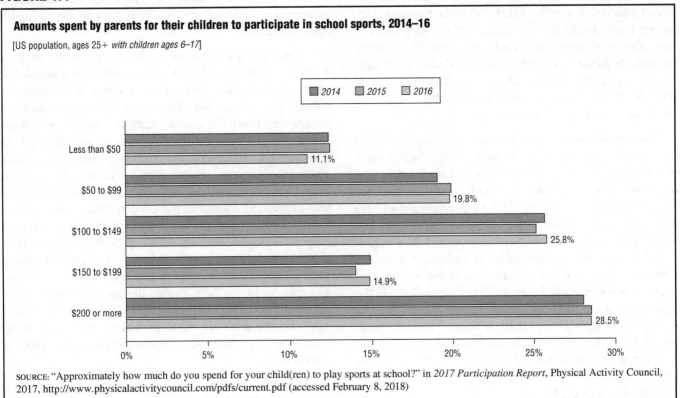

Amounts spent by parents for their children to participate in school sports, 2014–16

[US population, ages 25+ *with children ages 6–17*]

SOURCE: "Approximately how much do you spend for your child(ren) to play sports at school?" in *2017 Participation Report*, Physical Activity Council, 2017, http://www.physicalactivitycouncil.com/pdfs/current.pdf (accessed February 8, 2018)

FIGURE 1.5

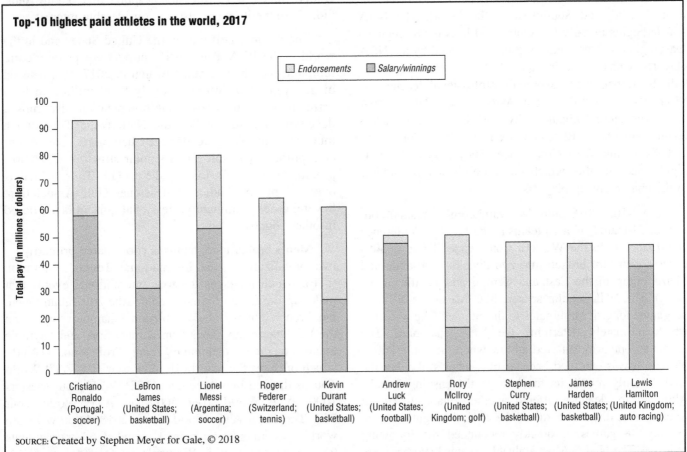

Top-10 highest paid athletes in the world, 2017

SOURCE: Created by Stephen Meyer for Gale, © 2018

Committee (IOC) to drop baseball from Olympic competition. Launched jointly by MLB and other baseball associations from around the world, the WBC was created to allow players to represent their home countries in global competition. Japan won the first two WBC championships, in 2006 and 2009, and the Dominican Republic won in 2013. In 2017, 16 teams competed for the WBC title, which was won by the United States.

The premier professional football league in the United States is the NFL, which has 32 teams (2018, https://www.nfl.com/teams) that are divided into two conferences: the American Football Conference (AFC) and the National Football Conference (NFC). The AFC and the NFC are each divided into four divisions (North, South, East, and West). NFL teams play a 16-game season, which begins around Labor Day in September. It ends with a single-elimination playoff series, culminating in the Super Bowl in late January or early February. The Super Bowl is the biggest television and broadcast sporting event in the country. In "Super Bowl XLIX Posts the Largest Audience in TV History" (CNN.com, February 2, 2015), Frank Pallotta reports that 114.4 million viewers watched Super Bowl XLIX in 2015, making it the most-watched television program in US history.

The NBA (2018, http://www.nba.com/teams) consists of 30 teams that are split into the Eastern Conference and the Western Conference, each with three divisions (Atlantic, Central, and Southeast in the East and Northwest, Pacific, and Southwest in the West). The NBA season begins in early November and lasts for 82 regular-season games. The regular season is followed by the NBA playoffs, which begin in April. Unlike football and baseball, basketball has a women's professional league, the Women's National Basketball Association (WNBA; http://www.wnba.com). Financed by the NBA, the women's league consists of 12 teams, six in the East Conference and six in the West Conference. They play a 34-game regular season, after which the top eight teams compete in the championship playoffs.

The NHL (2018, http://www.nhl.com/ice/teams) consists of 31 teams, with 16 teams in the Eastern Conference and 15 teams in the Western Conference. These conferences are in turn broken into two divisions (Atlantic and Metropolitan in the East and Central and Pacific in the West). The NHL regular season, like that of the NBA, is 82 games long. It culminates in the Stanley Cup playoffs, which ultimately determine the NHL champion. The league's popularity suffered a blow when the entire 2004–05 season was canceled because of a labor strike, but the NHL steadily rebuilt its fan base in the ensuing decade. Although the league suffered another financial setback when a labor dispute shortened the 2012–13 regular season to only 48 games, it quickly rebounded the following year. In "The NHL's Most Valuable Teams" (Forbes.com,

December 5, 2017), Mike Ozanian notes that the league generated revenues of approximately $4.4 billion during the 2016–17 season.

Although hockey remains the only league to have experienced a labor dispute that resulted in cancellation of an entire season, each of these sports is occasionally subject to conflicts that threaten their continuity and that sometimes result in cancellation of part of a season. Labor disagreements in professional sports often pit the league, which represents the interests of the team owners, against the players, who are represented by a labor union. In 2011 the NFL and the NBA saw long-standing collective bargaining agreements between owners and players expire. In the midst of the ensuing labor disputes, both leagues imposed lockouts, which prevented players from using team facilities and prohibited financial transactions such as trades and free agent signings. Although players and owners in the NFL eventually resolved their differences, the NBA's negotiations lasted well into the fall of 2011. By the time players and owners reached an agreement, the 2011–12 regular-season schedule was reduced to 66 games.

Detailed information on professional team sports is provided in Chapter 4.

Individual Sports

Team sports get most of the media attention in the United States, but professional sports that feature individual competitors are also of considerable interest.

The premier golf tour in the United States and in the world is the PGA Tour (2018, http://www.pgatour.com/tournaments/schedule.html), which in 2017–18 consisted of 52 events that offered roughly $350 million in total prize money. The PGA Tour organization also runs a developmental tour called the Nationwide Tour and a tour for senior players called the Champions Tour. Women's professional golf has a similar structure. The most prominent women's tour is the LPGA Tour, which is operated by the Ladies Professional Golf Association. Several other prominent professional golf tours are based in other countries.

Men's professional tennis is coordinated primarily by two organizations: the International Tennis Federation (ITF), which manages the four international events that make up the Grand Slam of tennis (the Australian Open, the French Open, the Wimbledon Championships, and the US Open), the Davis Cup competition, and Olympic tennis; and the Association of Tennis Professionals (ATP), which operates the worldwide ATP tour. The ATP World Tour is divided into three tiers: ATP World Tour Masters 1000, ATP World Tour 500, and ATP World Tour 250. The 2018 ATP World Tour (2018, http://www.atpworldtour.com/en/tournaments) included 64 tournaments throughout the world. Women's professional tennis is organized by the Women's Tennis Association (WTA), which runs the premier women's tour. According to the WTA (2018, http://www.wtatennis.com/calendar), the 2018 WTA tour included 63 tournaments worldwide.

Auto racing enjoyed a huge surge in popularity in the United States beginning in the mid-1990s. The most important racing circuit for stock cars (which resemble ordinary cars externally) is the National Association for Stock Car Auto Racing (NASCAR). NASCAR (2018, https://www.nascar.com) oversees three major racing series annually: the Monster Energy NASCAR Cup Series, the XFINITY Series, and the Camping World Truck Series.

The other major type of race car is the open-wheeled racer. The main open-wheeled racing circuit in the United States is the Indy Racing League (IndyCar). The 2018 IndyCar Series (2018, https://www.indycar.com) featured 17 races between March and September. A second prominent open-wheeled race series, the Champ Car Series, was merged into the Indy Racing League in 2008.

Boxing is unique among professional sports in that it has no single commission that regulates or monitors it nationwide. Professional boxing matches are sanctioned by a number of organizations, including the International Boxing Federation (http://www.ibf-usba-boxing.com), the World Boxing Association (http://www.wbaboxing.com), the World Boxing Council (http://www.wbcboxing.com), and the World Boxing Organization (http://www.wbobox ing.com). Each follows its own set of regulations, employs its own officials, and acknowledges its own champions. A fighter can be recognized as a champion by more than one organization simultaneously.

SPORTS AND THE MEDIA

For American sports enthusiasts, it is hard to separate sports from the media industry that covers professional and elite amateur events. Leagues, teams, promoters, organizations, and schools make money through lucrative media contracts that give television networks and cable outlets the rights to broadcast sporting events. For a full discussion of the intersection of sports and the media, see Chapter 3.

The History of Sports on Television

Sports programming on television began with the 1939 broadcast of a college baseball game between Columbia and Princeton Universities. Five years later the *Gillette Cavalcade of Sports*, which was televised by the National Broadcasting Company (NBC), became the first nationwide television sports show. When single-company sponsorship became too expensive during the mid-1960s, sports programming developed a new model in which different companies bought advertising spots throughout the program.

Since then, sports programming and the amount of money in televised sports has continued to grow. The Museum of Broadcast Communications notes in "Sports and Television" (2018, http://www.museum.tv/eotv/sport sandte.htm) that in 1970 the networks paid $50 million for the rights to broadcast NFL games, $18 million for MLB games, and $2 million for NBA games. By 1985 these totals had grown to $450 million, $160 million, and $45 million, respectively. During the 1980s the addition of cable television outlets extended the reach of televised sports even further. However, television ratings for the four major team sports generally declined during the 1990s as competition for the same audience arose from other viewing options.

Major Sports on Television

During the 1950s baseball was the most popular televised sport. Since then, however, it has lost a large share of its audience to other sports, particularly football. Television ratings for World Series broadcasts declined for several years, then rebounded after 2002, but sank again after peaking in 2004. The article "World Series Has Record-Low Rating" (Associated Press, October 30, 2012) indicates that the 2012 World Series between the Detroit Tigers and the San Francisco Giants garnered an average rating of only 7.6 (meaning that 7.6% of all television households were tuned in). According to the Baseball Almanac, in "World Series Television Ratings" (2018, http://www.baseball-almanac.com/ws/wstv.shtml), television viewership for the World Series rebounded in 2013, when the matchup between the Boston Red Sox and the St. Louis Cardinals drew an average rating of 8.9. The World Series drew average ratings of 8.2 and 8.6 in 2014 and 2015, respectively, before drawing an average rating of 12.9 for the 2016 matchup between the Chicago Cubs and the Cleveland Indians.

Well before the close of the 20th century, football had supplanted baseball as the reigning king of televised sports. As Table 1.1 shows, the five most-watched television programs of all time have been Super Bowl games. In "Update: Super Bowl on NBC Draws Record U.S. Television Audience" (Variety.com, February 2, 2015), Rick Kissell notes that Super Bowl XLIX between the New

TABLE 1.1

Most-watched telecasts in the United States, all time, as of February 2018

Program	Date	Network	Avg. # of viewers
Super Bowl XLIX	01-Feb-15	NBC	114.4 million
Super Bowl XLVIII	02-Feb-14	FOX	112.2 million
Super Bowl 50	07-Feb-16	CBS	111.9 million
Super Bowl XLVI	05-Feb-12	NBC	111.3 million
Super Bowl LI	05-Feb-17	FOX	111.3 million

SOURCE: Created by Stephen Meyer for Gale, © 2018

TABLE 1.2

NFL television contracts, by network or satellite provider, 2014–22

ESPN
Monday night
- 9 years, 2014–22
- $1.9 billion per year
- No Super Bowls

NBC
Sunday night
- 9 years, 2014–22
- $1 billion per year
- Super Bowls in 2015, 2018, and 2021

Fox
Sunday afternoon NFC
- 9 years, 2014–22
- $1.1 billion per year
- Super Bowls in 2014, 2017, and 2020

Thursday night
- 5 years, 2018–22
- $550 million per year
- 11 games per season

CBS
Sunday afternoon AFC, eight NFL night games
- 9 years, 2014–22
- $1.1 billion per year
- Super Bowls in 2016, 2019, and 2022

DirecTV Satellite
Sunday ticket
- 8 years, 2014–22
- $1.5 billion per year
- No Super Bowls

NFC = National Football Conference.
AFC = American Football Conference.
NFL = National Football League.

SOURCE: Created by Stephen Meyer for Gale, © 2018

England Patriots and the Seattle Seahawks, which took place on February 1, 2015, established a new record for a single telecast, attracting an average audience of more than 114.4 million viewers. This average viewership represented a 2.2 million increase over the previous record of 112.2 million, set the previous year in Super Bowl XLVIII between the Seattle Seahawks and the Denver Broncos.

The NFL signed new television deals in 2011, extending its existing contracts with the major broadcasters through 2022. (See Table 1.2.) Besides receiving $1.9 billion per year from ESPN for the rights to air Monday Night Football, the NFL also generates $5.25 billion in annual revenues from CBS, Fox, NBC, and DirecTV Satellite for various subsets of the NFL schedule.

Regular-season NBA basketball has never drawn as big a viewing audience as the NFL has—probably because there are so many more games—but viewership expands significantly during the playoffs. The NHL attracts fewer viewers than the other major sports, but it saw a steady resurgence of popularity in the years following the 2004–05 strike. Cam Tucker indicates in "2013 Stanley Cup Final Delivers Record Ratings for NBC" (NBCSports.com, June 25, 2013) that the 2013 Stanley Cup Finals between the Boston Bruins and the Chicago Blackhawks

attracted an average of 5.8 million viewers per game, making it the most-watched NHL playoff series in history. NASCAR also enjoyed a surge in its television audience during the early 21st century, including an increased female audience and broader viewership in the Pacific Northwest and other regions of the country that had not traditionally followed auto racing.

AMATEUR SPORTS

College Sports

Most college sports take place under the auspices of the NCAA. In "What Is the NCAA?" (2018, http://www.ncaa.org/about/resources/media-center/ncaa-101/what-ncaa), the NCAA describes itself as "a member-led organization dedicated to the well-being and lifelong success of college athletes." NCAA members include 1,117 colleges and universities, 100 athletic conferences, and 40 affiliated sports organizations.

The NCAA is divided into Divisions I, II, and III based on size, athletic budget, and related variables. Division I is further divided into three subdivisions: Division I–Football Bowl Subdivision (FBS, formerly Division I-A), Division I–Football Championship Subdivision (formerly Division I-AA), and the remaining Division I institutions that do not sponsor a football team (sometimes referred to informally as Division I-AAA). Within the NCAA many major sports colleges are grouped into conferences that function like the divisions and leagues in professional sports.

According to Erin Irick of the NCAA, in *NCAA Sports Sponsorship and Participation Rates Report: Student-Athlete Participation 1981–82—2016–17* (October 2017, http://www.ncaa.org/sites/default/files/2016-17 NCAA-0472_ParticRatesReport-FINAL_20171120.pdf), 491,930 student-athletes participated in championship sports at NCAA member schools during the 2016–17 school year. The average NCAA institution had 445 athletes—250 men and 195 women. Women's teams, however, outnumbered men's teams.

For most of the 20th century, men's college teams and athletes far outnumbered women's teams and athletes, and more money went into men's sports. However, the gap has been closing, largely because of the passage in 1972 of Title IX, a law mandating gender equality in federally funded education programs. Under Title IX, girls' sports are to be funded at the same rate as sports programs for boys. Since Title IX's mandatory compliance date of 1978, women's collegiate sports have experienced explosive growth.

Much to the discomfort of some in the academic world, college sports have become big business in the United States. Spending on sports programs has been rising at a faster rate than overall institutional spending across the NCAA. Although college sports generate substantial revenue, this revenue does not cover the cost of running the entire athletic program at the vast majority of schools, largely because only a few sports (mostly football and men's basketball programs) are actually profitable. Daniel L. Fulks of the NCAA notes in *Revenues & Expenses: 2004–15 NCAA Division I Intercollegiate Athletics Programs Report* (July 2016, http://www.ncaa publications.com/productdownloads/D1REVEXP2015.pdf) that Division I-FBS athletic programs had median (average) total generated revenues of $48 million and expenses of $66.3 million in 2015. "Generated revenues" are those produced by the athletic program itself through ticket sales, media contracts, merchandising, and direct fund-raising. Football and basketball accounted for a huge share of both revenues and expenses. Coaches' salaries often make up a substantial portion of these expenses. According to the *USA Today* report "NCAA Salaries" (2018, http://sports.usato day.com/ncaa/salaries/), of the 130 head coaches of Division I-FBS football teams, 78 earned annual salaries of $1 million or more in 2017.

High School Sports

The National Federation of State High School Associations (NFHS) annually conducts a detailed survey of high school sports participation. In *2016–17 High School Athletics Participation Survey* (2017, http://www.nfhs .org/ParticipationStatistics/PDF/2016-17_Participation_ Survey_Results.pdf), the NFHS indicates that nearly eight million students participated in high school sports during the 2016–17 school year. This total was a record high. Participation among boys was 4.6 million and among girls was 3.4 million. The top states by student-athlete participation during the 2016–17 school year were Texas (834,558), California (800,364), New York (367,849), Illinois (341,387), and Ohio (340,146).

For years, football has been the most popular high school sport for boys. According to the NFHS, just under 1.1 million boys played high school football during the 2016–17 school year. Outdoor track and field was the second-most popular sport for high school boys, with 600,136 participants, and basketball was third, with 550,305 participants. Among girls, outdoor track and field was the most popular sport, with 494,477 participants, followed by volleyball (444,779) and basketball (430,368).

The Olympics

The concept behind the Olympic movement is to bring the world together through sports in the spirit of common understanding and noble competition. The Olympic Games are based on an athletic festival that took place in ancient Greece from about 776 BC until AD 393. The Olympics were revived in their modern form in 1896. The Summer Olympics take place every four years. According to the IOC, in "Rio 2016" (2018, https://www.olympic.org/rio-2016), 11,238 athletes representing 207 countries competed in 306 sports events at the 2016 summer games in Rio de Janeiro, Brazil.

The Winter Olympics also take place every four years, halfway between the summer games. The winter games are smaller than the summer games. The IOC (2018, https://www.olympic.org/sochi-2014) notes that the 2014 Winter Olympics in Sochi, Russia, featured 2,780 athletes from 88 countries competing in 98 events, and presented a total of 102,000 hours of broadcast content across all television and digital platforms.

The IOC is the worldwide governing body for the Olympics. Each participating country has its own national Olympic committee (NOC), whose role is to support that nation's Olympic team and to coordinate bids by cities within the country to host the Olympics. The NOC in the United States is the US Olympic Committee, headquartered in Colorado Springs, Colorado.

Individual sports are governed worldwide by international federations, which make the rules for the events within their portfolio. Corresponding organizations on the national level are called national governing bodies (NGBs). Some of the NGBs in the United States include USA Gymnastics, USA Swimming, and USA Track and Field. These organizations choose which athletes will represent the United States in that sport in the Olympics. In the host country an organizing committee for the Olympic Games oversees the logistical preparations for the Olympics.

The Olympics generates billions of dollars through a handful of marketing programs. The biggest source of money is television broadcast revenue. Other sources include corporate sponsorships, ticket sales, and sales of licensed merchandise. Chapter 7 contains detailed information about Olympic Games revenue. It also includes descriptions of other Olympic-style meets, such as the Special Olympics, Paralympics, and Deaflympics.

SPORTS AND HEALTH

Participation in sports yields great health benefits. Many health benefits of physical activity have been well documented. Physical activity builds and maintains bones and muscles, reduces fat, lowers blood pressure, and decreases the risk of obesity and heart attacks. There is also substantial evidence that physical activity improves mental health and may help fend off depression. Several studies link sports participation with a better self-image and a healthier attitude toward one's own body.

However, there are also risks associated with sports. Children who are placed under severe pressure to succeed by parents, coaches, and other adults are at risk of psychological damage. The stress of ultracompetitive sports participation leads to high rates of burnout among young athletes. Pressure to perform also puts children and youth at elevated risk of physical injury, as demands are put on young bodies not yet developed enough to withstand the strain. In "Sports Safety Infographic" (October 28, 2013, https://www.safekids.org/infographic/sports-safety-infographic), Safe Kids Worldwide reveals that nearly 1.4 million US children and teens visited emergency rooms with sports-related injuries in 2012.

Chapter 8 explores both the health benefits and the health risks of athletic participation.

Doping

The use of prohibited substances to give an athlete an unfair advantage over other competitors is called doping. Doping has been around almost as long as sports have. Historical writings suggest that athletes were using concoctions made of herbs or psychoactive mushrooms to give themselves a competitive edge as early as the ancient Olympics.

The modern era of doping began in 1935, when injectable testosterone was first developed by scientists in Nazi Germany. Testosterone is a male hormone that occurs naturally in the body. Boosting its levels in the blood is thought to increase strength and aggressiveness.

Several decades later anabolic steroids (chemical variants of testosterone) were developed. John Benjamin Ziegler (1917–2000), the team physician for the US weightlifting squad, learned about steroids from his Soviet counterparts, and soon steroids were in wide use in the United States. By the late 1960s the IOC had compiled a list of officially banned substances, but it had no effective way to monitor steroid use. In the meantime, steroids soon spread to professional football and other sports requiring extreme strength and bulk.

One of the biggest doping scandals to date, the BALCO scandal, has been unfolding since 2003. BALCO, the Bay Area Laboratory Co-Operative, was a California-based drug distributor. The scandal erupted during the summer of 2003, when Trevor Graham (1962?–), a disgruntled track coach, provided authorities with a syringe containing a previously unknown steroid called tetrahydrogestrinone (commonly known as THG). Authorities raided BALCO facilities and uncovered not only large amounts of steroids but also documents implicating a number of high-profile athletes and trainers in football, baseball, and track and field.

Even in the post-BALCO era, baseball continued to reel from revelations of steroid use among its top players. Alex Rodriguez (1975–) of the New York Yankees, after reports of positive drug tests surfaced, admitted in 2009 to having used steroids in 2003. In 2013 Rodriguez found himself at the center of another performance-enhancing drug scandal, this one involving the Florida-based health clinic Biogenesis of America. In "A Miami Clinic Supplies Drugs to Sports' Biggest Names" (MiamiNewTimes.com, January 31, 2013), Tim Elfrink reports that Biogenesis records indicate the company provided performance-enhancing drugs to several MLB players, Rodriguez most prominent among them. An investigation by MLB corroborated the findings, and in August 2013 the league issued 50-game suspensions to a dozen major and minor league players. The league reserved its harshest punishment for two of its biggest stars: the former National League Most Valuable Player Ryan Braun (1983–), who was suspended for 65 games, and Rodriguez, who was suspended for an unprecedented 211 games. As a result, Rodriguez was forced to miss the entire 2014 baseball season.

Professional cycling has also been hit hard by steroid scandals. Floyd Landis (1975–), a 2006 Tour de France champion, tested positive for steroids, raising questions about the legitimacy of his victory. In September 2007 Landis was stripped of his 2006 Tour title. Three years later, in 2010, Landis publicly admitted that he had used a host of steroids during his career, including human growth hormone, testosterone, and erythropoietin. Bonnie D. Ford notes in "Landis Admits Doping, Accuses Lance" (ESPN.com, May 21, 2010) that Landis also accused other cyclists of using performance-enhancing drugs, notable among them Lance Armstrong (1971–). In "Lance Armstrong Team 'Ran Most Sophisticated Doping Ring in Sport'" (Guardian.com, October 10, 2012), Matt Seaton writes that in October 2012 the US Anti-Doping Agency released an exhaustive report detailing Armstrong's extensive use of erythropoietin, testosterone, and other banned substances throughout his cycling career. At the same time, the report revealed that Armstrong also coerced his teammates on the US Postal Service cycling squad to take banned substances. In the aftermath of the revelations, Armstrong was stripped of all seven of his Tour de France titles.

Steroid use has been linked to many potentially serious health problems, including liver and kidney tumors, high blood pressure, elevated cholesterol, severe acne, and in men, shrunken testicles. In 2009 the professional wrestler Edward Fatu (1973–2009) died of a heart attack at age 36. Soraya Roberts reports in "Former WWE Wrestler Edward 'Umaga' Fatu Dies of Heart Attack" (NYDailyNews.com, December 5, 2009) that Fatu had been caught purchasing a number of banned drugs from an online pharmacy, including the growth hormone somatropin, as recently as 2007. Steroid use is also associated with emotional disturbances, including violent mood swings commonly known as "'roid rage." In 2007, when the professional wrestler Chris Benoit (1967–2007) killed his wife and son before committing suicide, a toxicology report revealed that he had 10 times the normal amount of testosterone in his system. Speculation ran rampant that 'roid rage was to blame. However, the medical examiner determined that there was no indication that steroids played a role.

Chapter 9 includes more detailed information on the variety of anabolic steroids and other performance-enhancing substances that have been used over the years.

SPORTS AND GAMBLING

For millions of sports fans, the pleasure of watching a sporting event is enhanced by betting on its outcome. Although gambling on sports (not including horse and greyhound racing) is technically legal only in Nevada, Americans nevertheless find ways to engage in sports wagering in huge numbers, whether through small-scale office pools or via offshore internet gambling sites.

Legal Sports Betting

In Nevada legal sports betting is practiced through legitimate bookmaking operations, which are often affiliated with and located in a casino. Bookmakers set the margin of victory that is required to win the bet for each game. Football is the biggest betting draw among the major team sports, followed by basketball and baseball. Gambling on horse racing, dog racing, and jai alai (a handball-like sport that is popular in Florida) uses what is called the pari-mutuel system. In this type of betting, all the wagers go into a single pool, which is then split among the winners, with management taking a share off the top.

Illegal Sports Betting

Although both Nevada sports books and pari-mutuel gambling are lucrative industries, revenues from legal sports gambling represent just the tip of the sports-betting iceberg. Legal gambling in the United States is utterly dwarfed by illegal gambling. The American Gaming Association estimates in the press release "Americans to Wager More than $4.6 Billion Illegally on Super Bowl 52" (January 30, 2018, https://www.americangaming.org/newsroom/press-releasess/americans-wager-more-46-billion-illegally-super-bowl-52) that Americans placed roughly $4.6 billion in illegal wagers on the Super Bowl in 2018, compared with only $139 million wagered legally.

Chapter 10 offers a more in-depth analysis of the relationship between sports and gambling.

POLITICS AND SPORTS

At times throughout history, athletes have used their fame as a platform for expressing views on important political and social issues. In the United States these protests have often revolved around the question of race. In 1967, as the nation was escalating its involvement in the Vietnam War, heavyweight boxer Muhammad Ali (1942–2016) sparked controversy when he announced that he would not comply with an induction order from the US Armed Forces. In the editorial "Don't Remember Muhammad Ali as a Sanctified Sports Hero. He Was a Powerful, Dangerous Political Force" (LATimes.com, June 4, 2016), Dave Zirin quotes Ali's public statement on his refusal to fight:

> Why should they ask me to put on a uniform and go 10,000 miles from home and drop bombs and bullets on brown people in Vietnam while so-called Negro people in Louisville are treated like dogs and denied simple human rights? No, I'm not going 10,000 miles from home to help murder and burn another poor nation simply to continue the domination of white slave masters of the darker people the world over. This is the day when such evils must come to an end.

Ali was subsequently convicted on charges of draft evasion and prohibited from boxing until the US Supreme Court overturned the conviction in June 1971.

One of the most famous political demonstrations at an athletic competition occurred at the 1968 Summer Olympics in Mexico City. During the medal ceremony for the 200 meter running event, US sprinters Tommie Smith (1944–) and John Carlos (1945–), both African Americans, raised their fists and lowered their heads. Although their gesture was widely viewed as a symbol of the Black Power movement in the United States, Smith later explained that it was intended as a gesture of solidarity with the global fight for human rights. Smith and Carlos were subsequently expelled from the games, and upon their return home they faced media criticism and even death threats. In the ensuing decades, however, their gesture came to be viewed as an act of courage in the face of political oppression.

In the 21st century African American professional athletes have continued to use their status and fame to draw attention to racial injustice. One notable form of protest emerged in 2016, when San Francisco 49ers quarterback Colin Kaepernick (1987–) refused to stand for the national anthem prior to a game, in a gesture of protest against the systemic mistreatment of African Americans and other minorities in the United States. After consulting with former NFL player and US Army Green Beret Nate Boyer (1981–), Kaepernick altered his protest, instead taking a knee during the anthem. Kaepernick was soon joined by teammate Eric Reid (1991–), and the players continued the protest for the remainder of the 2016 season. A year later, when Kaepernick found himself unable to land a contract with an NFL team, he filed a lawsuit against the league, accusing it of colluding against him in retaliation for his protest. Meanwhile, in 2017 several players from other NFL teams began kneeling during the national anthem, sparking a fierce national debate between people who supported the gesture and people who believed that politics had no place in professional sports.

CHAPTER 2
SPORTS PARTICIPATION AND ATTENDANCE

For when the One Great Scorer comes

To write against your name,

He marks—not that you won or lost—

But how you played the game.

—American sportswriter Grantland Rice, "Alumnus Football," *Only the Brave, and Other Poems* (1941)

People have been playing games in one form or another ever since the first time a pair of humans decided to grapple for fun rather than for food. The number and variety of sports in which people have participated through the ages is impossible to calculate. In North America, Native Americans were playing lacrosse and many other organized sports before Europeans settled permanently on the continent. In addition, one need only think of gladiators doing battle at the Colosseum in ancient Rome (on the Italian Peninsula) to realize that people have been gathering to watch other people play sports for centuries. The following is a summary of sports participation and sports attendance in the United States, drawing information from government and industry publications.

SPORTS PARTICIPATION

There is no shortage of data available on sports participation in the United States. Participation is measured by market research firms, coordinating bodies of individual sports, and government agencies, among others. Sports participation is nevertheless a difficult thing to measure, and nobody has yet figured out how to measure it with complete accuracy. People who go for a casual walk or swim at the beach may not think of themselves as engaging in a sport, but those interested in selling walking shoes or studying the health benefits of physical activity might disagree. Table 2.1 presents an estimate of sports participation levels among various age groups and household incomes, while Table 2.2 provides

a breakdown of sporting goods purchases by age, sex, household income, and education level.

Sports & Fitness Industry Association Survey

Each year the Sports & Fitness Industry Association (SFIA; formerly the Sporting Goods Manufacturers Association) publishes reports on various aspects of sports participation in the United States based on extensive survey data of US children and adults aged six years and older. The SFIA's *2017 Sports, Fitness and Leisure Activities Topline Participation Report* outlines major trends in every category of sports participation and contains data from 24,134 online surveys that were conducted between late 2016 and early 2017.

TEAM SPORTS. Table 2.3 shows the total number of Americans participating in team sports between 2011 and 2016, by sport. Throughout this period basketball was consistently the most popular team sport. Approximately 22.3 million Americans aged six years and older reported that they played basketball at least once in 2016, compared with 23.4 million in 2015, a decrease of 4.6%. Football (17.3 million participants—5.5 million people who reported playing tackle football, 5.7 million who played touch football, and 6.2 million who played flag football), soccer (17 million participants—11.9 million people who played outdoor soccer and 5.1 million who played indoor soccer), volleyball (16 million participants—6.2 million people who played court volleyball, 4.3 million who played grass volleyball, and 5.5 million who played beach volleyball), and baseball (14.8 million) were the other team sports with the most participants in 2016.

INDIVIDUAL AND RACQUET SPORTS. Table 2.4 and Table 2.5 show data on participation in individual sports among US adults and children aged six years and older. As Table 2.4 shows, 45.9 million Americans bowled in 2016, making it the most popular of all competitive sports in the United States. This figure marked a 14.8%

TABLE 2.1

Participation in selected sports activities, by sex, age group, and income level, 2015

Activity	Total (number)	Sex		Age (years)								Household income (dollars)						
		Male	Female	7-17	18-24	25-34	35-44	45-54	55-64	65-74	75 and over	Under 25,000	25,000–34,999	35,000–49,999	50,000–74,999	75,000–99,999	100,000–149,999	150,000 and over
Total persons age 7 and older	290,841	142,627	148,214	45,567	31,464	43,517	40,513	43,459	40,078	34,599	11,644	68,639	29,375	38,100	49,443	33,447	38,973	32,865
Aerobic exercising[a]	45,138	15,835	29,303	4,185	5,229	9,504	7,881	6,623	5,376	5,354	985	6,514	3,258	5,105	8,193	5,930	7,568	8,568
Archery, target	8,353	5,469	2,884	2,316	1,352	1,463	1,111	1,244	546	240	80	1,381	838	1,175	1,403	1,170	1,326	1,059
Backpacking[b]	12,309	7,560	4,749	2,528	1,753	2,659	2,125	1,931	993	262	59	1,699	958	1,467	2,449	1,811	2,148	1,776
Baseball	11,786	9,491	2,295	5,730	1,141	2,051	1,489	889	393	93	—	1,495	920	1,454	2,201	1,822	2,139	1,755
Basketball	24,812	18,536	6,276	9,742	3,774	4,546	3,643	1,988	877	242	—	4,170	2,103	3,069	4,982	3,462	3,951	3,075
Bicycle riding[a]	36,008	20,430	15,578	10,528	3,083	5,137	4,553	5,691	4,112	2,568	337	5,143	2,969	3,847	7,046	5,507	6,031	5,464
Billiards/pool	21,465	13,586	7,879	2,310	3,257	4,548	4,340	3,614	2,145	1,036	216	4,006	2,278	2,261	4,104	2,854	3,078	2,884
Boating, motor/power	14,129	8,755	5,374	2,094	1,372	1,695	2,173	2,494	2,427	1,619	255	1,756	823	1,522	2,056	2,486	2,767	2,720
Bowling	35,219	18,810	16,409	7,931	4,121	6,885	6,139	5,319	3,030	1,523	271	5,508	3,122	3,904	7,434	4,844	5,816	4,591
Camping[c]	40,129	21,810	18,319	8,676	4,525	6,681	6,999	6,353	4,324	2,164	407	6,234	3,888	5,162	8,425	5,708	6,383	4,331
Cheerleading	3,739	334	3,405	2,675	473	314	152	126	—	—	—	277	216	514	865	535	811	520
Dart throwing	10,197	6,576	3,621	1,316	1,471	2,187	2,189	1,860	868	201	104	2,065	1,078	1,323	1,869	1,389	1,292	1,181
Exercise walking[a]	106,321	46,216	60,104	8,014	8,804	15,279	16,060	19,280	19,057	15,488	4,339	20,786	10,477	13,820	19,168	12,914	15,371	13,785
Exercise with equipment[a]	56,275	28,785	27,490	4,066	7,816	10,056	9,150	9,309	7,583	6,777	1,518	7,658	4,691	6,549	10,619	7,960	9,726	9,071
Fishing, fresh water	29,451	20,520	8,931	4,715	2,506	3,881	5,067	5,336	4,143	3,159	644	4,884	3,228	4,337	6,389	3,937	4,152	2,525
Fishing, salt water	9,716	7,063	2,653	1,209	709	1,661	1,572	2,026	1,440	924	176	1,369	752	1,089	1,850	1,390	1,466	1,801
Football, tackle	7,830	7,105	725	4,379	1,018	1,235	817	324	57	—	—	1,240	540	848	1,637	1,250	1,307	1,009
Golf	18,565	13,859	4,706	1,648	1,206	2,641	3,127	3,254	3,238	3,012	439	1,091	917	1,404	3,536	2,982	4,352	4,283
Gymnastics	5,769	1,298	4,471	3,508	557	862	464	222	55	75	25	712	436	525	1,164	1,073	1,126	734
Hiking	41,976	21,468	20,507	5,682	5,065	7,826	7,217	6,994	5,396	3,426	370	6,176	3,514	4,221	7,608	6,158	7,340	6,959
Hockey, ice	3,336	2,643	693	1,057	523	735	547	294	179	—	—	187	228	240	627	657	613	784
Hunting with bow & arrow	5,734	4,470	1,264	519	715	1,091	1,243	1,084	743	317	22	945	540	907	998	719	900	724
Hunting with firearms	17,656	14,701	2,955	1,639	1,843	2,700	3,130	3,601	2,991	1,441	311	3,208	1,418	2,702	3,575	2,317	2,378	2,057
In-line roller skating	4,895	2,136	2,759	2,271	755	637	682	357	141	53	—	683	443	625	983	810	834	517
Kayaking	9,225	5,039	4,186	1,251	1,080	2,066	1,454	1,461	1,239	582	93	891	390	529	1,491	1,443	1,939	2,543
Lacrosse	2,940	1,625	1,315	1,522	627	340	236	181	36	—	—	231	192	129	365	486	564	973
Mountain biking, off road	5,623	3,644	1,979	894	525	1,443	1,126	937	575	123	—	751	388	510	895	867	1,333	879
Muzzleloading	2,703	2,355	348	138	364	449	322	700	368	318	43	587	254	505	646	264	83	364
Paintball games	5,094	3,415	1,679	1,797	938	1,393	601	297	39	29	—	763	527	476	1,095	750	1,023	460
Running/jogging[a]	44,545	23,546	20,999	8,664	7,579	9,590	8,724	5,682	2,937	1,202	168	6,558	3,466	4,670	8,257	6,260	7,696	7,638
Skateboarding	5,656	3,808	1,848	2,830	1,297	750	501	230	49	—	—	1,451	359	719	944	689	925	569
Skiing, alpine	6,058	3,501	2,557	1,433	720	838	666	1,028	956	385	32	376	81	341	566	730	1,508	2,458
Skiing, cross country	2,428	1,282	1,146	414	159	489	542	340	349	119	16	185	78	152	299	396	504	814
Snowboarding	4,276	2,927	1,349	1,070	725	1,281	703	341	155	—	—	325	207	410	711	725	930	968
Soccer	14,112	9,027	5,085	7,364	1,926	2,311	1,689	583	185	36	17	2,054	1,016	1,390	2,717	2,210	2,596	2,130
Softball	9,751	4,943	4,808	3,971	1,009	1,450	1,420	1,161	646	95	—	974	746	873	2,316	1,379	1,797	1,667
Swimming[a]	46,278	23,322	22,956	12,806	4,052	6,505	6,062	6,036	5,693	4,402	722	5,454	4,031	5,239	8,699	6,607	8,528	7,721
Table tennis/ping pong	10,498	5,802	4,696	2,550	1,697	2,009	1,301	1,484	804	581	72	1,174	557	1,231	1,806	1,806	2,200	1,724
Target shooting, live ammunition	20,428	14,947	5,481	1,868	2,644	3,952	3,511	3,469	2,804	1,881	298	3,435	1,540	2,954	4,131	2,648	3,140	2,579
Target shooting, airgun	5,205	3,860	1,345	1,202	807	1,017	929	680	239	306	26	1,000	363	765	1,223	669	908	277
Tennis	12,771	6,597	6,174	2,946	1,197	2,987	1,923	2,136	977	492	114	847	834	1,096	2,302	2,307	2,749	2,637
Volleyball	10,699	4,423	6,276	4,453	1,673	1,908	1,310	947	335	53	21	1,336	785	1,067	2,310	1,595	2,116	1,491
Water skiing	3,487	1,991	1,496	943	571	728	577	341	273	54	—	243	119	371	586	830	598	740
Weightlifting[a]	34,483	23,235	11,568	3,155	5,381	7,354	5,995	5,681	3,685	2,776	776	5,174	2,589	3,795	6,312	4,593	6,042	6,298
Workout at club[a]	36,587	17,231	19,356	2,916	5,875	7,677	5,818	5,024	4,402	3,967	908	4,164	2,570	4,032	6,430	5,079	7,011	7,302
Wrestling	3,045	2,377	668	1,345	535	636	345	157	27	—	—	759	288	364	564	457	397	216
Yoga	30,696	7,253	23,443	2,522	4,790	8,393	5,536	4,150	2,992	1,937	376	5,660	2,475	3,358	5,370	4,111	5,073	4,648

TABLE 2.1

Participation in selected sports activities, by sex, age group, and income level, 2015 [CONTINUED]

—Represents zero.
[a]Participant engaged in activity at least six times in the year.
[b]Includes wilderness camping.
[c]Vacation/overnight.

SOURCE: "Table 1269. Participation in Selected Sports Activities: 2015," in *ProQuest Statistical Abstract of the United States, 2018*, ProQuest, LLC, 2018.

TABLE 2.2

Consumer sporting goods purchases, by selected demographic characteristics, 2015

[Shown as percent of dollar purchases.]

		Footwear					Equipment				
Characteristic	Total	Crosstrain/ fitness shoes	Gym shoes/ sneakers	Hiking shoes/ boots	Jogging/ running shoes	Walking shoes	Bicycles	Fitness trackers/ pedometers	Golf club sets	Hand- guns	Rod/reel combi- nation
Total	100.0	100.0	100.0	100.0	100.0	100.0	100.0	100.0	100.0	100.0	100.0
Age of user:											
Under 14 years old	17.8	3.9	11.8	2.9	5.1	4.4	11.7	0.9	3.9	0.2	3.9
14 to 17 years old	5.3	5.8	11.4	3.9	6.4	2.6	4.8	1.3	3.7	—	0.8
18 to 24 years old	9.9	11.2	11.4	6.6	11.0	5.2	8.1	8.1	0.5	5.8	4.8
25 to 34 years old	13.5	19.0	16.4	13.4	18.3	10.8	18.0	22.7	11.1	20.3	18.8
35 to 44 years old	12.7	15.2	12.1	15.5	18.0	12.0	13.8	16.3	9.7	14.7	20.4
45 to 64 years old	26.2	36.1	28.0	50.0	33.9	43.6	35.2	41.6	52.2	40.7	42.5
65 years old and over	14.5	8.8	8.9	7.7	7.3	21.4	8.4	9.1	18.9	18.3	8.8
Sex of user:											
Male	49.2	46.6	44.8	64.2	50.4	45.1	62.7	40.3	68.6	71.3	80.3
Female	50.8	53.4	55.2	35.8	49.6	54.9	37.3	59.7	31.4	28.7	19.7
Annual household income:											
Under $15,000	12.6	3.7	7.1	6.7	4.1	7.0	9.5	2.6	4.0	4.8	5.7
$15,000 to $24,999	11.0	5.4	9.0	5.8	4.4	8.5	4.3	3.5	0.4	4.3	8.6
$25,000 to $34,999	10.1	5.3	8.9	7.8	7.0	9.2	5.0	7.2	1.8	7.2	8.3
$35,000 to $49,999	13.1	10.7	12.0	11.5	10.6	12.4	10.1	10.9	3.5	13.9	15.6
$50,000 to $74,999	17.0	20.3	19.3	16.7	17.3	18.0	14.7	15.8	18.9	20.9	20.6
$75,000 to $99,999	11.5	15.8	12.1	14.8	15.7	14.0	13.9	16.0	14.8	12.3	12.9
$100,000 to $149,999	13.4	21.1	17.1	19.5	20.3	16.9	20.7	19.3	18.9	18.2	16.3
$150,000 and over	11.3	17.7	14.5	17.2	20.6	14.0	21.8	24.7	37.7	18.4	12.0
Education of household head:											
Less than high school	12.2	0.6	1.0	0.8	0.7	1.7	0.7	0.8	—	1.5	0.9
High school	29.6	10.2	14.9	10.9	9.6	15.0	8.7	8.1	5.1	13.3	19.4
Some college	28.4	26.2	32.8	31.5	26.5	29.0	26.1	24.3	10.3	28.5	32.5
College graduate	29.8	63.0	51.3	56.8	63.2	54.3	64.5	66.8	84.6	56.7	47.2

Notes: Data are based on an online survey of over 16,000 households. Because surveys prior to 2010 were conducted by mail, current data may not be fully comparable to past years.
—Represents or rounds to zero.

SOURCE: "Table 1270. Consumer Purchases of Sporting Goods by Consumer Characteristics: 2015," in *ProQuest Statistical Abstract of the United States, 2018*, ProQuest, LLC, 2018.

decline from 2011, when 53.9 million Americans bowled. Other popular individual sports in 2016 included golf (23.8 million), ice skating (10.3 million), and trail running (8.6 million).

As Table 2.5 shows, several racquet sports have seen an increase in popularity in the United States since 2011. Cardio tennis experienced the largest rise in participation, climbing from 1.3 million in 2011 to 2.1 million in 2016, an increase of 61.5%. Other racquet sports that experienced a rise in participation during this span included squash, which saw participation grow from 1.1 million in 2011 to 1.5 million in 2016, an increase of 36.4%; badminton, which rose from 7.1 million to 7.4 million, an increase of 4.2%; and tennis, which rose from 17.8 million to 18.1 million, an increase of 1.7%. By contrast, the number of Americans who played racquetball fell from 4.4 million in 2011 to 3.6 million in 2016, a decline of 18.2%, while participation in table tennis dropped from 18.6 million in 2011 to 16.6 million in 2016, a decrease of 10.8%.

Outdoor and Water Sports

Millions of Americans who refrain from competitive sports—individual or team—enjoy engaging in outdoor sports and water sports. Nearly 38.4 million US adults and children aged six years and older bicycled on roads or other paved surfaces in 2016, and another 8.6 million went mountain biking. (See Table 2.6.) Fishing is another immensely popular outdoor sport. A total of 56.8 million people went fishing in 2016, when the figures for fly, freshwater, and saltwater fishing are combined. Camping (42.4 million participants—15.9 million who camped in a recreational vehicle and 26.5 million who camped within a quarter-mile of their car or home); hiking (42.1 million participants); target shooting (30.2 million participants—16.2 million who shot targets with a handgun and 14 million who shot targets with a rifle); and hunting (27 million participants—4.4 million people who went bow hunting, 3.5 million who hunted with a handgun, 10.8 million who hunted with a rifle, and 8.3 million who hunted with a shotgun) also saw high levels of participation in 2016.

Some water sports have suffered declines in popularity since 2011, according to the *Topline Participation Report*. Table 2.7 shows that canoeing, jet skiing, rafting, snorkeling, wakeboarding, and waterskiing all experienced decreases in participation between 2011 and

TABLE 2.3

Team sports participation, 2011–16

[US population, ages 6+. All participation figures are in 000s.]

	Definition	2011	2012	2013	2014	2015	2016	Change 2015/2016	3 year AAG	5 year AAG
Baseball										
Total participation	1 + times	13,561	12,976	13,284	13,152	13,711	14,760	7.7%	3.6%	1.8%
Basketball										
Total participation	1 + times	24,790	23,708	23,669	23,067	23,410	22,343	−4.6%	−1.9%	−2.0%
Cheerleading										
Total participation	1 + times	3,049	3,244	3,235	3,456	3,608	4,029	11.7%	7.6%	5.8%
Field hockey										
Total participation	1 + times	1,147	1,237	1,474	1,557	1,565	1,512	−3.4%	0.9%	6.0%
Football (flag)										
Total participation	1 + times	6,325	5,865	5,610	5,508	5,829	6,173	5.9%	3.3%	−0.3%
Football (touch)										
Total participation	1 + times	7,684	7,295	7,140	6,586	6,487	5,686	−12.3%	−7.2%	−5.8%
Football (tackle)										
Total participation	1 + times	6,448	6,220	6,165	5,978	6,222	5,481	−11.9%	−3.6%	−3.1%
Gymnastics										
Total participation	1 + times	4,824	5,115	4,972	4,621	4,679	5,381	15.0%	3.1%	2.5%
Ice hockey										
Total participation	1 + times	2,131	2,363	2,393	2,421	2,546	2,697	5.9%	4.1%	4.9%
Lacrosse										
Total participation	1 + times	1,501	1,607	1,813	2,011	2,094	2,090	−0.2%	5.0%	7.0%
Paintball										
Total participation	1 + times	3,606	3,528	3,595	3,443	3,385	3,707	9.5%	1.2%	0.7%
Roller hockey										
Total participation	1 + times	1,237	1,367	1,298	1,736	1,907	1,929	1.2%	14.9%	10.0%
Rugby										
Total participation	1 + times	850	887	1,183	1,276	1,349	1,550	14.9%	9.5%	13.3%
Soccer (indoor)										
Total participation	1 + times	4,631	4,617	4,803	4,530	4,813	5,117	6.3%	2.3%	2.1%
Soccer (outdoor)										
Total participation	1 + times	13,667	12,944	12,726	12,592	12,646	11,932	−5.6%	−2.1%	−2.6%
Softball (fast–pitch)										
Total participation	1 + times	2,400	2,624	2,498	2,424	2,460	2,467	0.3%	−0.4%	0.7%
Softball (slow–pitch)										
Total participation	1 + times	7,809	7,411	6,868	7,077	7,114	7,690	8.1%	3.9%	−0.2%
Swimming on a team										
Total participation	1 + times	2,363	2,502	2,638	2,710	2,892	3,369	16.5%	8.6%	7.4%
Track and field										
Total participation	1 + times	4,341	4,257	4,071	4,105	4,222	4,116	−2.5%	0.4%	−1.0%
Ultimate frisbee										
Total participation	1 + times	4,868	5,131	5,077	4,530	4,409	3,673	−16.7%	−10.0%	−5.2%
Volleyball (beach/sand)										
Total participation	1 + times	4,451	4,505	4,769	4,651	4,785	5,489	14.7%	5.0%	4.4%
Volleyball (court)										
Total participation	1 + times	6,662	6,384	6,433	6,304	6,423	6,216	−3.2%	−1.1%	−1.3%
Volleyball (grass)										
Total participation	1 + times	4,211	4,088	4,098	3,911	3,888	4,295	10.5%	1.8%	0.5%
Wrestling										
Total participation	1 + times	1,971	1,922	1,829	1,891	1,978	1,922	−2.9%	1.7%	−0.4%

AAG = Average Annual Growth.

SOURCE: Adapted from "Team Sports," in *2017 Sports, Fitness, and Leisure Activities Topline Participation Report*, Sports & Fitness Industry Association, 2017, https://www.sfia.org/reports/512_2017-Sports%2C-Fitness%2C-and-Leisure-Activities-Topline-Participation-Report- (accessed February 12, 2018)

TABLE 2.4

Individual sports participation, 2011–16

[US population, ages 6+. All participation figures are in 000s.]

	Definition	2011	2012	2013	2014	2015	2016	Change 2015/2016	3 year AAG	5 year AAG
Adventure racing										
Total participation	1 + times	1,202	1,618	2,095	2,368	2,864	2,999	4.7%	12.9%	20.6%
Archery										
Total participation	1 + times	6,471	7,173	7,647	8,435	8,378	7,903	−5.7%	1.3%	4.3%
Bowling										
Total participation	1 + times	53,906	48,614	46,209	46,642	45,931	45,925	0.0%	−0.2%	−3.1%
Boxing for fitness										
Total participation	1 + times	4,631	4,831	5,251	5,113	5,419	5,175	−4.5%	−0.4%	2.4%
Boxing for competition										
Total participation	1 + times	747	959	1,134	1,278	1,355	1,210	−10.7%	2.7%	10.9%
Golf (on a golf course)										
Total participation	1 + times	25,682	25,349	24,720	24,700	24,120	23,815	−1.3%	−1.2%	−1.5%
Ice skating										
Total participation	1 + times	11,626	11,214	10,679	10,649	10,485	10,315	−1.6%	−1.1%	−2.4%
Martial arts										
Total participation	1 + times	5,037	5,075	5,314	5,364	5,507	5,745	4.3%	2.6%	2.7%
Mixed martial arts for competition										
Total participation	1 + times	713	749	977	1,235	1,290	1,133	−12.2%	6.2%	10.9%
Mixed martial arts for fitness										
Total participation	1 + times	1,697	1,977	2,255	2,455	2,612	2,446	−6.4%	3.0%	7.9%
Roller skating (2 × 2 wheels)										
Total participation	1 + times	7,851	7,274	6,599	6,914	6,646	6,500	−2.2%	−0.4%	−3.6%
Roller skating (inline wheels)										
Total participation	1 + times	7,451	6,647	6,129	6,061	6,024	5,381	−10.7%	−4.1%	−6.2%
Skateboarding										
Total participation	1 + times	6,318	6,227	6,350	6,582	6,436	6,442	0.1%	0.5%	0.4%
Trail running										
Total participation	1 + times	5,373	5,806	6,792	7,531	8,139	8,582	5.4%	8.1%	9.9%
Triathlon (non-traditional/off road)										
Total participation	1 + times	819	1,075	1,390	1,411	1,744	1,705	−2.2%	7.6%	16.7%
Triathlon (traditional/road)										
Total participation	1 + times	1,686	1,789	2,262	2,203	2,498	2,374	−5.0%	1.9%	7.7%

AAG = Average Annual Growth.

SOURCE: Adapted from "Individual Sports," in *2017 Sports, Fitness, and Leisure Activities Topline Participation Report*, Sports & Fitness Industry Association, 2017, https://www.sfia.org/reports/512_2017-Sports%2C-Fitness%2C-and-Leisure-Activities-Topline-Participation-Report- (accessed February 12, 2018)

2016. By contrast, participation in all forms of kayaking—recreational, sea and touring, and white water—rose significantly during this span. In 2011 a total of 11.1 million people in the United States kayaked; by 2016 this figure had grown to 15.7 million, an increase of 41.4%.

The *Topline Participation Report* reveals that strength and conditioning exercise programs maintained relatively steady popularity between 2011 and 2016. One activity that saw enormous growth during this span was yoga. In 2011 approximately 22.1 million Americans aged six years and older participated in yoga; by 2016 this number had grown to 26.3 million, an increase of 19%. (See Table 2.8.) Although large numbers of Americans participated in a variety of strength training activities between 2011 and 2016, overall participation still declined over this span. For example, use of weight and resistance machines fell from 39.5 million in 2011 to 35.8 million in 2016, a decrease of 9.4%. (See Table 2.9.)

As Table 2.10 shows, several aerobic activities grew in popularity between 2011 and 2016. Aerobic activities that saw increases in participation over this span included aquatic exercise, cardio kickboxing, elliptical motion trainer/cross-trainer activities, high impact/intensity training, stair climbing on a machine, group stationary cycling, and swimming for fitness. By contrast, aerobic activities that saw declines in participation between 2011 and 2016 included boot camp–style training, running and jogging, recumbent/upright stationary cycling, exercising on a treadmill, and walking for fitness.

TABLE 2.5

Racquet sports participation, 2011–16

[All participation figures are in 000s. US population, ages 6+.]

	Definition	2011	2012	2013	2014	2015	2016	Change 2015/2016	3 year AAG	5 year AAG
Badminton										
Total participation	1 + times	7,135	7,278	7,150	7,176	7,198	7,354	2.2%	0.9%	0.6%
Cardio tennis										
Total participation	1 + times	1,293	1,442	1,539	1,617	1,821	2,125	16.7%	11.5%	10.5%
Pickleball										
Total participation	1 + times				2,462	2,506	2,815	12.3%		
Racquetball										
Total participation	1 + times	4,357	4,070	3,824	3,594	3,883	3,579	−7.8%	−1.9%	−3.7%
Squash										
Total participation	1 + times	1,112	1,290	1,414	1,596	1,710	1,549	−9.5%	3.5%	7.3%
Table tennis										
Total participation	1 + times	18,561	16,823	17,079	16,385	16,565	16,568	0.0%	−1.0%	−2.2%
Tennis										
Total participation	1 + times	17,772	17,020	17,678	17,904	17,963	18,079	0.6%	0.8%	0.4%

AAG = Average Annual Growth.

SOURCE: Adapted from "Racquet Sports," in *2017 Sports, Fitness, and Leisure Activities Topline Participation Report*, Sports & Fitness Industry Association, 2017, https://www.sfia.org/reports/512_2017-Sports%2C-Fitness%2C-and-Leisure-Activities-Topline-Participation-Report- (accessed February 12, 2018)

Extreme Sports

As participation in traditional team sports such as baseball and basketball stagnates, especially among youth and young adults, a generation of sports participants is turning instead to a class of activities collectively known as "extreme" or "action" sports. This group of emerging sports is loosely identified by a degree of risk taking that is not associated with traditional sports. Among the best-known extreme sports are skateboarding, snowboarding, bungee jumping, ice climbing, free running, sand kiting, extreme skiing, mountain biking, BMX cycling, BASE jumping, wingsuit skydiving, windsurfing, and hang gliding, among others. The boldest of extreme sportspeople will engage in daredevilry such as riding a motorcycle off a ski jump. Many of these sports saw rapid growth in participation during the first decade of the 21st century and gained further recognition when sports such as BMX cycling and snowboarding were added to Olympic competitions.

SKATEBOARDING. Skateboarding is among the oldest of all the extreme sports. As Table 2.4 shows, more than 6.4 million Americans aged six years and older participated in skateboarding in 2016. Skateboarders tend to be a youthful group, but the sheer number of people participating indicates that skateboarding and other extreme sports are not just the domain of the young. The numbers suggest that as this youthful core group ages, these sports may continue to outgrow their "alternative" status and become more mainstream.

Skateboarding developed during the mid-20th century in California, where surfers attached small wooden platforms to roller skate wheels and began riding on sidewalks as a pastime when the surf was low. By the mid-1960s skateboards were being commercially manufactured, and by the 1970s improvements had been made in the design and materials so that riders gained increased speed and control over their maneuvers. During a severe drought in California in 1976, some skaters began practicing skateboard tricks in empty swimming pools, thus originating the vertical skating style that would eventually catapult the sport into international significance. Skate teams representing board companies performed and competed to promote their sponsors' products, and stars such as Tony Hawk (1968–) rose to fame during the late 1980s and early 1990s. By the early 21st century, designated skate parks had become a fixture in urban and suburban communities throughout the United States.

SNOWBOARDING. Snowsports Industries America (SIA) reports in *SIA Snow Sports Industry Insights Study* (November 30, 2017, https://www.snowsports.org/sia-research-industry-insights-study/) that snowboarding is among the most popular extreme sports in the United States, with 7.6 million participants in 2016–17. Like skateboarding, snowboarding developed in the United States during the mid-20th century. The first snowboards were crudely fashioned wood items made by high school shop students and home hobbyists, all inspired by the idea of surfing or skateboarding on snow. One such creation, the Snurfer, by Sherman Poppen (1930–) of Muskegon, Michigan, gained national distribution through a manufacturing deal with Brunswick during the mid-1960s. Snurf competitions were held, and other innovators, such as Jake Burton Carpenter (1954–), improved on the design

TABLE 2.6

Outdoor sports participation, 2011–16

[US population, ages 6+ . All participation figures are in 000s.]

	Definition	2011	2012	2013	2014	2015	2016	Change 2015/2016	3 year AAG	5 year AAG
Backpacking overnight more than 1/4 mile from vehicle/home										
Total participation	1+ times	7,722	7,933	9,069	10,101	10,100	10,151	0.5%	4.0%	5.8%
Bicycling (BMX)										
Total participation	1+ times	1,958	1,861	2,168	2,350	2,690	3,104	15.4%	12.8%	10.0%
Bicycling (mountain/non-paved surface)										
Total participation	1+ times	6,989	7,265	8,542	8,044	8,316	8,615	3.6%	0.4%	4.5%
Bicycling (road/paved surface)										
Total participation	1+ times	39,834	39,790	40,888	39,725	38,280	38,365	0.2%	−2.1%	−0.7%
Birdwatching more than 1/4 mile from home/vehicle										
Total participation	1+ times	13,067	13,535	14,152	13,179	13,093	11,589	−11.5%	−6.3%	−2.2%
Camping (recreational vehicle)										
Total participation	1+ times	16,282	15,903	14,556	14,633	14,699	15,855	7.9%	2.9%	−0.4%
Camping within 1/4 mile of vehicle/home										
Total participation	1+ times	31,961	31,454	29,269	28,660	27,742	26,467	−4.6%	−3.3%	−3.7%
Climbing (sport/indoor/boulder)										
Total participation	1+ times	4,445	4,355	4,745	4,536	4,684	4,905	4.7%	1.2%	2.1%
Climbing (traditional/ice/mountaineering)										
Total participation	1+ times	1,904	2,189	2,319	2,457	2,571	2,790	8.5%	6.4%	8.0%
Fishing (fly)										
Total participation	1+ times	5,581	5,848	5,878	5,842	6,089	6,456	6.0%	3.2%	3.0%
Fishing (freshwater/other)										
Total participation	1+ times	38,864	39,002	37,796	37,821	37,682	38,121	1.2%	0.3%	−0.4%
Fishing (saltwater)										
Total participation	1+ times	11,896	12,000	11,790	11,817	11,975	12,266	2.4%	1.3%	0.6%
Hiking (day)										
Total participation	1+ times	33,494	34,519	34,378	36,222	37,232	42,128	13.2%	7.1%	4.8%
Hunting (bow)										
Total participation	1+ times	4,271	4,354	4,079	4,411	4,564	4,427	−3.0%	2.9%	0.8%
Hunting (handgun)										
Total participation	1+ times	2,690	3,112	3,198	3,091	3,400	3,512	3.3%	3.3%	5.7%
Hunting (rifle)										
Total participation	1+ times	10,479	10,485	9,792	10,081	10,778	10,797	0.2%	3.3%	0.7%
Hunting (shotgun)										
Total participation	1+ times	8,370	8,426	7,894	8,220	8,438	8,271	−2.0%	1.6%	−0.2%
Shooting (sport clays)										
Total participation	1+ times	4,296	4,544	4,479	4,645	5,362	5,471	2.0%	7.1%	5.1%
Shooting (trap/skeet)										
Total participation	1+ times	3,453	3,591	3,784	3,837	4,368	4,600	5.3%	6.9%	6.0%
Target shooting (handgun)										
Total participation	1+ times	13,638	15,418	14,370	14,426	15,744	16,199	2.9%	4.1%	3.7%
Target shooting (rifle)										
Total participation	1+ times	13,032	13,853	13,023	13,029	13,720	14,039	2.3%	2.6%	1.6%
Wildlife viewing more than 1/4 mile from home/vehicle										
Total participation	1+ times	21,495	22,482	21,359	21,110	20,718	20,746	0.1%	−1.0%	−0.7%

AAG = Average Annual Growth.

SOURCE: Adapted from "Outdoor Sports," in *2017 Sports, Fitness, and Leisure Activities Topline Participation Report*, Sports & Fitness Industry Association, 2017, https://www.sfia.org/reports/512_2017-Sports%2C-Fitness%2C-and-Leisure-Activities-Topline-Participation-Report- (accessed February 12, 2018)

and incorporated boot bindings and laminate materials. Suicide Six in Woodstock, Vermont, became the first ski area to open itself to snowboarders in 1982, when it held the first national competition.

With many younger participants preferring snowboarding to the more expensive downhill skiing, slopes eventually welcomed snowboarders, and the sport increased in popularity. By 2018 nearly all ski areas in the United

TABLE 2.7

Water sports participation, 2011–16

[US population, ages 6+ . All participation figures are in 000s.]

	Definition	2011	2012	2013	2014	2015	2016	Change 2015/2016	3 year AAG	5 year AAG
Boardsailing/windsurfing										
Total participation	1+ times	1,384	1,372	1,324	1,562	1,766	1,737	−1.6%	9.8%	5.0%
Canoeing										
Total participation	1+ times	10,170	9,813	10,153	10,044	10,236	10,046	−1.9%	−0.3%	−0.2%
Jet Skiing										
Total participation	1+ times	7,574	6,996	6,413	6,355	6,263	5,783	−7.7%	−3.3%	−5.2%
Kayaking (recreational)										
Total participation	1+ times	7,347	8,187	8,716	8,855	9,499	10,017	5.5%	4.8%	6.4%
Kayaking (sea/touring)										
Total participation	1+ times	2,087	2,446	2,694	2,912	3,079	3,124	1.5%	5.1%	8.5%
Kayaking (white water)										
Total participation	1+ times	1,694	1,878	2,146	2,351	2,518	2,552	1.3%	6.0%	8.6%
Rafting										
Total participation	1+ times	4,141	3,756	3,836	3,781	3,883	3,428	−11.7%	−3.5%	−3.5%
Sailing										
Total participation	1+ times	3,797	3,841	3,915	3,924	4,099	4,095	−0.1%	1.5%	1.5%
Scuba diving										
Total participation	1+ times	2,866	2,781	3,174	3,145	3,274	3,111	−5.0%	−0.6%	1.9%
Snorkeling										
Total participation	1+ times	9,312	8,664	8,700	8,752	8,874	8,717	−1.8%	0.1%	−1.3%
Stand up paddling										
Total participation	1+ times	1,146	1,392	1,993	2,751	3,020	3,220	6.6%	18.2%	23.8%
Surfing										
Total participation	1+ times	2,481	2,545	2,658	2,721	2,701	2,793	3.4%	1.7%	2.4%
Wakeboarding										
Total participation	1+ times	3,517	3,368	3,316	3,125	3,226	2,912	−9.7%	−4.1%	−3.6%
Water skiing										
Total participation	1+ times	4,626	4,434	4,202	4,007	3,948	3,700	−6.3%	−4.1%	−4.4%

AAG = Average Annual Growth.

SOURCE: Adapted from "Water Sports," in *2017 Sports, Fitness, and Leisure Activities Topline Participation Report*, Sports & Fitness Industry Association, 2017, https://www.sfia.org/reports/512_2017-Sports%2C-Fitness%2C-and-Leisure-Activities-Topline-Participation-Report- (accessed February 12, 2018)

States allowed snowboarding; exceptions included Alta and Deer Valley in Utah and Mad River Glen in Vermont. Snowboarding became an Olympic sport in 1998, with giant slalom and half-pipe events during the winter games in Nagano, Japan. One of the most famous athletes in extreme board sports has been the Olympic gold medalist Shaun White (1986–). Instantly recognizable to spectators by his wild shock of flame-red hair, White is unique for having developed into a world-class performer in both skateboarding and snowboarding. Popular female snowboarders include Chloe Kim (2000–) and Jamie Anderson (1990–), who won gold medals in the snowboard halfpipe and snowboard slopestyle, respectively, for the United States at the 2018 Olympic Games in PyeongChang, South Korea.

SPORTS FANS

Enthusiasm for professional sports has witnessed a dramatic shift in the United States since the 1980s. In "Pro Football Is Still America's Favorite Sport" (January 26, 2016, https://theharrispoll.com/new-york-n-y-this-is-a-conflicting-time-for-football-fans-on-the-one-hand-with-the-big-game-50-no-less-fast-approaching-its-a-time-of-excite ment-especial/), Larry Shannon-Missal of Harris Insights and Analytics offers a breakdown of the favorite sports of adults who follow sports in select years between 1985 and 2015. Professional football increased in popularity during this 30-year span, with 24% of poll respondents naming it as their favorite sport in 1985 and 33% choosing football in 2015. During this same period professional baseball experienced a decline in popularity. In 1985, 23% of respondents named baseball as their favorite sport; in 2015 only 15% chose baseball.

Shannon-Missal also notes demographic variations of favorite sports among US adults. Professional football enjoyed its highest level of popularity among adult sports fans with annual household incomes between $75,000

TABLE 2.8

Conditioning activities participation, 2011–16

[US population, ages 6+. All participation figures are in 000s.]

	Definition	2011	2012	2013	2014	2015	2016	Change 2015/2016	3 year AAG	5 year AAG
Barre										
Total participation	1+ times			2,901	3,200	3,583	3,329	−7.1%	5.1%	
Bodyweight exercise & bodyweight accessory-assisted training*										
Total participation	1+ times				22,390	22,146	25,110	13.4%		
Pilates training										
Total participation	1+ times	8,507	8,519	8,069	8,504	8,594	8,893	3.5%	3.3%	1.0%
Rowing machine										
Total participation	1+ times	9,765	9,975	10,183	9,813	10,106	10,830	7.2%	2.2%	2.2%
Stretching/flexibility training/ warm up/cool down/mobility*										
Total participation	1+ times	34,687	35,873	36,202	35,624	35,776	33,771	−5.6%	−2.3%	−0.5%
Tai Chi										
Total participation	1+ times	2,975	3,203	3,469	3,446	3,651	3,706	1.5%	2.3%	4.6%
Yoga										
Total participation	1+ times	22,107	23,253	24,310	25,262	25,289	26,268	3.9%	2.6%	3.5%

AAG = Average Annual Growth.
*Merged or expanded definition.

SOURCE: Adapted from "Conditioning Activities," in *2017 Sports, Fitness, and Leisure Activities Topline Participation Report*, Sports & Fitness Industry Association, 2017, https://www.sfia.org/reports/512_2017-Sports%2C-Fitness%2C-and-Leisure-Activities-Topline-Participation-Report- (accessed February 12, 2018)

TABLE 2.9

Strength activities participation, 2011–16

[US population, ages 6+. All participation figures are in 000s.]

	Definition	2011	2012	2013	2014	2015	2016	Change 2015/2016	3 year AAG	5 year AAG
Free weights (barbells)										
Total participation	1+ times	27,056	26,688	25,641	25,623	25,381	26,473	4.3%	1.1%	−0.4%
Free weights (dumbbells/hand weights)*										
Total participation	1+ times			58,267	56,124	54,716	51,513	−5.9%	−4.0%	
Kettlebells										
Total participation	1+ times				10,240	10,408	10,743	3.2%		
Weight/resistance machines										
Total participation	1+ times	39,548	38,999	36,267	35,841	35,310	35,768	1.3%	−0.5%	−2.0%

AAG = Average Annual Growth.
*Merged or expanded definition.

SOURCE: Adapted from "Strength Activities," in *2017 Sports, Fitness, and Leisure Activities Topline Participation Report*, Sports & Fitness Industry Association, 2017, https://www.sfia.org/reports/512_2017-Sports%2C-Fitness%2C-and-Leisure-Activities-Topline-Participation-Report- (accessed February 12, 2018)

and $100,000. Among fans in this demographic, 48% named football as their favorite sport, the highest of any demographic category. By contrast, only 21% of adult sports fans with annual household incomes of $100,000 or more named professional football as their favorite sport.

Fantasy Sports Leagues

The rise of the internet during the 1990s and the first decade of the 21st century saw an explosion of interest in fantasy sports leagues, notably baseball and football. In fantasy sports an individual acts as the owner of an imagined team that consists of a roster of real professional athletes. A fantasy team's point total is based on the actual statistical performances of its individual players in real games or tournaments. For example, if a fantasy football team owner has a star National Football League (NFL) running back on his roster, and that running back rushes for 200 yards (183 m) and three touchdowns

TABLE 2.10

Aerobic activities participation, 2011–16

[US population, Ages 6+. All participation figures are in 000s.]

	Definition	2011	2012	2013	2014	2015	2016	Change 2015/2016	3 year AAG	5 year AAG
Aquatic exercise										
Total participation	1+ times	9,042	9,177	8,483	9,122	9,226	10,575	14.6%	7.8%	3.4%
Boot camp–style training										
Total participation	1+ times	7,706	7,496	6,911	6,774	6,722	6,583	−2.1%	−1.6%	−3.1%
Cardio kickboxing										
Total participation	1+ times	6,488	6,725	6,311	6,747	6,708	6,899	2.8%	3.1%	1.3%
Cross-training style workouts										
Total participation	1+ times				11,265	11,710	12,914	10.3%		
Dance, step, and other choreographed exercise to music										
Total participation	1+ times				21,455	21,487	21,839	1.6%		
Elliptical motion trainer/ cross-trainer*										
Total participation	1+ times	29,734	28,560	30,410	31,826	32,321	32,218	−0.3%	2.0%	1.7%
High impact/intensity & training*										
Total participation	1+ times	15,755	16,178	17,323	19,746	20,464	21,390	4.5%	7.4%	6.4%
Running/jogging										
Total participation	1+ times	50,061	51,450	54,188	51,127	48,496	47,384	−2.3%	−4.4%	−1.0%
Stair climbing machine										
Total participation	1+ times	13,409	12,979	12,642	13,216	13,234	15,079	13.9%	6.2%	2.6%
Stationary cycling (group)										
Total participation	1+ times	8,738	8,477	8,309	8,449	8,677	8,937	3.0%	2.5%	0.5%
Stationary cycling (recumbent/upright)										
Total participation	1+ times	36,341	35,987	35,247	35,693	35,553	36,118	1.6%	0.8%	−0.1%
Swimming for fitness										
Total participation	1+ times	21,517	23,216	26,354	25,304	26,319	26,601	1.1%	0.4%	4.5%
Treadmill										
Total participation	1+ times	53,260	50,839	48,166	50,241	50,398	51,872	2.9%	2.5%	−0.5%
Walking for fitness										
Total participation	1+ times	112,715	114,029	117,351	112,583	109,829	107,895	−1.8%	−2.8%	−0.8%

AAG = Average Annual Growth.
*Merged or expanded definition.

SOURCE: Adapted from "Aerobic Activities," in *2017 Sports, Fitness, and Leisure Activities Topline Participation Report*, Sports & Fitness Industry Association, 2017, https://www.sfia.org/reports/512_2017-Sports%2C-Fitness%2C-and-Leisure-Activities-Topline-Participation-Report- (accessed February 12, 2018)

---

during a real NFL game, then the fantasy owner receives credit for those statistics, typically in a head-to-head matchup against another fantasy team owner. Throughout the season, fantasy owners can conduct various transactions, including trades with other owners. The Fantasy Sports Trade Association (FSTA) indicates in the press release "Fantasy Sports Now a $7 Billion Industry" (June 20, 2017, https://fsta.org/press-release-fantasy-sports-now-a-7-billion-industry/) that by 2017 the number of people participating in fantasy sports leagues in the United States and Canada had grown to 59.3 million.

SPORTS ATTENDANCE

Attendance trends vary considerably from one sport to another, and in general one sport's loss, whether because of scandal or declining interest, translates into another sport's gain. Professional sports teams rely on revenue from ticket sales to cover much of the cost of the huge salaries they pay their players. At the college level, ticket sales are a big part of what keeps university athletic programs solvent (able to pay all legal debts).

Major Sports

BASEBALL. ProQuest, LLC, indicates in *ProQuest Statistical Abstract of the United States, 2018* (2018) that nearly 73.2 million spectators attended Major League Baseball (MLB) games during the 2016 regular season. This total represented a significant increase over attendance figures in 1995, when 50.5 million fans attended regular-season games. Interestingly, the National League has seen its attendance totals climb more dramatically than the American League during this span. In 1995 attendance at American League regular-season games was 25.4 million, slightly higher than the National League total of 25.1 million. By 2016 National League regular-season attendance totals reached 38.1 million, compared with slightly more than 35 million for the American League. One likely reason for this shift involved the number of teams in each league during these years. In 1998 the Milwaukee Brewers moved from the American League to the National League. For the next decade and a half, the National League consisted of 16 teams, while the American League had only 14, an imbalance that had an impact on overall attendance numbers for each league. Balance between the two leagues was restored in 2013, however, when the Houston Astros moved from the National League Central Division to the American League West Division.

According to ESPN (formerly known as the Entertainment and Sports Programming Network), in "MLB Attendance Report—2017" (2018, http://www.espn.com/mlb/attendance/_/year/2017), seven different teams had attendance figures that exceeded 3 million for home games in 2017. The Los Angeles Dodgers led all MLB organizations with an attendance total of 3.8 million; the Dodgers also led in attendance average, with 46,492 spectators per home game. The other leaders in terms of total attendance were the St. Louis Cardinals (3.5 million), the San Francisco Giants (3.3 million), the New York Yankees (3.1 million), the Toronto Blue Jays (3.2 million), the Chicago Cubs (3.2 million), and the Los Angeles Angels (3 million). The Tampa Bay Rays posted the lowest home attendance figures, attracting only 1.3 million fans in 2017, with an average of 15,670 people per game.

BASKETBALL. Professional basketball has been enjoying strong ticket sales since the turn of the 21st century. In "NBA Attendance Report—2017" (2018, http://www.espn.com/nba/attendance/_/year/2017), ESPN indicates that the league's overall attendance was just under 22 million in 2016–17. The Chicago Bulls led the league in home attendance that season, with an average of 21,680 spectators per game, followed by the Cleveland Cavaliers, with average attendance of 20,562 per home game. By contrast, the team with the lowest average attendance was the Denver Nuggets, with 14,770.

FOOTBALL. Professional football has enjoyed strong attendance figures in the early 21st century. According to Pro-Football-Reference.com, in "2017 NFL Attendance Data" (2018, https://www.pro-football-reference.com/years/2017/attendance.htm), regular-season NFL attendance reached nearly 17.3 million in 2017. ESPN indicates in "NFL Attendance—2017" (2018, http://www.espn.com/nfl/attendance) that the Dallas Cowboys led the league in attendance in 2017. The Cowboys attracted 741,775 fans

to its state-of-the-art stadium that year, with an average of 92,721 fans per game. New York City is a big enough market not only to have two NFL teams—the Jets and the Giants—but also to have these two teams place third (Jets) and fourth (Giants) in attendance. (Both the Jets and the Giants play their home games at MetLife Stadium in East Rutherford, New Jersey, just across the Hudson River from New York City.) The NFL franchise with the lowest home attendance total was the Los Angeles Chargers, which drew 202,687 spectators during the 2017 regular season, with an average of 25,335 per game.

HOCKEY. In "NHL Attendance Report—2016–17" (2018, http://www.espn.com/nhl/attendance/_/year/2017), ESPN reveals that attendance at regular-season NHL games was 21.5 million in 2016–17. The top draw was the Chicago Blackhawks, with 891,827 spectators over the course of the season and an average of 21,751 per home game. Only two other teams—the Montreal Canadiens and the Detroit Red Wings—drew an average of more than 20,000 fans per game that season. The team with the lowest attendance in 2016–17 was the Carolina Hurricanes, with an average of only 11,776 spectators per home game.

SOCCER. As soccer emerges as a major sport in the United States, its popularity among fans is steadily growing. According to ESPN, in "Statistics" (2018, http://www.espnfc.us/mls/19/statistics/performance?season=2017), average attendance at Major League Soccer (MLS) games was 22,112 during the 2017 season, an increase of 1.9% over the previous season's average of 21,692 spectators per game. Soccer Stadium Digest notes in "2017 MLS Attendance" (2018, https://soccerstadiumdigest.com/2017-mls-attendance/) that Atlanta United FC attracted an average of 48,200 fans to its home games in 2017, while the Seattle Sounders attracted an average of 43,666 fans to its home games. Atlanta and Seattle were by far the biggest-drawing MLS teams in 2017. By comparison, the team with the third-highest attendance, Toronto FC, drew an average of 27,647 spectators to its home games in 2017.

AUTO RACING. Auto racing enjoyed a surge in popularity during the first years of the 21st century. The most prominent auto racing event in the United States is the Indianapolis 500 (Indy 500), a 200-lap, 500-mile (805-km) race that is held on Memorial Day weekend each year at the Indianapolis Motor Speedway. Although the Indy 500 does not release official attendance figures, the seating capacity at the Indianapolis Motor Speedway is listed at 257,325, making it the largest sports venue in the world, according to World Stadiums in "100 000+ Stadiums" (2018, http://www.worldstadiums.com/stadium_menu/stadium_list/100000.shtml). In "5 Reasons to Watch the 2015 Indianapolis 500" (Forbes.com, May 24, 2015), Maury Brown notes that the speedway also provides additional space for an estimated 150,000 spectators in the infield. The total annual attendance at the Indy 500 is estimated to be roughly 400,000.

However, the Indy Racing League (IndyCar) is only one segment of the broader auto racing scene. There is also the National Association for Stock Car Auto Racing (NASCAR), which has become such a phenomenon that its male followers (also known as "NASCAR dads") are now viewed by political analysts as a powerful voting bloc alongside so-called soccer moms. In 2016 roughly 359,000 racing fans attended NASCAR events regularly, while another 1.7 million racing fans attended them occasionally. (See Table 2.11.)

BOSTON MARATHON. It can be assumed that what draws these hundreds of thousands of spectators to auto races such as the Indy 500 each year is the speed—the experience of watching people hurtle around a track at well over 200 miles per hour (322 km/h). However, people also jam the streets of Boston, Massachusetts, each year to watch a race in which the fastest entrant averages a mere 12 miles per hour (19 km/h). That race is the Boston Marathon, the most famous 26.2-mile (42.2-km) footrace in the world. John S. Kiernan reports in "Boston Marathon Facts: Records, Money & More" (WalletHub.com, April 12, 2017) that approximately 500,000 spectators turn out to witness the historic race each year. Few other sporting events in the world are witnessed live by as many people as is the Boston Marathon.

Indeed, the sheer magnitude of these crowds poses a formidable security challenge in the age of global terrorism, as the deadly marathon explosions of April 15, 2013, starkly revealed. On that day Tamerlan Tsarnaev (1986–2013) and Dzhokhar Tsarnaev (1993–), brothers of Chechen descent, detonated two homemade bombs near the marathon's finish line, killing three people and wounding more than 260 others. James Alan Fox explains in "Marathon Bombings Could Impact Outdoor Events" (USAToday.com, April 15, 2013) that the bombings exposed the inherent dangers involved with attending high-profile sporting events, while calling into question the extent to which law enforcement officials can keep spectators safe at large outdoor gatherings. In "Boston Marathon Heightens Security Measures after Bombing Attack" (Reuters.com, February 27, 2014), Eric M. Johnson reports that Boston Marathon organizers introduced a range of heightened security measures for the 2014 race, including a new rule prohibiting runners from bringing backpacks onto the course.

Despite these efforts, extremists continued to pose a threat at global sporting events. During the coordinated attacks that occurred at various locations in Paris on November 13, 2015, terrorists detonated three bombs outside the Stade de France, where France and Germany's soccer teams were engaging in a friendly match. The bombs killed three people and injured numerous others. Yair Galily et al. note in "Terrorism and Sport: A Global

TABLE 2.11

Adult attendance at sporting events, by frequency, 2016

Event	Attend regularly		Attend on occasion	
	Number (1,000)	Percent	Number (1,000)	Percent
Alpine skiing and ski jumping	168	0.07	808	0.33
Auto racing—NASCAR	359	0.15	1,741	0.71
Auto racing—other	401	0.16	1,459	0.60
Baseball:				
College	494	0.20	1,459	0.60
Pro (MLB) regular season	1,975	0.81	13,292	5.44
Pro (MLB) playoffs/ World Series	400	0.16	1,685	0.69
Basketball:				
College	947	0.39	3,598	1.47
NCAA tournament	270	0.11	684	0.28
Pro (NBA) regular season	477	0.20	3,602	1.47
Pro (NBA) playoffs	266	0.11	961	0.39
Pro (WNBA)	162	0.07	384	0.16
Bicycle racing	194	0.08	560	0.23
Bowling	346	0.14	1,071	0.44
Boxing	247	0.10	693	0.28
Bull riding (Pro)	91	0.04	551	0.23
Equestrian events	200	0.08	710	0.29
Extreme sports—Summer	190	0.08	439	0.18
Extreme sports—Winter	111	0.05	460	0.19
Figure skating	120	0.05	418	0.17
Fishing	471	0.19	1,120	0.46
Football:				
College	2,997	1.23	8,192	3.35
Pro (NFL) Monday or Thursday night games	583	0.2	2,557	1.1
NFL weekend games	1,015	0.42	5,059	2.07
NFL playoffs/Super Bowl	247	0.10	1,020	0.42
Golf:				
PGA	147	0.06	943	0.39
LPGA	98	0.04	445	0.18
Other golf	108	0.04	538	0.22
Greyhound racing	76	0.03	246	0.10
Gymnastics	269	0.11	625	0.26
High school sports	4,046	1.65	7,902	3.23
Horse racing (track or OTB)	352	0.14	1,487	0.61
Ice hockey:				
NHL regular season	891	0.36	4,231	1.73
NHL playoffs and Stanley Cup finals	253	0.10	984	0.40
Lacrosse (MLL)	195	0.08	320	0.13
Marathon, triathlon & other endurance events	219	0.09	827	0.34
Mixed martial arts (MMA)	138	0.06	434	0.18
Motorcycle racing	209	0.09	690	0.28
Olympics—Summer	52	0.02	218	0.09
Olympics—Winter	27	0.01	217	0.09
Poker	114	0.05	424	0.17
Rodeo	274	0.11	1,533	0.63
Soccer:				
MLS	340	0.14	1,741	0.71
World Cup	146	0.06	673	0.28
Tennis:				
Men's	206	0.08	527	0.22
Women's	126	0.05	615	0.25
Track & field	401	0.16	793	0.32
Truck and tractor pull/mud racing	58	0.02	473	0.19
Volleyball (Pro beach)	69	0.03	255	0.10
Weightlifting	130	0.05	272	0.11
Wrestling:				
WWE	180	0.07	851	0.35
Other Pro	109	0.04	362	0.15

Perspective" (*American Behavioral Scientist*, vol. 60, no. 9, 2016) that in the days following the Paris attack, officials canceled soccer games in Hannover, Germany, and Brussels, Belgium, because of security concerns.

TABLE 2.11

Adult attendance at sporting events, by frequency, 2016 [CONTINUED]

Notes: In thousands (168 represents 168,000), except percent. For fall 2016. Percent is based on total projected population of 244,525,000. Data not comparable to previous years.

Pro = professional.
NASCAR = National Association for Stock Car Auto Racing.
MLB = Major League Baseball.
NCAA = National Collegiate Athletic Association.
NBA = National Basketball Association.
WNBA = Women's National Basketball Association.
NFL = National Football League.
PGA = Professional Golfers' Association.
LPGA = Ladies Professional Golf Association.
OTB = Off-Track Betting.
NHL = National Hockey League.
MLL = Major League Lacrosse.
WWE = World Wrestling Entertainment.

SOURCE: "Table 1266. Adult Attendance at Sports Events by Frequency: 2016," in *ProQuest Statistical Abstract of the United States, 2018*, ProQuest, LLC, 2018.

CHAPTER 3
SPORTS AND THE MEDIA

Sports and the media are so thoroughly intertwined in the United States that it is difficult to think of them as two distinct industries. The financial relationship is complex and reciprocal. Media enterprises, mostly broadcast and cable television stations but also web based, pay the sports leagues millions of dollars for the rights to broadcast their games. Leagues distribute this money to their member teams—the distribution formula varies from sport to sport—which then transfer most of this money to their players in the form of salaries. The media outlets try to recoup their huge expenditures by selling advertising time during sports broadcasts to companies that believe their products will appeal to the kinds of people who like to watch sports on television. These consumer product companies also pay large sums to individual athletes to endorse their products, or in some cases to teams to display their company logo on their uniforms or cars. Consumers then purchase these products, providing the money the companies use to buy advertising and pay for celebrity endorsements. The more people who watch a sport, the more the station can charge for advertising. The more the station can charge for advertising, the more it can offer the league for broadcast rights. The more the league gets for broadcast rights, the more the teams can pay their players.

THE HISTORY OF SPORTS ON TELEVISION

In "Sports and Television" (2018, http://www.muse um.tv/eotv/sportsandte.htm), the Museum of Broadcast Communications quotes Harry Coyle, a pioneering television sports director, who explained that "television got off the ground because of sports. Today, maybe, sports need television to survive, but it was just the opposite when it first started. When we (NBC) put on the World Series in 1947, heavyweight fights, the Army-Navy football game, the sales of television sets just spurted."

Although it may be an exaggeration to credit the explosive growth of television in its early days solely to sports, sports certainly played a significant role. The first-ever televised sporting event was a baseball game between Columbia and Princeton Universities in 1939. It was covered by one camera that was positioned along the third-base line. The first network-wide sports broadcast came five years later with the premier of the National Broadcasting Company's (NBC) *Gillette Cavalcade of Sports*, the first installment of which featured a featherweight championship boxing match between Willie Pep (1922–2006) and Chalky Wright (1912–1957). Sports quickly became a staple of prime-time network fare, accounting for up to one-third of prime-time programming, but other genres began to catch up during the 1950s, perhaps spurred on by an increase in female viewers. The *Gillette Cavalcade of Sports* remained on the air for 20 years, before giving way to a new model in which sports programs were sponsored by multiple buyers of advertising spots rather than by a single corporation, as the cost of sponsorship became prohibitively expensive during the mid-1960s.

The amount of money involved in televising sports was growing fast by the 1970s. According to the Museum of Broadcast Communications, in 1970 the networks paid $50 million for the rights to broadcast National Football League (NFL) games, $18 million for Major League Baseball (MLB) games, and $2 million for National Basketball Association (NBA) games. By 1985 these numbers reached $450 million for football, $160 million for baseball, and $45 million for basketball. This explosive growth was fueled by a combination of increasing public interest, better—and therefore more expensive—coverage of events by the networks, and an effort on the part of the networks to lock in their position of dominance in sports programming in the face of challenges from emerging cable television networks. These skyrocketing fees did not cause much of a problem during the 1970s, because the networks were able to pass the high cost of producing sports programs along to their advertisers. Nevertheless, things began to change during the early 1980s. The Museum of Broadcast Communications notes that between 1980 and 1984 professional football lost 7% of its viewing audience and baseball lost 26% of its viewers. Meanwhile, advertisers became hesitant to pay increasing prices for commercials that would be seen by fewer people. The networks responded by airing more hours of sports. By 1985 the three major networks (NBC, the American Broadcasting Company [ABC], and the Columbia Broadcasting System [CBS]) broadcast a total of 1,500 hours of sports, about twice as many hours as in 1960. By the mid-1980s, however, the market for sports programming appeared saturated, and the presence of more shows made it harder for the networks to sell ads at top prices.

The first half of the 1980s marked the rise of sports coverage on cable. The all-sports station Entertainment and Sports Programming Network (ESPN), first launched in 1979, was reaching 4 million households by the mid-1980s. National stations such as WTBS (Atlanta) and WGN (Chicago), as well as the premium channel Home Box Office (HBO), were also airing a substantial number of sporting events. By 1986, 37 million households were subscribing to ESPN.

Between the early 1990s and the first decade of the 21st century broadcast television ratings for the four major professional sports generally trended downward. There is no real consensus as to why this happened. In "Pro Leagues' Ratings Drop; Nobody Is Quite Sure Why" (Scott R. Rosner and Kenneth L. Shropshire, eds., *The Business of Sports*, 2004), Jere Longman points to "a growing dislocation between fans and traditional sports, as players, coaches and teams move frequently, as athletes misbehave publicly, as salaries skyrocket, and as ticket prices become prohibitively expensive," as possible contributing factors in the decline of ratings during that period.

SPORTS AND SOCIAL MEDIA

As sports television ratings declined, however, other media forms were attracting the interest of sports fans. The early 21st century saw an explosion of new platforms that enabled people to follow sports over the internet, from league and team websites to social networking sites such as Facebook and Twitter. The introduction of video streaming technology enabled fans to view a wide range of live sporting events from anywhere in the country. Professional sports leagues created online streaming services that enabled subscribers to view nearly all of a league's games for a monthly or annual fee. The only exception involved games that featured local teams. Typically, these broadcasting rights remained under the control of regional networks.

At the same time, digital technology changed the way that people engaged with sports. The Nielsen Company notes in *Year in Sports Media Report: 2014* (February 6, 2015, http://www.nielsen.com/content/dam/corporate/us/en/reports-downloads/2015-reports/2014-ye-sports-media-report-february-2015.pdf) that between 2012 and 2014 the number of Americans who used smartphones to follow sports grew from 50.9 million to 72.3 million, an increase of 42%. According to Sarah Groarke, in "The Power of Live Content: World Cup 2014 Social Media Winners and Losers" (NextWeb.com, July 16, 2014), nearly three-quarters (72.4%) of the global television audience for the 2014 Men's World Cup soccer tournament in Brazil were simultaneously sharing posts about the games on social media sites. During the semifinal match between Germany and Brazil, fans posted 35.6 million "tweets" on Twitter; this was a record for a single World Cup game.

The 2015 Women's World Cup in Canada also generated a considerable rise in social media activity. The Fédération Internationale de Football Association (FIFA) notes in "Key Figures from the FIFA Women's World Cup Canada 2015" (July 7, 2015, http://www.fifa.com/womensworldcup/news/y=2015/m=7/news=key-figures-from-the-fifa-women-s-world-cup-canada-2015tm-2661648.html) that the number of visitors to the FIFA Women's World Cup Facebook page rose to 662,000 over the course of the tournament, an increase of 130%. Meanwhile, the official FIFA YouTube site set a new record for hits in the month of June during the Women's World Cup, with 28 million views; by comparison, 19 million viewers visited the FIFA YouTube site in June 2014 during the Men's World Cup. In "Carli Lloyd Adds 50K Twitter Followers during Final" (ESPN.com, July 7, 2015), Darren Rovell indicates that the US midfielder Carli Lloyd (1982–), whose three goals in the final against Japan helped deliver the United States its first World Cup title since 1999, saw her number of Twitter followers increase by 50,000 over the course of the match.

Social media also provides an enormous marketing advantage to sports advertisers. Groarke notes that the athletic footwear and equipment giant adidas used the 2014 Men's World Cup to launch a new advertising campaign specifically designed to capitalize on the growing popularity of Twitter and other networking platforms. Featuring video spots of international soccer stars, the campaign inspired 1.6 million individual tweets mentioning the adidas brand, more than any other company during the 2014 World Cup. In addition, the adidas hashtag slogan #allin appeared in 570,000 tweets, making it the most popular brand hashtag of the tournament.

Social media also enhances the sports viewing experience by providing sports fans with a platform for expressing their allegiance to certain teams or sports stars. In "The 25 Most Popular Athletes of 2017" (BusinessInsider.com,

December 23, 2017), Sam Belden indicates that the Portuguese soccer star Cristiano Ronaldo (1985–) was by far the most popular athlete on social media, with 122.6 million Facebook likes, 117 million Instagram followers, and 66.7 million Twitter followers as of December 2017. Among US athletes, the NBA star LeBron James (1984–) was the most popular, with 23.2 million Facebook likes, 34.3 million Instagram followers, and 40 million Twitter followers as of December 2017.

The key challenge for all the major sports leagues—beyond the obvious challenge of attracting as many viewers and listeners as possible—is to balance exposure and distribution of their product against consumer demand. In other words, in an era witnessing the emergence of new media such as the internet, satellite radio, and live feeds to mobile devices, at what point does the coverage of a sport available for consumption outstrip the public's interest in that sport, thereby becoming a losing financial proposition?

BASEBALL AND TELEVISION: THE CONVERGENCE OF TWO NATIONAL PASTIMES

The first televised professional baseball game, between the Brooklyn Dodgers and the Cincinnati Reds, took place in August 1939. The broadcast used two cameras: one positioned high above the home plate and a second one along the third-base line. Such a broadcast would appear primitive by 21st-century standards. To cover the World Series in 2017, Fox Sports used 41 cameras—30 of which were high definition and one aerial—to capture each play from multiple angles. In addition, early broadcasts offered none of the additional features that contemporary viewers take for granted, including color, instant replays, and statistics superimposed on the screen.

NBC was the network that first brought televised baseball to the American public. Because NBC used home-team announcers to call the World Series, and because the New York Yankees were in the World Series nearly every year, the Yankees announcer Mel Allen (1913–1996) became the first coast-to-coast voice of baseball. The Hall of Fame pitcher Dizzy Dean (1910–1974) became the first nationwide television baseball announcer when NBC premiered the *Game of the Week* in 1953, thus initiating the long line of former ball players who have transformed themselves into commentators when their playing careers have ended.

By the 1960s baseball had lost a large share of its audience to other sports, particularly football. Baseball nevertheless remains a solid ratings draw, especially when teams with well-known stars located in large markets square off during the postseason. The overall ratings, however, for World Series broadcasts have been declining for years. The article "World Series Has Record-Low Rating" (Associated Press, October 30, 2012) notes that ratings for the 2012 World Series, in which the San Francisco Giants triumphed over the Detroit Tigers in four games, attracted a record-low viewership for the fall classic. The series averaged a 7.6 rating (meaning that 7.6% of all households were tuned in) and a 12 share (meaning that 12% of those watching something were watching the World Series). Viewership for the World Series improved slightly over the next three years, before spiking in 2016, when the broadcast averaged a 12.9 rating and a 22 share. This jump was likely attributable to the historic nature of the series, which featured the Chicago Cubs (who had not won a title since 1908) against the Cleveland Indians (who last won the World Series in 1948). The World Series broadcast also produced solid numbers in 2017, when the matchup between the Houston Astros and the Los Angeles Dodgers averaged a 10.6 rating and a 20 share.

Meanwhile, professional baseball has increased its media income substantially in recent years. According to Mark Newman, in "MLB, ESPN Agree on Record Eight-Year Deal" (MLB.com, August 28, 2012), the league signed a new broadcasting contract with ESPN in August 2012. The eight-year deal was worth a total of $5.6 billion, roughly double the existing contract between the MLB and the network, which was due to expire in 2013. Under the terms of the agreement, ESPN would have the rights to air 90 regular-season baseball games per year, as well as one of two wild-card playoff games. The league reached similar agreements with Fox and Turner Broadcasting in October 2012. Newman reports in "MLB Reaches Eight-Year Agreement with Fox, Turner" (MLB.com, October 2, 2012) that the combined value of the three television deals was worth $12.4 billion through the 2021 season. Baseball has expanded its radio presence in recent years as well. The league's new television agreement with ESPN also included radio broadcast rights, both in the United States and overseas. In August 2013 the MLB renewed its contract with Sirius XM Radio, granting the broadcaster the right to air all regular-season and playoff baseball games through the 2021 season.

Since the start of the 21st century the MLB has been working to expand its presence on the internet. In 2000 the league formed MLB Advanced Media as a way of consolidating the online businesses of individual teams into a single centralized location: MLB.com. In "Baseball Team Values 2017" (Forbes.com, April 11, 2017), Mike Ozanian indicates that MLB Advanced Media had an overall value of roughly $12 billion by 2017.

FOOTBALL: BIGGEST ATHLETES, BIGGEST AUDIENCE

Professional Football

It is not an exaggeration to say that television put football where it is today. Before the era of televised sports, baseball was much more popular than football. Stirring television moments such as the 1958 NFL Championship, a thrilling overtime victory by the Baltimore Colts over the New York Giants, helped establish professional football as a big-time spectator sport. A few years later, when *Time* placed the Green Bay Packers coach Vince Lombardi (1913–1970) on its cover in 1962—accompanied by the pronouncement that football was "The Sport of the '60s"—it was clear that the sport had come of age as a media phenomenon.

In September 2011 the NFL extended its broadcasting agreement with ESPN, granting the network the right to air *Monday Night Football* through 2022, at a cost of $1.9 billion per year. (See Table 1.2 in Chapter 1.) In December of that year the league also extended its *Sunday Night Football* contract with NBCUniversal in a deal worth $1 billion annually between 2014 and 2022. Under the terms of the agreement, NBC would also receive the right to broadcast the Super Bowl in 2015, 2018, and 2021. Also in December 2011 the NFL forged new agreements with Fox and CBS, granting the networks the rights to air weekly regular-season games and three Super Bowls each.

Football is by far the most popular sport to watch on television in the United States. The entertainment that accompanies NFL broadcasts is also a source of widespread appeal. For more than two decades, *Monday Night Football* broadcasts began with Hank Williams Jr. (1949–) singing a modified version of his country hit "All My Rowdy Friends Are Coming Over Tonight." ESPN abruptly terminated Williams's contract in 2011, after the singer made some controversial public remarks comparing President Barack Obama (1961–) to Adolf Hitler (1889–1945). Between 2007 and 2012 the country singer Faith Hill (1967–) performed the opening song to NBC's *Sunday Night Football*; she was replaced by the country singer Carrie Underwood (1983–) before the 2013 season. Likewise, the NFL's showcase event, the Super Bowl, which combines the league's championship game with elaborate pregame and halftime programming, owns the record for the most-watched broadcast in television history.

The United States' fascination with the Super Bowl extends far beyond the actual contest on the field. Every year, companies produce highly original, memorable television advertisements to air during the big game, pouring millions of dollars into 30- and 60-second spots. Andrew Gould reports in "Super Bowl Ads 2018: Latest Info on Cost of 2018 Super Bowl Commercials" (Bleacher Report.com, February 4, 2018) that a television advertisement spot for Super Bowl LII cost $5 million for 30 seconds. This figure represents an increase of more than 163% compared with advertising prices during Super Bowl XXXVI in 2002, when a 30-second television spot cost $1.9 million.

College Football

Televised college sports have nearly as much appeal as professional sports for American audiences, and since the 1980s they have become the subject of large media contracts as well. During the early days of televised sports, the National Collegiate Athletic Association (NCAA) determined which college teams could play on television. Officially, the NCAA's goal in making these decisions was to protect the schools from the loss of ticket-buying fans who were lured by the glowing screen in a warm home. The NCAA's dominance over the right to broadcast football games went virtually unquestioned for years.

By the 1970s several universities with top football programs had become frustrated with the limits the NCAA was placing on their television exposure. In 1977 five major conferences, along with a handful of high-profile independents, formed their own group, the College Football Association (CFA), to fight for their interests within the NCAA. A few years later the CFA signed its own television agreement with NBC, the second-largest sports television contract ever signed up to that time. Naturally, the NCAA was unhappy about this development and moved to ban the teams involved from all championship events. The University of Georgia and the University of Oklahoma sued the NCAA, and the case was eventually decided by the US Supreme Court in *NCAA v. Board of Regents of the University of Oklahoma* (468 US 85 [1984]). In the end, the NCAA was found to be in violation of antitrust laws.

In the wake of the Supreme Court decision, the CFA took on the role of coordinating the television coverage of most of the nation's leading football conferences. Still, some teams found the arrangement too restrictive. Following the defection of a handful of teams and conferences, the CFA folded in 1994, and the conferences were on their own to negotiate television contracts with the networks. The dollars began to flow in an ever-greater volume during this period. In 1990 the Southeastern Conference (SEC) signed a contract that brought in $16 million to be divided among its members. In "SEC, ESPN Agree to Milestone Contract" (TampaBay.com, August 25, 2008), Antonya English notes that in 2008 the SEC signed broadcast contracts with CBS and ESPN that extended for 15 years and guaranteed participating schools such as the University of Alabama, the University of Florida, and Louisiana State University an estimated $20 million each per year.

With so much money at stake, the nation's leading college conferences also began exploring possibilities for expansion. Dennis Dodd reports in "Whenever Big Ten Expands, College Football Will Feel Trickle-Down Effect" (CBSSports.com, April 21, 2010) that in 2010 the Big 10 Conference and the SEC were by far the two largest conferences in the United States, together accounting for roughly 50% of the nation's college football television audience. As the two conferences jockeyed for dominance, they began exploring ways to attract more teams. In 2011 the University of Nebraska officially joined the Big 10 Conference. Three years later, in 2014, the Big 10 added the University of Maryland and Rutgers University to its ranks, bringing the total number of schools in the conference to 14.

With about a thousand universities participating in more than 150,000 sporting events each year, competition for the right to put these events on television is fierce. In 2003 a network devoted strictly to collegiate athletics was launched under the name College Sports Television. College Sports Television was purchased by CBS in January 2006 and rebranded as College Sports Live. According to the article "BCS, ESPN Reach Deal to Air Games from 2011–14" (Associated Press, November 18, 2008), in 2008 ESPN entered into an agreement with the NCAA to cover Bowl Championship Series (BCS) football games from 2011 to 2014, in a deal worth $125 million per year. Jerry Hinnen reports in "ESPN Reaches 12-Year Deal to Air College Football Playoffs" (CBSSports.com, November 21, 2012) that the network reached a new deal with college football in 2012. Under the new contract, which was worth an estimated $5.6 billion and which spanned from 2014 to 2025, ESPN would have the exclusive right to broadcast the new playoff games, as well as several traditional bowl games.

The highlight of the college football season comes each December, when the annual bowl game season gets under way. Traditionally, the most prestigious bowl games included the Rose Bowl, the Orange Bowl, and the Sugar Bowl. In recent years, however, the college bowl game schedule has expanded significantly. According to FBSchedules.com, in "College Football Bowl Schedule: 2018–19 Bowl Games" (2018, http://cdn.fbschedules.com/ncaa/college-football-bowl-schedule.php), there were 41 bowl games slated for the 2018–19 season, beginning in December. Corporate sponsorship has also become an integral aspect of the bowl game lineup, as events such as the Capital One Orange Bowl, the Allstate Sugar Bowl, and the Goodyear Cotton Bowl have emerged as some of college football's signature events. Only the Rose Bowl has retained its original name in this new era of commercialization.

Until 2014 the college bowl game season concluded with the BCS National Championship Game, which determined the top college football team in the country. This format changed during the 2014–15 season, when the NCAA introduced a four-team playoff that culminated with the College Football Playoff (CFP) championship. Under the new system, two of the traditional bowl events became semifinal playoff games to determine which two teams would compete for the CFP title. In the inaugural year of the four-team playoff, the University of Oregon defeated Florida State University in the Rose Bowl, while Ohio State University upset the University of Alabama in the Allstate Sugar Bowl. On January 12, 2015, at the AT&T Stadium in Arlington, Texas, Oregon and Ohio State faced off in the first CFP National Championship game. Ohio State emerged victorious, 42–20, becoming the first college football title winner under the new system.

The new playoff format proved to be a huge success with television audiences. In *Year in Sports Media Report: 2014*, the Nielsen Company indicates that between 2013–14 and 2014–15 average viewership for the Rose Bowl rose from 18.6 million to 28.2 million, an increase of 51.1%. The Allstate Sugar Bowl saw an even more dramatic spike in ratings, as the television audience grew from 16.3 million to 28.3 million, an increase of 73%. The CFP National Championship game also outperformed the previous season's BCS title game, as television viewership for the title matchup rose nearly 31%, from 25.6 million in 2013–14 to 33.4 million in 2014–15. The Nielsen Company notes in *Year in Sports Media Report: U.S. 2017* (February 15, 2018, http://www.nielsen.com/content/dam/corporate/us/en/reports-downloads/2018-reports/year-in-sports-media-2017.pdf) that ratings for all three games fell in 2017–18, with the CFP National Championship matchup between Alabama and Georgia drawing an average viewership of 28.8 million, a decline of nearly 14% compared with 2014–15.

BASKETBALL

NBA regular-season games have never drawn the kind of television audiences that NFL games routinely attract. In basketball, viewership increases significantly during the playoffs and is greatly influenced by the specific teams or personalities involved in a game. Fueled by stars such as LeBron James, Stephen Curry (1988–), Kevin Durant (1988–), and James Harden (1989–), the NBA saw television ratings surge in 2016–17. In "TV Ratings: NBA Finals Is Most Watched since 1998" (Variety.com, June 13, 2017), Daniel Holloway reports that the season's NBA Finals matchup between the Cleveland Cavaliers and the Golden State Warriors drew an average television audience of 20.4 million over five games, making it the most-viewed NBA title series since 1998, when the Chicago Bulls defeated the Utah Jazz. NBA television viewership continued to rise during the first half of the 2017–18 regular season. According to the article "NBA's Good Times Continue into 2018" (SportsMediaWatch.com, January 5, 2018), NBA broadcasts on ABC, ESPN, and Turner Network Television (TNT) averaged 2.2 million viewers through early January 2018, an increase of 18% compared with an average viewership of 1.8 million during the 2016–17 regular season.

Table 3.1 shows the history of the NBA's television contracts since 1953. The rate at which the money involved has increased is striking. The most recent contracts, signed in 2014 with ABC/ESPN and TNT, cover nine years (from the 2016–17 season to the 2024–25 season) and have a total value of $24 billion. Under these contracts ABC airs 17 regular-season games and the entire NBA finals, along with several early-round playoff games. ESPN broadcasts up to 87 regular-season games and one of the conference finals, as well as some early-round playoff games. TNT airs 67 regular-season games, the All-Star Game, and playoff games, including one of the conference finals.

In 2003 Time Warner Cable, Cox Communications, and Cablevision Systems teamed up on a multiyear agreement with the NBA for distribution of NBA TV, the league's own 24-hour network. In January 2008 Turner Sports, part of Time Warner, took over management of all of the NBA's digital assets, including both NBA TV and NBA.com, under a deal to run through 2016. Turner Sports' rights to these assets were extended through 2025 as part of the previously discussed television deal that was signed in 2014.

College basketball also attracts a wide viewing audience. In 2010 the NCAA signed a 14-year, $10.8 billion deal with Turner Broadcasting and CBS to provide expanded television coverage of its annual Division I basketball tournament known as March Madness. Brad Wolverton explains in "NCAA Agrees to $10.8-Billion Deal to Broadcast Its Men's Basketball Tournament" (Chronicle.com, April 22, 2010) that the agreement would generate a minimum of $740 million for member colleges and universities each year. According to the Nielsen Company, in *Year in Sports Media Report: U.S. 2017*, the second round of the NCAA Men's Basketball Tournament drew an average of 5.6 million viewers. Television audiences grew considerably as the tournament progressed, with an average of 16.8 million viewers tuning in for the Final Four games, while an average of 23 million viewers watched the University of North Carolina defeat Gonzaga University in the title game.

HOCKEY

According to Steve Keating, in "NBC and NHL Agree to 10-Year TV Rights Deal" (Reuters.com, April 19, 2011), in April 2011 NBC and the NHL signed a new 10-year, $2 billion deal that granted the network the right to broadcast 100 regular-season games per year. As part of the agreement, the cable channel Versus, which had broadcast professional hockey games since 2005 and had since been acquired by NBC, would continue to televise the NHL throughout the regular season and the playoffs as the NBC Sports Network. Austin Karp indicates in "NHL Regular-Season Viewership Sees Sharp Drop on TV, but Streaming Sets New Record" (SportsBusinessDaily.com, April 14, 2017) that NBC averaged just over 1.2 million viewers per nationally televised NHL game in 2016–17, a 20% decline from an average viewership of more than 1.5 million in 2015–16. Meanwhile, the NBC Sports Network averaged 336,000 viewers per game in 2016–17, its lowest figure since it drew an average viewership of 332,000 in 2011–12. By contrast, the network's NHL live streaming service attracted a record 923,000 views in 2016–17, totaling roughly 126 million minutes of live viewing time.

AUTO RACING

In "NASCAR Makes Changes to Ramp Up Racing, Boost TV Ratings" (USAToday.com, February 24, 2017), Brant James reports that television ratings for National Association for Stock Car Auto Racing (NASCAR) events fell sharply between 2005 and 2016. During this period viewership for NASCAR races fell 45%, from an average of 9 million viewers in 2005 to 4.6 million viewers in 2016. Attendance at races also dropped during this span. Justin Fox notes in "4 Reasons for NASCAR's Big Skid" (Bloomberg.com, July 28, 2017) that ticket revenues reported by the three leading NASCAR racetrack corporations—International Speedway, Speedway Motorsports, and Dover Motorsports—fell from a peak of $467.4 million in 2007 to $221 million in 2016,

TABLE 3.1

National Basketball Association television contracts, by cable channel or broadcast network, 1953–2025

Seasons	Station	Contracts amount
NBA cable television contracts		
1979–80 to 1981–82	USA	$1.5 million/3 years
1982–83 to 1983–84	USA/ESPN	$11 million/2 years
1984–85 to 1985–86	TBS	$20 million/2 years
1986–87 to 1987–88	TBS	$25 million/2 years
1988–89 to 1989–90	TBS/TNT	$50 million/2 years
1990–91 to 1993–94	TNT	$275 million/4 years
1994–95 to 1997–98	TNT/TBS	$397 million/4 years
1998–99 to 2001–02	TNT/TBS	$840 million/4 years
2002–03 to 2007–08	TNT	$2.2 billion/6 years
NBA network television contracts		
1953–54	DUMONT	$39,000/13 games
1954–55 to 1961–62	NBC	N/A
1962–63 to 1972–73	ABC	N/A
1973–74 to 1975–76	CBS	$27 million/3 years
1976–77 to 1977–78	CBS	$21 million/2 years
1978–79 to 1981–82	CBS	$74 million/4 years
1982–83 to 1985–86	CBS	$91.9 million/4 years
1986–87 to 1989–90	CBS	$173 million/4 years
1990–91 to 1993–94	NBC	$601 million/4 years
1994–95 to 1997–98	NBC	$892 million/4 years
1998–99 to 2001–02	NBC	$1.1616 billion/4 years
2002–03 to 2007–08	ABC/ESPN	$2.4 billion/6 years
Current contracts, combined cable and network		
2008–09 to 2015–16	ABC/ESPN and TNT	$7.44 billion/8 years
2016–17 to 2024–25	ABC/ESPN and TNT	$24 billion/9 years

SOURCE: Created by Stephen Meyer for Gale, © 2018

a decline of 52.7%. Despite sagging ratings, NASCAR extended its existing contract with Fox Sports in 2012, which would continue broadcasting races from the first half of the Sprint Cup season. In 2013 NASCAR struck a 10-year, $8.2 billion television deal with the NBC Sports Network to air late-season Sprint Cup events. According to the article "NBC Wins NASCAR TV Rights, Signs 10-Year Deal to Replace ESPN, Turner" (Sporting News.com, July 23, 2013), the new deals run from 2015 to 2024 and are worth a combined $8.2 billion.

ADVERTISING

Plunkett Research, Ltd., estimates in "Sports Industry Statistics and Market Size Overview" (2018, https://www.plunkettresearch.com/statistics/sports-industry/) that sports in the United States was a $498.4 billion industry in 2015. Furthermore, approximately $34.9 billion was spent by US companies on sports advertising that year. In "NFL's Regular Season Ad Revenue Fell 1.2%, as Makegoods Overtook Unit Rate Increases" (AdWeek.com, January 25, 2018), Jason Lynch indicates that the NFL alone generated just over $2.4 billion in television advertising during the 2017 regular season. This figure actually represented a slight decline from 2016, when ad revenues approached $2.5 billion during the NFL regular season.

SPORTS VIEWING AND GENDER

Although female athletes generally fail to generate the same television ratings as male athletes, during the first decade of the 21st century there were signs that the audience for women's sports was growing. The article "Women's Basketball Sees Higher Attendance, TV Ratings" (Reuters.com, September 16, 2008) reports that in 2007 the Women's National Basketball Association (WNBA) signed an eight-year, $30 million deal to extend its television contract with ABC and ESPN2, as the league continued to expand its fan base. According to the article "ESPN, WNBA Extend Agreement" (ESPN.com, March 28, 2013), in March 2013 the league extended its television partnership with ESPN through the 2022 season. Meanwhile, the WNBA continued to grow in popularity among television viewers. The league reports in the press release "Dramatic WNBA Finals Leads League to Highest Postseason Attendance in Seven Years" (October 9, 2017, http://www.wnba.com/news/dramatic-wnba-finals-leads-league-highest-postseason-attendance-seven-years/) that the 2017 finals series between the Minnesota Lynx and the Los Angeles Sparks drew an average television audience of 559,000 viewers per game, the third-highest finals viewership in league history. It also notes that fans viewed 47 million WNBA videos on social media platforms during the postseason that year, an increase of 109.6% compared with the 2016 playoffs.

Nowhere was the increasing popularity of women's sports more apparent than during the US soccer team's run to the Women's World Cup final in 2015. According to the article "Women's World Cup Final Has Record TV Ratings" (CBSNews.com, July 6, 2015), 26.7 million Americans watched the United States defeat Japan 5–2 in the title match; it was the largest television audience for a Women's World Cup event in US history. Of these, 25.4 million watched the English-language broadcast on Fox, while another 1.3 million watched the game in Spanish on Telemundo. By comparison, the 2014 Men's World Cup final between Germany and Argentina attracted a total US television audience of 26.5 million.

GAMING

Not long ago there were only two options for sports enthusiasts: playing a sport oneself or watching others play it live or onscreen. In recent years, a third way has emerged in the form of sports gaming.

Sports-oriented video games have been around for years, but until the mid-1980s the graphics were mediocre and the action unexciting for a true sports buff. A big change took place during the late 1980s, when Electronic Arts (EA), at the time a relatively new company making interactive entertainment software, introduced the first-ever football video game to offer realistic 11-on-11 action. To make the game as realistic as possible, the company consulted extensively with John Madden (1936–), a former NFL coach and former football commentator. EA eventually named the game after Madden, and in 1989 the first version of *John Madden Football* was released for Apple II computers. The game was an instant sensation.

Over the next few years the gaming industry grew exponentially, split about evenly between computer games and television-based systems. By the release of the 1995 version of the game *Madden NFL '95*, EA had hashed out licensing deals with the NFL and the NFL Players Association, allowing it to use the likenesses of real players and team logos and uniforms. *Madden NFL* was eventually made available for every major gaming system. Andrew Goldfarb reports in "Madden NFL 13 Sales Pass 1.6 Million" (IGN.com, September 6, 2012) that within a week of its release on August 28, 2012, *Madden NFL 13* sold nearly 1.7 million copies, a record for EA. *Madden NFL* continued to dominate the video game market over the next half decade. In "Madden NFL 18 Sells an Estimated 938,000 Units First Week at Retail-Sales" (VGChartz.com, October 12, 2017), William D'Angelo notes that sales of *Madden NFL 18* exceeded 938,000 units in the week following its release on August 25, 2017, making it the highest-selling product in the industry over that span.

During these years another popular EA game, the *FIFA* soccer series, emerged as the best-selling sports video game in Europe. Robert Workman indicates in "FIFA 18 Reaches Outstanding New Sales Record" (ComicBook.com, January 10, 2018) that during the three months following its release on September 29, 2017, *FIFA 18* sold more than 10 million copies worldwide, with Europe accounting for roughly three-quarters (7.7 million) of these sales.

CURRENT ISSUES IN SPORTS AND MEDIA
Violence and Athlete Role Models

Violence in sports is often a focus of media scrutiny and academic research because the behavior of high-profile athletes can have an impact on fan behavior, according to social scientists. In "Violence in Sports Reflects Society, Says IU Professor" (Newsinfo.iu.edu, July 3, 2002), Lynn Jamieson of Indiana University explains that "sport tends to reflect society, and we live in a violent era. We have a violent society where people use violence to solve problems instead of using other means.... The violence issue is not limited to professional sports. It filters down to the high schools and even to recreational activities.... This is because if it occurs at the professional level, it is likely to be imitated at the lower levels like Little League and city recreational programs."

Some sports include a measure of violence that is held in check by the rules of fair play and by officials who can enforce penalties or regulate the players' behavior to some extent. The violence below the surface, however, can often erupt, and violent events involving professional athletes—either on or off the playing field—become major stories that are covered by news and entertainment organizations in addition to the sports media. The 2004–05 NBA season was marred by a huge brawl during a game between the Detroit Pistons and the Indiana Pacers; the fracas spilled into the stands, resulting in the involvement of both spectators and players. Several players received long suspensions, and the entire season took place under the cloud of the melee.

Basketball is not alone in contending with image problems stemming from extended media coverage of the actions of its players. In August 2007 Michael Vick (1980–) of the Atlanta Falcons was suspended by the NFL after he pleaded guilty to felony charges stemming from his involvement in an illegal dog-fighting ring. According to Michael MacCambridge, in *America's Game: The Epic Story of How Pro Football Captured a Nation* (2005), such incidents result from the unique position athletes are afforded within US society. In "Goodell Is Keeping the N.F.L. Inbounds" (NYTimes.com, September 16, 2007), Judy Battista quotes MacCambridge, who stated, "There is a tremendous amount of money, free time and scrutiny in the lives of most pro football players, and the combination is more pronounced and more combustible than

it was a generation ago." Vick's suspension indicated a no-nonsense response from Roger Goodell (1959–), who during his first year as commissioner of the NFL instituted a strict code of conduct for players and coaches. Goodell reinstated Vick following completion of his sentence in 2009, and Vick joined the Philadelphia Eagles, returning to play in September 2009.

One of the most shocking incidents of violence involving a professional athlete occurred in June 2013, when Aaron Hernandez (1989–2017) of the New England Patriots was arrested in connection with the murder of the semiprofessional football player Odin Lloyd (1985–2013). Shortly after the arrest, the celebrity news site TMZ released an iPhone photograph of Hernandez holding a Glock automatic pistol; the self-portrait was reportedly taken in 2009, while Hernandez was still playing at the University of Florida. Jay Busbee reports in "Police Locate Gun Used in Double Homicide with Alleged Connections to Aaron Hernandez" (Yahoo.com, August 19, 2013) that in August 2013 Hernandez became the subject of a second murder investigation, after police recovered a handgun from the vehicle of a woman who was associated with Hernandez. Investigators later discovered that the weapon was likely used in a 2012 double homicide in Boston. In April 2015 a jury found Hernandez guilty of first-degree murder in the Lloyd case. Two years later, in April 2017, Hernandez was acquitted in the 2012 double murder in Boston. Less than a week after the acquittal the former NFL tight end hanged himself in his prison cell. An autopsy later revealed that Hernandez had suffered from chronic traumatic encephalopathy, a progressive brain disease known to occur in football players and other athletes who experience repeated blows to the head.

Incidents in college sports also abound. In a Conference USA basketball game in January 2009, the University of Houston's Aubrey Coleman (1987–) stepped on the face of the University of Arizona's Chase Budinger (1988–). The video of the incident spread quickly around the internet. Ultimately, Coleman was suspended for one game. During the first weekend of the 2009 college football season, LeGarrette Blount (1986–) of the University of Oregon punched Byron Hout (1990–) of Boise State University and was suspended for the rest of the season. Blount, however, was eventually reinstated after 10 games. In June 2015 Florida State University's De'Andre Johnson punched a woman in the face during an altercation at a nightclub in Tallahassee, Florida. He was eventually dismissed from the team after video footage of the incident became public.

Even more concerning to college officials is the rise in criminal behavior among student-athletes. In "Out of Bounds: College Athletes and Crime" (CBSNews.com, March 2, 2011), Armen Keteyian examines the results of an investigation into the criminal backgrounds of top college athletes. Of 2,837 total players on the rosters of the nation's top-25 football teams, 200 (7%) had been arrested or cited for a crime. More than 25% (56) of these incidents involved violent crimes, including assault and battery, rape, and robbery. The University of Pittsburgh held the dubious distinction of having 22 student-athletes with criminal records, the most for any American college or university. Keteyian points out that only two of the 25 universities surveyed performed any kind of criminal background check on its athletic recruits, and none conducted research into the juvenile records of their players. Paula Lavigne reports in "Lawyers, Status, Public Backlash Aid College Athletes Accused of Crimes" (ESPN.com, June 15, 2015) that university administrations and athletic departments often become directly involved in criminal charges involving student-athletes. Lavigne notes that a high percentage of student-athletes accused of crimes end up not being charged. For example, of the 80 student-athletes at the University of Florida accused of crimes between 2009 and 2014, more than half (56%) were never prosecuted. By contrast, 28% of all college-aged males accused of crimes in Gainesville, Florida, during that span ended up avoiding charges.

ATHLETES AND DOMESTIC VIOLENCE. Domestic violence is also a cause of concern in professional sports. Numerous examples of violence are reported in the media. One of the most notorious incidents of domestic violence involving a professional athlete occurred on February 15, 2014, when the Baltimore Ravens running back Ray Rice (1987–) punched his fiancée, Janay Palmer, in the elevator of an Atlantic City casino, knocking her unconscious. Four days later, on February 19, TMZ released footage showing Rice dragging Palmer's body out of the elevator. The article "Key Events in the Ray Rice Story" (CNN.com, September 16, 2014) reports that Goodell spent months determining a punishment for Rice, finally handing him a two-game suspension in July 2014. The leniency of the suspension sparked widespread criticism. For example, Kavitha Davidson, a sports writer for *Bloomberg News*, told Scott Simon in "NFL Faces Criticism over Ray Rice Suspension from Ravens" (NPR.org, July 26, 2014) that Goodell's failure to impose a harsher punishment for Rice's assault risked alienating the league's female fans. "The NFL has sent a really damaging message to its female fans, to all women," Davidson said. "To all victims of domestic abuse, really." Davidson explained that the two-game suspension was particularly upsetting in light of the fact that the NFL routinely issued four-game suspensions to players caught violating the league's substance abuse policy.

In August 2014 Goodell revised the league's policy toward domestic violence incidents, implementing mandatory six-game suspensions for first-time offenders. The following month the Baltimore Ravens cut Rice from the team and the NFL suspended him indefinitely. Jill Martin

and Steve Almasy report in "Ray Rice Wins Suspension Appeal" (CNN.com, November 30, 2014) that with the support of the NFL Players Association Rice subsequently sued the NFL to be reinstated, winning his appeal in November 2014. Despite his legal victory, Rice never signed with another NFL franchise.

Meanwhile, in May 2014 Adrian Peterson (1985–) of the Minnesota Vikings was charged with child abuse after it was discovered that he had injured his four-year-old son while whipping him with a wooden switch. In "Adrian Peterson Avoids Jail Time in Child Abuse Case" (USA Today.com, November 4, 2014), Eric Prisbell and Brent Schrotenboer indicate that Peterson was indicted by a grand jury in September 2014. He was suspended indefinitely by the Vikings, with pay, pending the trial. In the end, Peterson was placed on probation and sentenced to community service. By the following year, the running back had rejoined the Vikings.

INAPPROPRIATE SEXUAL BEHAVIOR AND SPORTS. As with domestic violence, cases of sexual assault and sexual harassment are prevalent in both professional and amateur sports. In one notable scandal, players on the Baylor University football team were accused of sexually assaulting female students during a period between 2012 and 2016. Lavigne reports in "Baylor Faces Accusations of Ignoring Sex Assault Victims" (ESPN.com, July 13, 2017) that a subsequent investigation revealed that university officials had known about at least one instance of sexual assault in 2013, but failed to disclose the information to legal authorities. In the aftermath of the revelations Art Briles (1955–), the head football coach, was fired, and Ken Starr (1946–), the president of Baylor University, resigned. Lavigne further notes that as of July 2017 the US Department of Education had opened investigations into 161 colleges and universities, on grounds that they had mishandled sexual assault cases. Meanwhile, in 2016 Darren Sharper (1975–), a former Pro Bowl NFL safety, was sentenced to 20 years in prison after pleading guilty to drugging and raping three women in New Orleans. According to Mike Perlstein, in "Ex-NFL Star Darren Sharper Sentenced to 20 Years in Louisiana Rape Case" (USAToday.com, August 25, 2016), the verdict followed a plea deal in which Sharper pleaded guilty to sexually assaulting a total of 16 women in four states.

An even more staggering case of sexual abuse emerged in 2017, when Larry Nassar (1963–), a longtime USA Gymnastics doctor, stood trial for molesting hundreds of female gymnasts, many of them underage, over a span of several decades. In "How Larry Nassar Abused Hundreds of Gymnasts and Eluded Justice for Decades" (IndyStar.com, April 4, 2018), Tim Evans et al. indicate that police investigated Nassar on similar charges on two prior occasions, once in 2004 and again in 2014, but no charges were ever filed. Besides the sexual assault charges, Nassar also faced federal charges for possession of child pornography. In December 2017 Nassar was sentenced to 60 years in prison after pleading guilty to the child pornography charges. The following month he received another prison sentence of 40 to 175 years for his sexual abuse crimes. At the time of his second sentencing in January 2018, Nassar stood accused of sexually assaulting at least 265 women and girls.

In the wake of the #MeToo movement, which emerged in 2017 in reaction to pervasive sexual abuse in all segments of American society, sexual harassment has also been exposed at the highest levels of the sports industry. Chris Isidore reports in "NFL Network, ESPN Suspend Marshall Faulk, Other Stars after Sexual Harassment Lawsuit" (CNN.com, December 13, 2017) that several former NFL players, including the Hall of Famers Marshall Faulk (1973–) and Warren Sapp (1972–), were suspended by ESPN and the NFL Network in the wake of a sexual harassment lawsuit filed by the wardrobe stylist Jami Cantor. Isidore notes that the harassment occurred repeatedly over a period of several years and involved instances of lewd and suggestive behavior as well as inappropriate physical contact.

CHAPTER 4
PROFESSIONAL TEAM SPORTS

For decades baseball, football, basketball, and hockey have been considered the four major professional team sports in the United States. Although other sports such as auto racing and soccer are gaining ground in terms of popularity, it most likely will be some time before major league sports in the United States means anything other than the four core sports.

Besides being popular spectator events, professional league sports are also major industries that generate huge amounts of money—for team owners and managers, companies that sponsor teams, equipment and athletic gear manufacturers, and the athletes themselves.

MAJOR LEAGUE BASEBALL

Major League Baseball (MLB) is no longer as popular as professional football and is losing ground to other sports, yet it remains firmly ingrained in the American imagination, retaining the title of "national pastime." At the same time, baseball has had more than its share of bad publicity since the 1990s, largely because of steroid scandals. Baseball's steroid problem was magnified in 2007, as Barry Bonds (1964–), the player most closely associated with the scandal, approached the all-time home-run record held by Hank Aaron (1934–) since 1974. Bonds broke Aaron's record on August 7, 2007, eliciting an ambivalent response from fans and the national media. The steroid problem flared up again in 2009, when information was leaked that in 2003 a number of elite players had tested positive for steroids during a round of testing the players union had agreed to under a set of conditions that included anonymity. Among the top players revealed to have tested positive were Alex Rodriguez (1975–) of the New York Yankees, Manny Ramirez (1972–) of the Los Angeles Dodgers, and David Ortiz (1975–) of the Boston Red Sox. Ramirez served a 50-game suspension in 2009 as a result of his steroid violations. In 2011 Ramirez once again

tested positive for steroid use; he decided to retire from the game rather than face another suspension.

Rodriguez found himself at the center of a performance-enhancing drug controversy in 2013, when he was linked to Biogenesis of America, a health clinic in Florida that was accused of providing human growth hormone and other banned substances to more than a dozen MLB players. T. J. Quinn reports in "Whistle-Blower: Not Only MLB Players" (ESPN.com, August 11, 2013) that the controversy arose when Porter Fischer, a former employee of Biogenesis, released a large number of the clinic's documents to reporters at the *Miami New Times*. According to Quinn, these documents revealed the names of more than a dozen MLB players who had received performance-enhancing drugs from Biogenesis. In "Baseball Union Says League Interviewing Players in New Drug Probe" (NBCSports.com, June 5, 2013), Erin McClam notes that the Biogenesis allegations posed a unique dilemma for the MLB Players Association (MLBPA). Although obligated to provide legal defense for players accused of using performance-enhancing drugs, the association was also committed to cooperating with league officials in their efforts to eradicate drug use in baseball. McClam reports that Michael S. Weiner (1961–2013), the president of the MLBPA, said in a public statement, "The Players Association has every interest in both defending the rights of players and in defending the integrity of our joint program."

According to Tim Brown, in "MLB's Biogenesis Investigation Leads to 13 More Suspensions" (Yahoo.com, August 5, 2013), Ryan Braun (1983–) of the Milwaukee Brewers was the first player to be punished as a result of the Biogenesis investigation. In July 2013 Braun was suspended for the remainder of the 2013 season, including the playoffs. Two weeks later, a dozen more players received 50-game bans; among the players suspended were Bartolo Colon (1973–) of the Oakland Athletics, Nelson Cruz

(1980–) of the Texas Rangers, and Jhonny Peralta (1982–) of the Detroit Tigers, all former All-Stars. Rodriguez, who had already admitted to using performance-enhancing drugs in the past, was suspended for the remainder of the 2013 season and the entire 2014 season, for a total of 211 games.

MLB Structure and Administration

Technically speaking, "Major League Baseball" refers to the entity that operates the National League and the American League, the two top professional baseball leagues in North America. The MLB operates these two leagues under a joint organizational structure that was established in 1920 with the creation of the Major League Constitution. This constitution has been overhauled many times since then. MLB team owners appoint a commissioner, under whose direction the MLB hires and maintains umpiring crews, negotiates marketing and television deals, and establishes labor agreements with the MLBPA.

As of 2018, the MLB consisted of 30 teams. (See Table 4.1.) These teams are divided into two leagues: 15 in the American League and 15 in the National League. Each of these leagues is further split into three divisions—East, Central, and West—that are loosely based on geography. The MLB season normally runs from early April through late September and consists of 162 games. Following the regular season, the champions of each division (three teams in each league) plus two wild-card teams (the two teams with the best record among those not winning their division) from each league compete in the playoffs. The playoffs consist of four rounds: a one-game playoff between the two wild-card teams in each league; two best-of-five Division Series in each league; a best-of-seven Championship Series in each league; and finally the World Series, a best-of-seven game series between the champions of each league, to determine the major league champion team.

According to Mike Ozanian, in "Baseball Team Values 2017" (Forbes.com, April 11, 2017), the MLB took in just over $9 billion in revenues in 2016. Figure 4.1 shows the values and revenues of select MLB teams in 2017. The New York Yankees were worth $3.7 billion that year. This sum was 32% greater than the value of the second-most-valuable team, the Los Angeles Dodgers, which was worth $2.8 billion in 2017. Other teams worth $2 billion or more that year included the Boston Red Sox ($2.7 billion), the Chicago Cubs ($2.7 billion), the San Francisco Giants ($2.6 billion), and the New York Mets ($2 billion). The Yankees also dwarfed the rest of the league in revenues, at $526 million. According to the article "MLB Salaries 2017: Earnings Flatten Out, While Clayton Kershaw Leads Pack" (USAToday.com, April 2, 2017), the average MLB player salary topped $4.5 million in 2017. By comparison, the average MLB player salary in 1989 was $512,804, according to CBS Sports, in "MLB Salaries" (2018, http://www.cbssports.com/mlb/salaries/avgsalaries).

MLB History

The first professional baseball team was the Cincinnati Red Stockings, founded in 1869. That year the team—which still exists as the Cincinnati Reds—embarked on a 57-game national tour and went undefeated against local amateur teams. The team's success led to the creation in 1871 of the first professional baseball league, the nine-team, eight-city National Association of Professional Baseball Players. Various other competing leagues were formed over the next decade, including a precursor to the modern National League. The American League was founded in 1901. The champions of the American League and the National League faced off in what became the first World Series in 1903. The popularity of professional baseball continued to grow over the next several years. A crisis unfolded in 1919, when several members of the Chicago White Sox were paid by gamblers to throw the World Series in the so-called Black Sox scandal. In the wake of the scandal, club owners hired baseball's first commissioner, Kenesaw Landis (1866–1944), to clean up the game.

Baseball's golden era took place between the two world wars, which was marked by the rise of all-time greats such as Babe Ruth (1895–1948), Ty Cobb (1886–1961), and Lou Gehrig (1903–1941). The major leagues survived the Great Depression (1929–1939) by introducing night games, which soon became the norm for games played during the week; weekend games were still played during the day. From its beginnings through World War II (1939–1945), the MLB was racially segregated.

TABLE 4.1

Major League Baseball teams and divisions

American League	National League
East Division	**East Division**
Baltimore Orioles	Atlanta Braves
Boston Red Sox	Miami Marlins
New York Yankees	New York Mets
Tampa Bay Rays	Philadelphia Phillies
Toronto Blue Jays	Washington Nationals
Central Division	**Central Division**
Chicago White Sox	Chicago Cubs
Cleveland Indians	Cincinnati Reds
Detroit Tigers	Milwaukee Brewers
Kansas City Royals	Pittsburgh Pirates
Minnesota Twins	St. Louis Cardinals
West Division	**West Division**
Houston Astros	Arizona Diamondbacks
Los Angeles Angels of Anaheim	Colorado Rockies
Oakland Athletics	Los Angeles Dodgers
Seattle Mariners	San Diego Padres
Texas Rangers	San Francisco Giants

SOURCE: Created by Stephen Meyer for Gale, © 2018

FIGURE 4.1

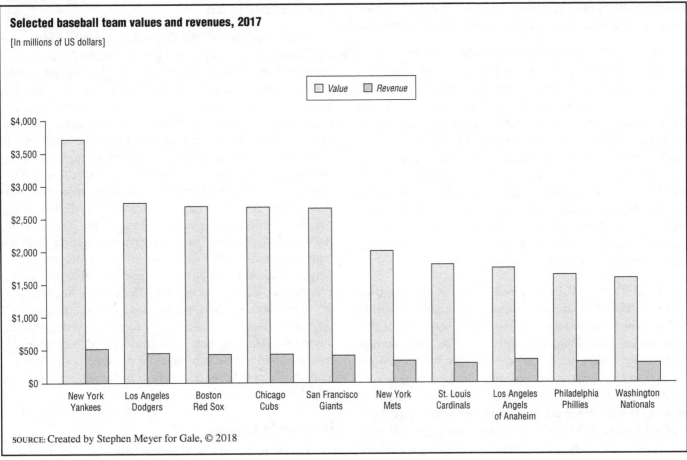

Selected baseball team values and revenues, 2017

[In millions of US dollars]

SOURCE: Created by Stephen Meyer for Gale, © 2018

That changed in 1947, when the African American player Jackie Robinson (1919–1972) joined the Brooklyn Dodgers. Legends such as Willie Mays (1931–) and Hank Aaron followed over the next decade, and by the mid-1950s African American players were fairly common on major league rosters.

After 50 years of stability, the 1950s brought changes to the MLB in response to demographic shifts in the United States. The Boston Braves moved to Milwaukee in 1953. Two New York teams moved to the West Coast in 1957: the Brooklyn Dodgers departing to Los Angeles and the New York Giants to San Francisco.

The MLBPA was formed in 1966. The association's main goal was to end the reserve clause, a contractual provision that essentially gave teams ownership of players, meaning they were bound to a particular team until they were traded or released. The reserve clause was finally overturned in 1975, ushering in the era of free agency in baseball, wherein players were free to negotiate with any team they wanted once their existing contract had expired. Labor squabbles continued over the next 20 years, and parts of several seasons were lost to work stoppages. The worst of these took place in 1994, when the final third of the season, including the World Series, was canceled.

The sport survived in spite of these distractions, however, thanks partly to a handful of individual accomplishments. These included Cal Ripken Jr. (1960–) breaking Gehrig's long-standing record for consecutive games played, and Mark McGwire's (1963–) and Sammy Sosa's (1968–) 1998 competition to break the record for home runs in a season—a record that was broken again by Bonds just three years later. Since then, enthusiasm over these feats has been muted by ongoing scandals involving performance-enhancing drugs, which have called into question the accomplishments of Bonds, McGwire, Sosa, and others who just a few years earlier had been credited with reviving public interest in the sport.

The Labor History of the MLB: Players versus Owners

The MLB's first major strike took place in 1981. Team owners wanted to receive compensation when one of their players was signed by another team. The players went on strike in protest, and more than 700 games were canceled before the two sides agreed on a limited form of compensation for free-agent signings.

In 1990 owners proposed a sort of salary cap and the elimination of the arbitration system in place for resolving salary disputes. A 32-day lockout followed, resulting in the cancellation of spring training that year. The owners finally dropped their demands, and the full regular season took place, although its start was postponed by one week.

In "The Baseball Strike of 1994–95" (*Monthly Labor Review*, vol. 120, no. 3, March 1997), Paul D. Staudohar of California State University explains that in June 1994 the owners proposed a salary cap that would have limited the players to 50% of total industry revenues. This represented a pay cut of about 15% for the players; not surprisingly, they declined the offer and went on strike in August. This strike resulted in the cancellation of the 1994 postseason, including the World Series. A ruling by the federal judge Sonia Sotomayor (1954–) ended the strike in March 1995. Sotomayor reinstated the 1990 contract, and the 1995 and 1996 seasons were played under the terms of the expired agreement.

In 2002 the MLB appeared to be on the brink of another strike, the causes of which were mainly rooted in imbalances between teams in large and small markets that resulted in some financial disparities. The team owners lobbied for salary caps, but the players were opposed. Instead, the owners came up with the idea of a luxury tax, which would be imposed on any team that spent more than a predetermined amount on player salaries. A strike was thus averted. The impact of the luxury tax, however, has been questionable. For example, the New York Yankees continued to spend vast sums to lure top players; in 2005 the Yankees became the first team in the history of sports to spend more than $200 million on salaries in a season. Indeed, Cork Gaines indicates in "The MLB Luxury Tax Should Really Be Called 'The Yankees Tax'" (BusinessInsider.com, April 6, 2011) that between 2003 and 2011 the Yankees accounted for 91.6% of all MLB luxury tax expenditures, paying a total of $192.2 million during this span. Nonetheless, in "Penny-Pinching in Pinstripes? Yes, the Yanks Are Reining in Pay" (NYTimes.com, March 11, 2013), David Waldstein reports that beginning in 2013 Yankees management adopted a more conservative attitude toward player salaries, with the aim of getting the franchise's payroll below the MLB luxury tax threshold of $189 million for the 2014 season. According to Baseball Prospectus (2018, http://www.baseball prospectus.com/compensation/?team=NYA), the Yankees management did manage to trim its payroll to $198.5 million in 2014, before allowing it to rise to $217.8 million in 2015 and to $227.9 million in 2016. New York's payroll subsequently dropped to $196.4 million in 2017. Meanwhile, the Los Angeles Dodgers emerged as the biggest spender in baseball during this period. Baseball Prospectus (2018, https://legacy.baseballprospectus.com/compensation/?cyear=2018&team=LAN&pos=) indicates that in 2015 the club's payroll topped $282.2 million, before gradually decreasing to $250 million in 2016 and to $241.1 million

in 2017. By contrast, the average MLB payroll was $136.6 million in 2017.

The other part of the 2002 deal was increased revenue sharing, meaning that a greater share of each team's revenue was put into a pot to be divided among all the major league teams. The biggest difference between baseball's revenue-sharing system and football's is that baseball teams earn significant revenue from local television broadcasts, whereas almost all football coverage is national. The MLB's 2002 contract brought a sharp increase in the amount of local revenue that teams must share. The 2002 collective bargaining agreement ran through the 2006 season; a new agreement, signed during the fall of 2006 and running through the 2011 season, preserved the luxury tax and revenue-sharing systems with only minor alterations. In 2011 MLB owners and players entered into a new five-year collective bargaining agreement that ran through the 2016 season. According to the agreement, by 2016 teams playing in the league's 15 largest markets would no longer receive revenue-sharing payments. The number of teams deemed ineligible for revenue sharing was subsequently reduced from 15 to 13, as part of a new labor deal forged in December 2016 and scheduled to expire in 2021.

Diversity in Baseball

Diversity has long been an issue in major league sports in the United States. The MLB was entirely white until Jackie Robinson crossed the color line in 1947. Over the next few decades the number of prominent African American players grew, and baseball took on the appearance of an inclusive sport (at least on the field; managerial jobs for African Americans remained scarce). The trend, however, has reversed itself. Once again, MLB teams have few African Americans on their rosters, although the number of Hispanic players has increased dramatically. The Baseball Almanac notes in "Major League Baseball Players by Birthplace during the 2017 Season" (2018, http://www.baseball-almanac.com/players/birthplace.php?y=2017) that the country that has produced the greatest number of players born outside the United States is the Dominican Republic, with 170 players in 2017. Venezuela was second with 112. In recent years the MLB has also earned praise for hiring minorities to management and front office positions. In *The 2017 Racial and Gender Report Card: Major League Baseball* (April 18, 2017, http://nebula.wsimg.com/d96daf1e011b077b2fd9ff4cfe4 bf1bc?AccessKeyId=DAC3A56D8FB782449D2A&disposition=0&alloworigin=1), Richard Lapchick et al. indicate that the University of Central Florida's Institute for Diversity and Ethics in Sport gave professional baseball a B for racial diversity in its hiring practices. It also, however, gave the league a C+ for gender diversity in its hiring practices.

NATIONAL FOOTBALL LEAGUE

The National Football League (NFL) is the premier US professional sports league, both in terms of popularity and monetary value. As Figure 4.2 reveals, all but five of the NFL's 32 teams were worth more than $2 billion during the 2017 season.

NFL Structure and Administration

As of 2017, there were 32 teams in the NFL, 16 each in the American Football Conference (AFC) and the National Football Conference (NFC). (See Table 4.2.) Each conference is divided into four divisions—East, North, South, and West—and each division has four teams. The NFL teams play a 16-game regular season, which begins the weekend of Labor Day. Each team also has a week off, or bye week, during the season; therefore, the full regular season lasts 17 weeks. Sunday afternoons have long been the traditional time for professional football games. The exceptions have been one game per week on Sunday night and another on Monday night (double-headers also occasionally occur), although in recent years the league has also begun scheduling games on Thursday nights, and on Saturday nights late in the season. In addition, three games are played annually on Thanksgiving Day. Two teams, the Dallas Cowboys and the Detroit Lions, always host a game on the holiday.

At the end of the regular season, six teams from each conference qualify for the playoffs: the four division champions and two wild-card teams. The champions of the two conferences square off in the Super Bowl.

The NFL is administered by the Office of the Commissioner. The first commissioner of the NFL was Elmer Layden (1903–1973), who had been a star player and later a coach at the University of Notre Dame. Layden held the post from 1941 to 1946, guiding the league through the difficult years of World War II, when most able-bodied American men had either joined or were drafted into the armed services. Layden was succeeded by Bert Bell (1895–1959), a cofounder of the Philadelphia Eagles. Under Bell, whose term as commissioner lasted until his death in 1959, NFL attendance grew every year. Bell is famous for his oft-quoted statement, "On any given Sunday, any team can beat any other team."

Nevertheless, it was Bell's successor, Pete Rozelle (1926–1996), who led the league through its period of dramatic growth during the 1960s and 1970s. Rozelle introduced the concept of long-term network broadcast contracts and applied sophisticated marketing techniques to sell the NFL brand to the American public. He oversaw the merger between the American Football League (AFL) and the NFL and guided the league to what is

FIGURE 4.2

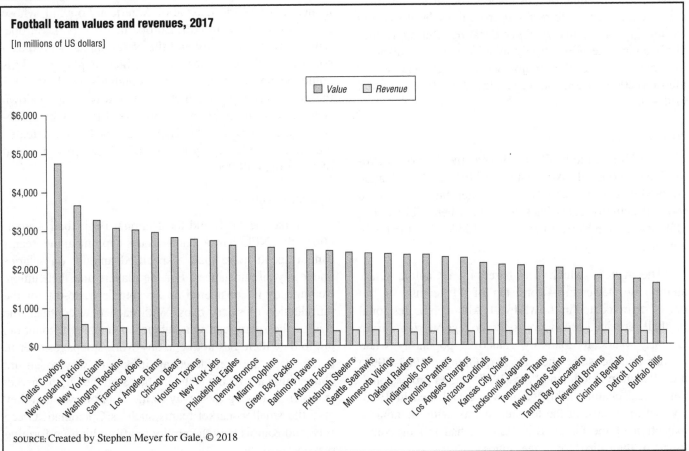

Football team values and revenues, 2017

[In millions of US dollars]

SOURCE: Created by Stephen Meyer for Gale, © 2018

TABLE 4.2

National Football League teams and divisions

American Football Conference (AFC)	National Football Conference (NFC)
East Division	**East Division**
Buffalo Bills	Dallas Cowboys
Miami Dolphins	New York Giants
New England Patriots	Philadelphia Eagles
New York Jets	Washington Redskins
North Division	**North Division**
Batimore Ravens	Chicago Bears
Cincinnati Bengals	Detroit Lions
Cleveland Browns	Green Bay Packers
Pittsburgh Steelers	Minnesota Vikings
South Division	**South Division**
Houston Texans	Atlanta Falcons
Indianapolis Colts	Carolina Panthers
Jacksonville Jaguars	New Orleans Saints
Tennessee Titans	Tampa Bay Buccaneers
West Division	**West Division**
Denver Broncos	Arizona Cardinals
Kansas City Chiefs	Los Angeles Rams
Los Angeles Chargers	San Francisco 49ers
Oakland Raiders	Seattle Seahawks

SOURCE: Created by Stephen Meyer for Gale, © 2018

generally considered a victory over the players union during the 1987 labor strike. Rozelle retired in 1989 and was replaced by Paul Tagliabue (1940–). Under Tagliabue the NFL was marked by a great deal of team movement between cities, as owners sought to maximize the revenue they could generate from the sale of stadium naming rights and luxury skybox seating. During Tagliabue's tenure the NFL largely avoided the labor disputes that plagued the other major sports. Tagliabue retired after the 2005 season and was replaced by Roger Goodell (1959–).

NFL History

The NFL came to life in 1920 as the American Professional Football Association (APFA). The league adopted its current name two years later, but professional football actually dates back to 1892, when a Pittsburgh club paid Pudge Heffelfinger (1867–1954) $500 to play in a game.

The APFA—which was based in a Canton, Ohio, automobile dealership—consisted of 11 teams, all but one of them located in the Midwest. Although professional football remained secondary to the college version during its early years, it gradually gained in popularity when former college stars such as Red Grange (1903–1991) and Benjamin Friedman (1905–1982) turned professional. An annual championship game was established in 1933. By that time most of the league's teams, with the notable exception of the Green Bay Packers, had left the small towns of their birth for bigger cities.

Professional football began to challenge college football's dominance in the years following World War II, as a faster-paced, higher-scoring style drew new fans. The NFL expanded to the West Coast in 1945, when the Cleveland Rams relocated to Los Angeles. By the 1950s professional football was firmly entrenched as a major sport in the United States, as television effectively captured the heroics of stars such as Bobby Layne (1926–1986), Paul Hornung (1935–), and Johnny Unitas (1933–2002). The explosive growth of professional football led to the creation of a rival league, the AFL, in 1960, which resulted in a costly bidding war for the services of top players. By the mid-1960s professional football had eclipsed baseball as the nation's favorite sport. In 1970 the two football leagues merged. The AFL's 10 teams plus three NFL teams became the American Football Conference; the remaining 13 NFL teams became the National Football Conference. The champions of the two conferences would meet in the newly created Super Bowl to determine the world champion of professional football.

The NFL was the biggest spectator sport in the United States during the 1970s and 1980s. In most years the Super Bowl was the most watched television show of any kind, and *Monday Night Football* set a new standard for sports broadcasting with its innovative mixture of sports and entertainment. Since the 1990s the popularity of football has spread internationally. In 1993 the NFL launched the World League of American Football, whose name was changed to NFL Europe in 1997. NFL Europe, with teams in Germany and the Netherlands, served as a sort of development league in which a player's skills could be honed to reach NFL standards. In June 2007 the NFL abruptly announced that it was shutting down NFL Europe. Its final game, the World Bowl Championship match in which the Hamburg Sea Devils defeated the Frankfurt Galaxy by a score of 37–28, drew a crowd of more than 48,000.

The NFL Salary Cap

Unlike the MLB and the National Basketball Association, the NFL has a hard salary cap, meaning teams cannot spend more than a specified amount on salaries under any circumstances. For the players and their union, free agency is considered an acceptable trade-off for the introduction of salary caps. With each new contract, the size of the salary cap is a subject of intense negotiation, but to date there has not been any work stoppages over it. Salary caps are considered an important way to ensure competition across the league: They stop the larger-market teams from buying their way to the Super Bowl, and they give the smaller-market teams such as Cincinnati, Green Bay, and Kansas City the ability to afford high-performing players.

Labor Disputes in the NFL

The NFL Players Union was formed in 1956, when players on the Green Bay Packers and the Cleveland Browns used a collective approach to demand minimum salaries, team-paid uniforms and equipment, and other benefits from owners. The owners refused to respond to any of these demands. The union threatened to sue, a threat that was strengthened by *Radovich v. National Football League* (352 US 445 [1957]), in which the US Supreme Court ruled that the NFL did not enjoy the same special status as the MLB did with regard to antitrust laws. The owners eventually gave in to most of the players' demands but did not formally recognize the union for collective bargaining purposes. The NFL Players Association (NFLPA), as it was by then named, did not become the official bargaining agent for players until 1968, following a brief lockout and strike.

After the merger of the NFL and the AFL, the NFLPA focused on antitrust litigation that challenged the so-called Rozelle Rule, which required a team signing a free agent to compensate the team losing the player, thereby severely limiting players' ability to benefit from free agency. The union succeeded in getting the Rozelle Rule eliminated in 1977.

When the NFLPA went on strike for a month in 1987, the owners responded by carrying on with the schedule by using replacement players and a handful of veterans who chose to cross the picket line. With support weakening, the union ended its strike in October 1987. Free agency finally came to the NFL in 1992, and this was balanced by the introduction of salary caps during the mid-1990s. The owners and the NFLPA established a new collective bargaining agreement in March 2006, which was supposed to be active through the 2011 season. The owners, however, abruptly opted out of the agreement in 2008, setting the stage for the NFL's first genuine labor strife since the mid-1990s.

In August 2008, with a standoff between players and owners looming on the horizon, the NFLPA executive director Gene Upshaw (1945–2008) died of cancer. The following March the NFLPA unanimously elected DeMaurice Smith (1964–), a District of Columbia lawyer, as Upshaw's successor. As the expiration of the collective bargaining agreement approached, a number of key issues dividing players and owners materialized. At the heart of the dispute was the question of revenue sharing. With the league generating roughly $9 billion in annual revenues by decade's end, the stakes for both sides were high. Owners also wanted to expand the regular-season schedule by two games, from 16 to 18, something the players adamantly opposed. The players, for their part, wanted to increase pensions and expand medical benefits for retired players, while also implementing stricter safety provisions for active players.

Serious negotiations between the NFLPA and NFL owners began in February 2011, shortly after Super Bowl XLV. As talks faltered, it emerged that the league had included a clause in its latest round of television contracts that guaranteed the owners $4 billion in broadcast revenues, regardless of whether a single game was played during the 2011 season. In the eyes of many, this guaranteed money put the owners at a significant advantage in the talks. The NFLPA strenuously objected to this provision in the television contracts, arguing that the league was legally required to provide benefits for both owners and players when entering into any contract. According to the article "Federal Judge: NFL Can't Keep TV Revenue" (CBSSports.com, March 2, 2011), on March 1, 2011, the US district judge David Singleton Doty (1929–) ruled in favor of the players, deeming that the television contracts were in violation of the former collective bargaining agreement. As discussions intensified, the owners and the players agreed to extend the collective bargaining agreement expiration date by more than a week, in the hope of forging a deal. The two sides, however, were unable to resolve their differences, so on March 11 the players union voted to decertify. Through decertification, the union effectively disbanded, giving NFL players greater latitude to sidestep existing labor laws and file suit against the league.

On March 12 the NFL owners imposed a lockout, which prohibited players from using team facilities or signing new contracts. That same day the players filed an antitrust suit against the league in federal court, seeking an injunction against the lockout. The case was titled *Brady v. National Football League* (No. 11-1898), after Tom Brady (1977–), the star quarterback of the New England Patriots and one of the league's high-profile players. On April 25 Judge Susan Richard Nelson (1952–) of the US Court of Appeals for the Eighth Circuit ruled in favor of the players and ordered the owners to lift the lockout. The NFL owners subsequently filed for a stay (delay) of Judge Nelson's order, pending an appeal; the stay was eventually granted by the US Court of Appeals for the Eighth Circuit.

Talks continued intermittently into the summer, but with little progress. Finally, on July 14 the two sides came to an agreement on a new wage scale for rookie players, which would lower the cap on contract amounts for top draft picks. The following week, on July 21, the owners ratified a new collective bargaining agreement. Mark Maske reports in "NFL Back in Business after Player Leaders Recommend Ratification of CBA" (Washington Post.com, July 25, 2011) that the players unanimously approved the new collective bargaining agreement on July 25. Key provisions of the 10-year agreement included a new revenue-sharing split, which granted the owners 53% of total revenues and the players 47%; a fund of between

$900 million and $1 billion for retired players, $620 million of which was earmarked for the Legacy Fund, a newly formed program aimed at assisting players who retired prior to 1993; and a protection benefit for injured players, with a value of up to $1.5 million over two years. With the new collective bargaining agreement in place, the four-and-a-half-month lockout ended and the 2011 NFL season was saved.

Bountygate and Deflategate

Shortly after reaching the new deal between players and owners, the NFL once again found itself at the center of controversy. In March 2012 reports emerged that coaches for the New Orleans Saints had paid some of the team's defensive players to injure their opponents during games. According to the NFL, in "NFL Announces Management Discipline in Saints' 'Bounty' Matter" (July 26, 2012, http://www.nfl.com/news/story/09000d5d 827c15b2/article/nfl-announces-management-discipline-in-saints-bounty-matter), these "bounties" involved payments for hits such as "cart-offs" and "knock-outs," which were aimed at hurting opposing players badly enough to force them out of the game. The bounties were paid during the course of the previous three seasons, including 2009, when the Saints won the Super Bowl. The New Orleans coaching staff also came under fire for willfully concealing the program from league officials, as well as misleading investigators. As a result of these actions Sean Payton (1963–), the head coach for the Saints, was suspended for the 2012 season, and Gregg Williams (1958–), the defensive coordinator, was suspended indefinitely. The Saints also paid a $500,000 fine and lost the second-round picks during the 2012 and 2013 NFL drafts.

Another scandal developed in January 2015, after evidence emerged that the New England Patriots had deliberately used underinflated footballs during the team's 45–7 win over the Indianapolis Colts in the AFC Championship Game. The controversy, which became known as "Deflategate," dominated the media coverage leading up to New England's Super Bowl matchup against the Seattle Seahawks, as allegations that the Patriots had cheated appeared in news outlets throughout the country. Although the Patriots quarterback Tom Brady denied any knowledge of footballs having been deflated, Commissioner Roger Goodell hired Theodore V. Wells Jr. (1950–) to spearhead an official investigation. In May 2015, three months after New England's dramatic 28–24 victory in Super Bowl XLIX, the NFL released *Investigative Report Concerning Footballs Used during the AFC Championship Game on January 18, 2015* (https://www.documentcloud.org/documents/2073728-ted-wells-report-deflategate.html). The report suggests that New England personnel did in fact regularly alter footballs at Brady's request, concluding that it was "more probable than not" that the

quarterback knew that the footballs had been under-inflated. In response to the report's findings, Goodell suspended Brady for four games, while also fining the team $1 million and forcing it to forfeit two draft picks. Brady appealed the following month, but ultimately, in late July 2015, Goodell decided to uphold the four-game suspension. The NFLPA subsequently filed another appeal in federal court.

On September 3, 2015, after hearing arguments from both sides, the US district judge Richard M. Berman (1943–) ruled in Brady's favor, nullifying the league's four-game suspension. In "Tom Brady Ruling: Judge Richard Berman Explains Decision to Overturn Suspension" (SportingNews.com, September 3, 2015), Rana L. Cash quotes Judge Berman, who found that "Brady had no notice that he could receive a four-game suspension for general awareness of ball deflation by others or participation in any scheme to deflate footballs, and non-cooperation with the ensuing Investigation. Brady also had no notice that his discipline would be the equivalent of the discipline imposed upon a player who used performance enhancing drugs." The NFL promptly appealed the ruling. In April 2016 the US Court of Appeals for the Second Circuit reversed the lower court's ruling, reinstating Brady's suspension. Although Brady subsequently filed for a second hearing, the court denied his appeal. In July of that year Brady announced that he would accept the suspension, and he missed the first four games of the 2016 NFL regular season.

Issues Surrounding Retired Players

Since the beginning of the 21st century greater attention has been focused on the well-being of former players suffering from physical problems resulting from the pounding their bodies took during their active playing careers. Many players with disabilities severe enough to prevent them from working have faced financial hardships besides physical pain. One story that received a great deal of media attention is the case of Mike Webster (1952–2002), a Hall of Fame–caliber player for the Pittsburgh Steelers. Webster died homeless and destitute at the age of 50 after years of drug addiction and dementia that he believed was caused by the many concussions he suffered during his 17-year career. The NFL denied that Webster's injuries were football-related and withheld assistance. A court later ordered the league to pay Webster's estate more than $1 million. Webster's case was subsequently dramatized in the movie *Concussion* (2015). The film features Will Smith (1968–) in the role of Dr. Bennet Omalu, the forensic neuropathologist who discovered symptoms of chronic traumatic encephalopathy (CTE; a degenerative brain disease) when performing Webster's autopsy. *Concussion* also sparked controversy in its depiction of the NFL's repeated efforts to suppress Omalu's findings concerning the dangers inherent in the sport.

In June 2007 congressional hearings revealed that the NFL's disability compensation system provided assistance to a shockingly low number of former players who had suffered debilitating injuries, ranging from multiple concussions to severe arthritis necessitating joint replacement. In 2007, in response to this problem, a number of former players—led by Jerry Kramer (1936–) and Mike Ditka (1939–)—formed the Gridiron Greats Assistance Fund, a nonprofit foundation that provides financial assistance to former players who need help with medical or domestic issues.

Nevertheless, many former players remained angry about their treatment by the league. In July 2011, as owners and players were finalizing terms on the new collective bargaining agreement, a group of 75 former players filed a lawsuit against the league. The article "Ex-Players Sue NFL over Concussions" (ESPN.com, July 20, 2011) indicates that the retired players accused the NFL of deliberately withholding information about the harmful effects of concussions for decades. As a result, the players were seeking unspecified compensation from the league. Over the next two years several more lawsuits followed. In "Portis, Culpepper among 83 Players Suing NFL over Concussions" (NBCSports.com, August 14, 2013), Michael David Smith reports that by August 2013 more than 4,500 former players were involved in "dozens" of lawsuits seeking damages from the NFL for football-related brain injuries.

During this time the risk of suffering permanent brain damage was causing many active players to reconsider pursuing their football careers. Tony Manfred reports in "NFL Players Giving Up Millions and Retiring out of Nowhere before Age 30 Is Becoming a Trend" (BusinessInsider.com, March 17, 2015) that in March 2015 four NFL players unexpectedly announced their early retirement. Among them was the 24-year-old San Francisco 49ers linebacker Chris Borland (1990–), who was leaving the league after only one season. In discussing his decision, Borland cited concerns about head injuries as a major factor. "I'm concerned that if you wait 'til you have symptoms, it's too late," Borland said in a March 17, 2015, interview with ESPN's (formerly the Entertainment and Sports Programming Network) *Outside the Lines* (https://www.youtube.com/watch?v=F-BU9lK5iqs). "I just want to live a long, healthy life, and I don't want to have any neurological diseases or die younger than I would otherwise."

In subsequent years other NFL players also announced their early retirement on the same grounds. Notable among these players were the Cleveland Browns tight end Jordan Cameron (1988–), who left football in March 2017, and the Baltimore Ravens offensive lineman John Urschel (1991–), who retired in July of that year.

Urschel's retirement came days after the publication of "Clinicopathological Evaluation of Chronic Traumatic Encephalopathy in Players of American Football" (*Journal of the American Medical Association*, vol. 318, no. 4, July 25, 2017) by Jesse Mez et al., a groundbreaking study that established a strong link between professional football and incidences of CTE. According to Ken Belson, in "C.T.E. Is Found in 110 of 111 Donated N.F.L. Brains" (NYTimes.com, July 26, 2017), of 111 former NFL players who had donated their brain to scientists at Boston University, 110 were revealed to have symptoms of CTE.

NATIONAL BASKETBALL ASSOCIATION

Kurt Badenhausen notes in "NBA Team Values 2018: Every Club Now Worth at Least $1 Billion" (Forbes.com, February 7, 2018) that by 2018 the average National Basketball Association (NBA) team was worth nearly $1.7 billion. Figure 4.3 shows the values and revenues of select NBA teams for the 2017–18 season. Of all NBA teams, only the New York Knicks ($3.6 billion), the Los Angeles Lakers ($3.3 billion), and the Golden State Warriors ($3.1 billion) were valued at $3 billion or more that season. Five more teams—the Chicago Bulls ($2.6 billion), the Boston Celtics ($2.5 billion), the Brooklyn Nets ($2.3 billion), the Houston Rockets ($2.2 billion), and the Los Angeles Clippers ($2.1 billion)—were valued at $2 billion or more in 2017–18.

NBA Structure and Administration

The 30-team NBA is divided into two conferences: the Eastern Conference, which consists of the Atlantic, Central, and Southeast Divisions; and the Western Conference, which consists of the Southwest, Northwest, and Pacific Divisions. (See Table 4.3.) Each division contains five teams.

The NBA regular season begins in early November. A season consists of 82 games for each team, divided evenly between home and away games. Teams play each of the other teams in their own division four times per season; they play teams in the other divisions of their own conference three or four times; and they play teams in the other conference twice each. To date, the NBA is the only one of the major sports leagues in which all teams play each other over the course of the regular season.

The NBA playoffs begin in late April. Eight teams from each conference qualify: the winners of each of the three divisions plus the five teams with the next-best records. Each round of the playoffs is a best-of-seven series. The third round of the playoffs is for the Conference Championship, and the winners of these two series

FIGURE 4.3

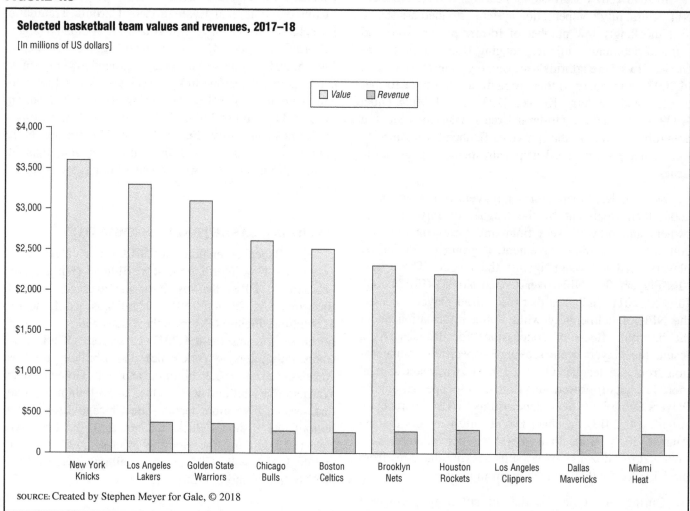

Selected basketball team values and revenues, 2017–18

[In millions of US dollars]

□ Value   ▪ Revenue

SOURCE: Created by Stephen Meyer for Gale, © 2018

TABLE 4.3

National Basketball Association teams and divisions

Eastern Conference	Western Conference
Atlantic Division	**Southwest Division**
Boston Celtics	Dallas Mavericks
Brooklyn Nets	Houston Rockets
New York Knicks	Memphis Grizzlies
Philadelphia 76ers	New Orleans Pelicans
Toronto Raptors	San Antonio Spurs
Central Division	**Northwest Division**
Chicago Bulls	Denver Nuggets
Cleveland Cavaliers	Minnesota Timberwolves
Detroit Pistons	Oklahoma City Thunder
Indiana Pacers	Portland Trail Blazers
Milwaukee Bucks	Utah Jazz
Southeast Division	**Pacific Division**
Atlanta Hawks	Golden State Warriors
Charlotte Hornets	Los Angeles Clippers
Miami Heat	Los Angeles Lakers
Orlando Magic	Phoenix Suns
Washington Wizards	Sacramento Kings

SOURCE: Created by Stephen Meyer for Gale, © 2018

compete against each other in the NBA Finals, the winner receiving the Larry O'Brien Trophy.

NBA History

Basketball was invented in 1891 by James Naismith (1861–1939), a Canadian physical education instructor and physician. Working at a Young Men's Christian Association (YMCA) in Springfield, Massachusetts, Naismith was directed by the head of the physical education department to create an indoor athletic game that would keep a class of young men occupied during the winter months. In two weeks Naismith had developed the game, including the original 13 rules of basketball. Among them: "A player cannot run with the ball" and "The referee shall be judge of the ball and shall decide when the ball is in play, in bounds, to which side it belongs, and shall keep the time." Although he never sought recognition for his invention, Naismith was present at the 1936 Olympic Games in Berlin, Germany, basketball's first appearance as an Olympic event.

Basketball was first played professionally in 1896, when members of a YMCA team in Trenton, New Jersey, left to form a squad that would play for money. Two years later a group of New Jersey sports journalists founded the National Basketball League (NBL), which consisted of six teams based in Pennsylvania and New Jersey. The NBL petered out after several years, but during the mid-1930s a new league with the same name was founded. A second professional league, the Basketball Association of America (BAA), was formed by a group of New York entrepreneurs. The BAA, which was in direct competition with the NBL, had teams in New York, Boston, Philadelphia, Chicago, and Detroit. Right before the start of the 1948–49 season, four NBL teams—Minneapolis, Rochester, Fort Wayne, and Indianapolis—joined the BAA, and the following year the NBL's six surviving teams followed suit. The BAA was then divided into three divisions and renamed the National Basketball Association. One division was eliminated the following year, leaving the two that became the forerunners of the modern Eastern Conference and Western Conference of the NBA.

The NBA had no serious competition for the next two decades. That changed in 1967 with the formation of the American Basketball Association (ABA). The ABA lured fans, and quite a few players, away from the NBA with a flashier style of play that featured a red, white, and blue ball. The ABA disbanded in 1976, and several of its teams became part of the NBA. By the late 1970s, however, professional basketball's popularity was sagging. Revenue and television ratings were down, and the game had become dull. The league received a huge boost with the emergence of two new stars: Magic Johnson (1959–) of the Los Angeles Lakers and Larry Bird (1956–) of the Boston Celtics, who together are credited with ushering in a new era of popularity and prosperity to the NBA. Behind Johnson and Bird, the Lakers and the Celtics dominated the NBA throughout the 1980s. During the 1990s the game's biggest star was Michael Jordan (1963–) of the Chicago Bulls. With the charismatic Jordan leading the way, the NBA continued to thrive through most of the decade.

After the 1997–98 season, tensions between players and owners began to heighten, as the salary cap and other issues came to a head. The owners instituted a player lockout, and the two sides did not reach an agreement until January 1999, by which time more than a third of the regular season had been canceled.

At the turn of the 21st century there was a dramatic increase in the number of foreign-born players in the NBA. According to the league, in "NBA Rosters Feature 108 International Players from Record 42 Countries and Territories" (October 17, 2017, http://www.nba.com/article/2017/10/17/nba-international-players-2017-18-season-record-countries), players from 42 countries and territories were on NBA rosters at the beginning of the 2017–18 season, a new league record. Overall, 108 foreign-born players were on NBA rosters at that time, a slight drop from the record 113 foreign-born players who were in the league at the beginning of the 2016–17 season.

Current Issues in the NBA

Basketball has a soft salary cap, meaning the amount a team can spend on salaries is limited, but there are loopholes and complications. As a result, there are still great disparities in how much the teams spend. According to Basketball-Reference.com, in "NBA Contracts Summary" (2018, https://www.basketball-reference.com/contracts/), the Golden State Warriors was due to pay $137.5 million on player salaries during the 2017–18 season, the most in the league. By comparison, the Dallas Mavericks was on track to pay its players a total of only $85.9 million. As of April 2018, only seven NBA teams were below the roughly $99.1 million salary cap for the 2017–18 season. Table 4.4 shows the history of the NBA salary cap since 1984.

Beginning in the late 1980s it became increasingly common for top college players to leave school before graduating and enter the NBA draft. By the mid-1990s the best high school players were forgoing college altogether and moving straight into the professional ranks. The NBA has long sought to discourage players from making the jump from high school to the pros. Toward

TABLE 4.4

National Basketball Association salary cap per season, 1984–85 to 2017–18

NBA season	NBA salary cap
1984–85	$3.6 million
1985–86	$4.233 million
1986–87	$4.945 million
1987–88	$6.164 million
1988–89	$7.232 million
1989–90	$9.802 million
1990–91	$11.871 million
1991–92	$12.5 million
1992–93	$14 million
1993–94	$15.175 million
1994–95	$15.964 million
1995–96	$23 million
1996–97	$24.363 million
1997–98	$26.9 million
1998–99	$30 million
1999–2000	$34 million
2000–01	$35.5 million
2001–02	$42.5 million
2002–03	$40.271 million
2003–04	$43.84 million
2004–05	$43.87 million
2005–06	$49.5 million
2006–07	$53.135 million
2007–08	$55.63 million
2008–09	$58.68 million
2009–10	$57.7 million
2010–11	$58.044 million
2011–12	$58.044 million
2012–13	$58.044 million
2013–14	$58.679 million
2014–15	$63.065 million
2015–16	$70 million
2016–17	$94.143 million
2017–18	$99.093 million

SOURCE: Created by Stephen Meyer for Gale, © 2018

that end, in 1995 the league enacted a salary limit for rookies, in the hopes of making the move less enticing.

In June 2005, as another labor dispute seemed possible, the league and the players union reached a new collective bargaining agreement. In "The NBA's New Labor Deal: What It Means, Who It Impacts" (SportsBusinessDaily.com, June 27, 2005), Liz Mullen and John Lombardo explain that the agreement's key provisions included a new rule that prevented players from entering the NBA straight out of high school, increased drug testing, set a 3% increase in the salary cap, and reduced the maximum length of free-agent contracts from seven to six years. This deal remained in effect through the 2010–11 season, after which NBA players and owners once again found themselves in negotiations over a new collective bargaining agreement.

Chris Sheridan reports in "Sources: NBA, Union to Meet Monday" (ESPN.com, July 28, 2011) that NBA players wanted a six-year deal and agreed to reduce their share of league revenues from 57% to 54.6%, a pay cut of roughly $100 million per season. Owners, for their part, insisted on implementing a hard salary cap, like the one that was adopted by the NFL. In July 2011, after the two sides failed to forge a deal, the league imposed a lockout. Negotiations dragged over the next several months, and summer training camps, exhibition games, and the first month of regular-season games were canceled. Finally, in late November 2011 players and owners came to an agreement. In "Breaking Down Changes in New CBA" (ESPN.com, November 28, 2011), Larry Coon indicates that the new collective bargaining agreement granted players 51.2% of all basketball-related income, which was a sizable decrease from the 57% they received under the previous agreement. Furthermore, the new agreement mandated that teams spend at least 85% of the salary cap on player salaries during the 2011–12 and 2012–13 seasons, and 90% thereafter; under the old agreement, a team could spend as little as 75% of the cap on its players. In principle, the new agreement would be effective for 10 years, although either side had the option of opting out in 2017. After reaching the deal, the league announced that the 2011–12 season would consist of 66 games, beginning on Christmas Day.

WOMEN'S NATIONAL BASKETBALL ASSOCIATION

The Women's National Basketball Association (WNBA) started play in June 1997 following the celebrated gold medal run of the US women's basketball team during the 1996 Olympics. There had been other professional women's basketball leagues before, but the WNBA was launched with the full support of the NBA, making it much more viable than other upstart leagues. At its inception, the WNBA already had television deals in place with the National Broadcasting Company (NBC), ESPN, and the Lifetime network.

During its first season the WNBA had eight teams. By 1999 four more teams had joined the league. That same year the players and the league signed the first collective bargaining agreement in the history of women's professional sports. Four more teams were added in 2000. Following the 2002 season, the league's ownership structure was changed. Previously, the NBA owned all the teams in the WNBA. In 2002, however, the NBA sold the women's teams either to their NBA counterparts in the same city or to outside parties.

As of 2018, there were 12 teams in the WNBA: six in the East Conference and six in the West Conference. (See Table 4.5.) Each team plays a 34-game regular-season schedule, with the top-four teams in each conference competing in the playoffs. The first and second rounds of the playoffs are best-of-three series, while the WNBA Finals are best of five. The WNBA season starts in the summer, when the NBA season ends.

Although the WNBA has gained in popularity, it has been slow to achieve financial success. The league did reach a significant milestone in 2010, when the Connecticut Sun became the first team in WNBA history to turn a profit. Pat Eaton-Robb indicates in "WNBA Hoping to Take Lessons from Sun's Profit" (Associated Press, June 6, 2011) that Laurel J. Richie (1959?–), the incoming league president, saw the Sun as a valuable model for all WNBA franchises. "I think the league, as well as the teams themselves, are always looking for best practices and successes that can be replicated," Richie was quoted as saying. "One of the lessons that I take from Connecticut that it's important having a good venue that attracts a lot of people, that is easy to fill, that is easy to get to." In "WNBA: Basketball Courts Full of Women" (Forbes.com, October 22, 2012), Alana Glass reports that by 2012 three WNBA teams—the Connecticut Sun, the Minnesota Lynx, and the San Antonio Stars—had become profitable. Nevertheless, according to Richard Sandomir, in "After Two Decades, W.N.B.A. Still Struggling for Relevance" (NYTimes.com, May 28, 2016), as of 2016 half of the league's 12 teams continued to lose money each year.

TABLE 4.5

Women's National Basketball Association teams and divisions

East Conference	West Conference
Atlanta Dream	Dallas Wings
Chicago Sky	Los Angeles Sparks
Connecticut Sun	Minnesota Lynx
Indiana Fever	Phoenix Mercury
New York Liberty	San Antonio Stars
Washington Mystics	Seattle Storm

SOURCE: Created by Stephen Meyer for Gale, © 2018

NATIONAL HOCKEY LEAGUE

In "The NHL's Most Valuable Teams" (Forbes.com, December 5, 2017), Ozanian notes that the NHL's revenues topped $4.4 billion during the 2016–17 season. The league's most-valuable team, the New York Rangers, was worth $1.5 billion in 2017–18. (See Figure 4.4.) Only three other teams—the Toronto Maple Leafs ($1.4 billion), the Montreal Canadiens ($1.3 billion), and the Chicago Blackhawks ($1 billion)—were worth $1 billion or more that year.

NHL Structure and Administration

The 31-team NHL is divided into the Eastern Conference and the Western Conference. (See Table 4.6.) Each conference consists of two divisions. The Eastern Conference is split into the Atlantic Division and the Metropolitan Division, each consisting of eight teams. The Western Conference consists of the seven-team Central Division and the eight-team Pacific Division. NHL teams play an 82-game regular season that is split evenly between home and away games.

At the conclusion of the regular season, the three top teams in each division, plus the two teams in each conference with the next-best records, compete in the Stanley Cup Playoffs. The structure is similar to that of the NBA: a single-elimination tournament consisting of four rounds of best-of-seven series, culminating in the Stanley Cup Finals, which is usually played in late spring.

NHL History

Although hockey in North America started in Canada, the first professional version of the game was launched in the United States. In 1904 the International Pro Hockey League was founded in the iron-mining areas of Michigan's Upper Peninsula. That league lasted only a few years, but in 1910 a new league, the National Hockey Association (NHA), arose. The Pacific Coast League was founded soon after the NHA. It was arranged that the champions of the two leagues would play a championship series, the winner gaining possession of the coveted Stanley Cup, a trophy named for Frederick Arthur Stanley (1841–1908), a former British governor-general of Canada.

World War I (1914–1918) put a temporary halt to the fledgling sport, but when the war ended professional hockey reorganized itself as the National Hockey League. At first, the NHL was strictly a Canadian affair. The league initially consisted of five teams: Montreal Canadiens, Montreal Wanderers, Ottawa Senators, Quebec Bulldogs, and Toronto Arenas (later renamed the Maple Leafs). The first game took place in December 1917. During the 1920s the NHL expanded into the United States, adding the Boston Bruins in 1924; the New York

FIGURE 4.4

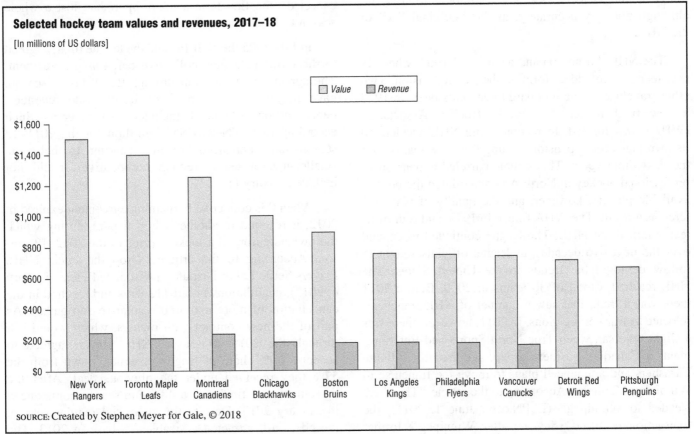

Selected hockey team values and revenues, 2017–18

[In millions of US dollars]

SOURCE: Created by Stephen Meyer for Gale, © 2018

TABLE 4.6

National Hockey League teams and divisions

Eastern Conference	Western Conference
Atlantic Division	**Central Division**
Boston Bruins	Chicago Blackhawks
Buffalo Sabres	Colorado Avalanche
Detroit Red Wings	Dallas Stars
Florida Panthers	Minnesota Wild
Montreal Canadiens	Nashville Predators
Ottawa Senators	St. Louis Blues
Tampa Bay Lightning	Winnipeg Jets
Toronto Maple Leafs	
Metropolitan Division	**Pacific Division**
Carolina Hurricanes	Anaheim Ducks
Columbus Blue Jackets	Arizona Coyotes
New Jersey Devils	Calgary Flames
New York Islanders	Edmonton Oilers
New York Rangers	Los Angeles Kings
Philadelphia Flyers	San Jose Sharks
Pittsburgh Penguins	Vancouver Canucks
Washington Capitals	Vegas Golden Knights

SOURCE: Created by Stephen Meyer for Gale, © 2018

Americans and the Pittsburgh Pirates in 1925; and the New York Rangers, the Chicago Blackhawks, and the Detroit Cougars (which later became the Red Wings) in 1926. By the end of the 1930–31 season there were 10 teams in the NHL. The Great Depression and World War II took their toll on the league, however, and by its 25th anniversary the NHL was reduced to six teams. Those six teams—the Canadiens, Maple Leafs, Red Wings, Bruins, Rangers, and Blackhawks—are commonly referred to, although not very accurately, as the "Original Six" of the NHL.

The NHL did not expand again until 1967, when six new teams were added, forming their own division. Two other franchises came on board three years later. In 1972 a new rival league, the World Hockey Association (WHA), was formed. In response, the NHL accelerated its own plans for expansion, adding four new teams over the next three years. This double-barreled expansion of professional hockey in North America diluted the pool of available players, however, and the quality of play suffered as a result. The WHA folded in 1979, and four of its teams joined the NHL. The league continued to expand over the next two decades, as league officials sought to follow demographic trends in the United States. The NHL reached a total of 30 teams in 2000. Before 2011 there was a trend that saw a number of NHL franchises relocate to warmer locations. In 2011, however, there was a slight reversal, when True North Sports and Entertainment, a Canadian business group, acquired the Atlanta Thrashers and announced plans to move the franchise to Winnipeg, Manitoba. According to the article "Thrashers Headed to Winnipeg" (ESPN.com, June 1, 2011), the transaction occurred 15 years after Winnipeg's former

NHL team, the Jets, moved to Phoenix, Arizona, to become the Coyotes. Soon after moving the Thrashers to Winnipeg, True North officially renamed the team the Jets. In June 2016 league owners approved the addition of a new expansion team, the Vegas Golden Knights, which began play during the 2017–18 season.

Labor Issues in the NHL: A Season on Ice

In its long history the NHL has been interrupted only three times by labor strife. The first, a 1992 strike by the NHL Players Association (NHLPA), lasted only 10 days and was short enough for all missed games to be made up. A lockout at the start of the 1994–95 season was more disruptive. It lasted three months and resulted in the cancellation of 36 games, nearly half of the regular season.

With the 1995 deal moving toward its 2004 expiration date, negotiations between players and owners turned bitter. Unlike the 1994 lockout, which came at a time when the NHL was enjoying strong fan support and rising popularity, interest in the league had been waning for several years by 2004. As in other major sports, one of the biggest points of contention was proposed limits on the amount teams could spend on player salaries. The league proposed what it called cost certainty, which the NHLPA argued was just a fancy term for a salary cap. The union rejected the idea and instead proposed a luxury tax. Not surprisingly, the owners were opposed. The two sides failed to reach an agreement, and the entire 2004–05 season, from preseason training through the Stanley Cup Finals, was canceled—the first time a major sport had lost a whole season to labor unrest.

In July 2005 the NHLPA and the league finally agreed to the terms of a new collective bargaining agreement. The agreement, which ran through the 2011–12 season, gave players 54% to 57% of league-wide revenues, depending on the total. It included a salary cap—which according to ESPN was $64.3 million for the 2011–12 season—and enhanced revenue sharing to help the smaller-market teams remain competitive. It did not include a luxury tax.

When this collective bargaining agreement expired in 2012, it resulted in another labor dispute, during which the owners enforced a lockout prior to the 2012–13 season. According to the article "Drop the Puck: NHL, Players Settle Labor Dispute" (Associated Press, January 6, 2013), negotiations lasted 113 days and resulted in the cancellation of more than 480 regular-season games. As part of the new contract with owners, which would last through the 2019–20 season, NHL players agreed to accept a 50% share of league revenues, down from the 57% they received under the previous deal. After the agreement was finalized, a 48-game season commenced in January 2013. Despite the shortened regular season, the NHL still attracted a sizable fan base in 2013. The

NBC Sports Group notes in the press release "Regular-Season NHL Viewership on NBC Sports Network Is Best on Cable in Nearly Two Decades" (April 30, 2013, http://nbcsportsgrouppressbox.com/2013/04/30/regular-season-nhl-viewership-on-nbc-sports-network-is-best-on-cable-in-nearly-two-decades) that an average of 1.5 million viewers tuned into NHL broadcasts on NBC during the 2012–13 season, a 15% increase over the previous season. According to Austin Karp, in "NBC, NBCSN See Viewership Figures Decline for '14–15 NHL Regular Season" (SportsBusinessDaily.com, April 15, 2015), average viewership for NHL broadcasts on NBC rose to 1.7 million in 2013–14, before dropping to a little over 1.5 million in 2014–15. In "Sabres Lead Way in NHL Local Ratings, but Some Strong Markets See Declines" (SportsBusiness Daily.com, April 24, 2017), John Ourand and Ian Thomas report that in 2016–17 NHL broadcasts on NBC drew an average viewership of 1.2 million, the lowest figure on record and a 20% decline from the previous year.

MAJOR LEAGUE SOCCER

Major League Soccer (MLS), the premier professional soccer league in the United States, was launched in April 1996. The MLS has a unique ownership and operating structure that is unlike those of other major US sports leagues. Whereas the other leagues are confederations of independent franchise owners, the MLS has a single-entity structure, which allows investors to own a share of the league as well as individual teams.

As of the 2018 season, the MLS consisted of 22 teams that were equally divided into the Eastern and Western Conferences. (See Table 4.7.) Teams compete through a season that runs from April through the MLS Cup championship in November. Each team plays 34 regular-season games, which are evenly divided between home and away matches. Eight teams advance to the MLS Cup Playoffs, which begin in mid-October and culminate in the crowning of a new MLS Cup champion.

TABLE 4.7

Major League Soccer teams and divisions

Eastern Conference	Western Conference
Atlanta United FC	Colorado Rapids
Chicago Fire	FC Dallas
Columbus Crew SC	Houston Dynamo
D.C. United	LA Galaxy
Montreal Impact	Minnesota United
New England Revolution	Portland Timbers
New York City FC	Real Salt Lake
New York Red Bulls	San Jose Earthquakes
Orlando City FC	Seattle Sounders FC
Philadelphia Union	Sporting Kansas City
Toronto FC	Vancouver Whitecaps

SOURCE: Created by Stephen Meyer for Gale, © 2018

Plans to start up the MLS were first announced in December 1993. Twenty-two cities submitted bids to secure teams, of which 10 were selected. A player draft was conducted in February 1996, and the league's first game took place that April. Two additional teams were added in 1998. The following year the Columbus Crew, based in Columbus, Ohio, built the first major league stadium ever constructed specifically for soccer in the United States. The Crew ended up leading the league in attendance for the year.

In 2002 the league was forced to cut two teams for financial reasons, returning the MLS to its original 10-team size. Two new teams were added in 2005, bringing the league to 12 teams once again. The addition of the Toronto Football Club (FC) before the 2007 season made the league 13 strong. The San Jose Earthquakes morphed into the expansion Houston Dynamo in 2005, but a new version of the Earthquakes was formed in San Jose in 2008. The Seattle Sounders joined the league in 2009, followed by the Philadelphia Union in 2010, the Portland Timbers and the Vancouver Whitecaps FC in 2011, and the Montreal Impact in 2012. After the Chivas USA squad was dissolved following the 2014 season, two new franchises joined the league in 2015: the New York City FC and the Orlando City FC. Two additional teams, the Atlanta United FC and the Minnesota United FC, began competing in the MLS in 2017.

Women's Professional Soccer

Women's professional soccer in the United States has not met with great success, but players and fans are hopeful that its most recent incarnation, the National Women's Soccer League, will catch on. The first women's professional outdoor league to be sanctioned by US Soccer, the Women's United Soccer Association, was launched in 2001. It featured stars from the popular 2000 US Olympic team, including Mia Hamm (1972–), Brandi Chastain (1968–), and Julie Foudy (1971–). Faced with financial struggles, the association suspended operations in September 2003.

In 2004 a new nonprofit organization, the Women's Soccer Initiative, was established with the goal of reviving women's professional soccer in the United States. In September 2007 the Women's Soccer Initiative announced plans to relaunch a professional women's league in 2009. Women's Professional Soccer opened its inaugural season in March 2009, with seven teams each playing 20 regular-season games. After the league disbanded in 2012, the National Women's Soccer League (NWSL) was formed. Consisting of eight teams, the league launched its inaugural season in 2013. As of 2018, the NWSL consisted of 10 teams, each of which played 24 games between mid-April and late September.

THE STADIUM SCRAMBLE

Since the early 1990s there has been an unprecedented boom in the construction of new stadiums for US sports teams. The main reason is that team owners believe they can make more money selling skyboxes to wealthy corporate customers than they can by selling cheaper seats to the masses, and many older stadiums lack luxury accommodations. A skybox can sell for more than $300,000 per season. An additional incentive is that the revenue from sales of these luxury skyboxes is exempt from the revenue-sharing formulas of both the MLB and the NFL, meaning that teams get to keep all the money that is generated from skybox sales.

Public Funding for Stadiums

The use of public funds in the construction of professional sports venues remains highly controversial. Steven Malanga reveals in "The Public Dollars Fueling the NFL Dispute" (RealClearMarkets.com, June 1, 2011) that the NFL built or renovated 13 stadiums between 1993 and 1999 at a cost of $3.3 billion. Of this, $2.4 billion (73%) came from public funds. Even after the league created a stadium loan program, known as the G-3 fund, in 1999, public financing continued to play a major role in the construction and renovation of new NFL venues. According to Malanga, the NFL built or renovated 12 more stadiums between 1999 and 2011, at a total cost of nearly $8 billion; of this sum, roughly 40% came from public funding. One of the most impressive NFL venues ever built, Cowboys Stadium (now called AT&T Stadium) in Arlington, Texas, opened in 2009 at a total cost of $1.2 billion, according to Ballparks.com (2015, http://football .ballparks.com/NFL/DallasCowboys/newindex.htm). To help finance construction, the Dallas Cowboys received $325 million from the city of Arlington. As a result, sales tax in the city rose 0.5%, while the hotel tax rose 2% and the car rental tax rose 5%.

NFL owners usually argue that a new stadium will generate additional tax revenue because as fans flock to the new facility they will spend vast sums of money at nearby businesses. Opponents, however, of public funding for stadiums have challenged this view. In "Do Economists Reach a Conclusion on Subsidies for Sports Franchises, Stadiums, and Mega-Events?" (*Econ Journal Watch*, vol. 5, no. 3, September 2008), Dennis Coates and Brad R. Humphreys report on survey data and economic research measuring the benefits of subsidies for sports facilities and conclude that from an economic standpoint, most research does not support subsidies.

Corporate Sponsorship of Stadiums

Another source of revenue from stadiums comes from the sale of naming rights. Whereas in the past most stadiums had straightforward names such as Tiger Stadium or the Houston Astrodome, in the 21st century an increasing number of facilities bear the name of a corporate sponsor that has paid millions of dollars for the privilege. Badenhausen reports in "Warriors, Chase Bank Tie-Up Ranks among Biggest Stadium Naming Rights Deals Ever" (Forbes.com, January 28, 2016) that the following were the three most lucrative stadium naming deals as of 2018:

- MetLife Stadium in East Rutherford, New Jersey, home of football's New York Giants and New York Jets ($450 million for 25 years)

- AT&T Stadium in Arlington, home of football's Cowboys ($400 million for 20 years)

- Citi Field in Flushing, New York, home of baseball's New York Mets ($400 million for 20 years)

Sometimes these deals backfire. For example, in 1999 Enron, a US energy company, signed a 30-year, $100 million deal with the Houston Astros. In 2001 Enron filed for bankruptcy following an accounting scandal. The collapse of the company forced the Astros to buy their way out of the deal to get Enron's name off their stadium. In 2002 a new sponsor was found, and the stadium was rechristened Minute Maid Park.

CHAPTER 5
OTHER PROFESSIONAL SPORTS

As important as professional team sports are in the United States, Americans' sports obsession extends well beyond them. Not every sports enthusiast is engrossed by the hoopla of *Monday Night Football* or the high-flying acrobatics of the National Basketball Association. Some fans prefer the quiet beauty of a perfect putt or the battle of wills that takes place across the Centre Court net at Wimbledon. Others are attracted to the "sweet science" of boxing or the raw speed of the National Association for Stock Car Auto Racing. This chapter considers several sports that fall below the top tier of US sports in terms of audience or revenue but are nevertheless important components of the nation's professional sports culture.

GOLF

Professional golf in the United States is coordinated by the Professional Golfers' Association (PGA) of America, a nonprofit organization that promotes the sport while enhancing golf's professional standards. The PGA of America (https://www.pga.com/pga-america) states that in 2018 there were nearly 29,000 PGA professionals in the United States, both men and women, making it the largest working sports organization in the world. Nevertheless, most of these members were primarily golf instructors; only a small fraction competed in high-profile tournaments. According to R&A Championships Limited, in *Golf around the World 2017* (March 13, 2017, https://www.randa.org/~/media/Files/DownloadsAndPublications/Golf-around-the-world-2017.ashx), as of year-end 2016, there were 33,161 golf courses in 208 countries worldwide. Of these, 45% were in the United States. One of the most celebrated courses in the world is the Augusta National Golf Club in Augusta, Georgia, the site of the annual Masters Tournament. First opened in 1932 by the golfing legend Bobby Jones (1902–1971), Augusta National is distinctive for its natural beauty, with flowering dogwood, camellia, and azalea bushes scattered throughout the course and fairways lined with enormous pine trees. Other notable US courses include Pebble Beach Golf Links in Pebble Beach, California; Shinnecock Hills Golf Club in Southampton, New York; and Pinehurst Resort in Pinehurst, North Carolina.

The PGA of America traces its roots to 1916, when a group of golf professionals and serious amateurs in the New York area got together at a luncheon that was sponsored by the department store magnate Lewis Rodman Wanamaker (1863–1928). The purpose of the meeting was to discuss forming a national organization to promote golf and elevate the occupation of golf professionals. The meeting led to the organization of the first PGA Championship tournament, which was played later that year. The PGA Championship has grown to become one of professional golf's four major championships, along with the Open Championship (formerly the British Open), the Masters, and the US Open. Together, these four tournaments make up the unofficial Grand Slam of Golf. (See Table 5.1.) Besides the PGA Championship, the PGA of America sponsors three other top golf events: the Senior PGA Championship; the Ryder Cup, which every two years pits a team of top US golfers against their European counterparts; and the PGA Grand Slam of Golf, an annual event in which the winners of the four major championships compete head to head. Besides these championships, the PGA of America also conducts about 40 tournaments for PGA professionals. In October 2009 the International Olympic Committee voted to include golf in the 2016 Summer Olympics.

Worldwide, professional golf is organized into several regional tours, each of which usually holds a series of tournaments over the course of a season. There are approximately 20 of these tours around the world, each run by a national or regional PGA or by an independent tour organization. Joining a tour usually requires that a golfer achieve some specified level of success, often by

TABLE 5.1

Golf Grand Slam events

Event	Location	Scheduled time
Masters Tournament	Augusta, Georgia	April
US Open	Location varies	June
Open Championship	United Kingdom (location varies)	July
PGA Championship	Location varies	August

SOURCE: Created by Stephen Meyer for Gale, © 2018

performing well in a qualifying tournament. A player can be a member of multiple tours.

The History of the PGA

According to WorldGolf, in "A History of the PGA Tour" (2018, http://www.worldgolf.com/wglibrary/history/tourhist.html), the first US Open took place in 1895 in Newport, Rhode Island. Ten professionals and one amateur competed in the event. Four years later the Western Open made its debut in Chicago, Illinois. Tournaments were initiated throughout the country at about this time, although there was no coordination or continuity among them. British players dominated the competition in US tournaments. As interest in golf continued to grow, US players improved. Enthusiasm for the sport began to increase after Johnny McDermott (1891–1971) became the first US-born player to win the US Open in 1911. By the 1920s professional golf had spread to the West Coast and southward to Florida, and the prize money was becoming substantial.

The PGA Tour was formally launched in late 1968, when the Tournament Players Division of the PGA broke away from the parent organization. The tour grew during the 1970s and 1980s, with its total annual revenue increasing from $3.9 million in 1974 to $229 million in 1993. In "PGA Tour's Investments Suffer in '08" (SportsBusiness Daily.com, September 7, 2009), Jon Show reports that although the PGA Tour lost financial value due to the economic downturn (which lasted from late 2007 to mid-2009), the "combined revenue from tournaments and supporting business" was still "creeping closer to the $1 billion mark" by 2008.

To a large extent, PGA revenues during these years were driven by the popularity of Tiger Woods (1975–), the world's premier golfer of the early 21st century. Indeed, Woods's impact on tournament television ratings and attendance was enormous. Michael McCarthy notes in "Financial Impact for Golf Felt All Around with Tiger Woods Gone" (USAToday.com, January 28, 2010) that when Woods missed the 2008 PGA Championship due to a knee injury, the tournament's final round attracted roughly 4 million television viewers. When Woods returned to competition the following year, television viewership for the final round of the PGA Championship

rose to 10.1 million. In December 2009, amid revelations that he had been cheating on his wife, Elin Nordegren (1980–), Woods announced that he was taking an indefinite hiatus from the game. His absence hurt the tour almost immediately. According to McCarthy, when Woods withdrew from the Chevron World Challenge, tournament organizers refunded $20,000 worth of tickets and reduced the price on 2010 tickets by 20%. In the aftermath of his infidelity scandal, Woods himself lost lucrative sponsorship deals with Accenture, AT&T, and Gillette.

By 2013 Woods appeared to have once again claimed his place as the top-ranked golfer in the world. He won five titles that year, while earning the 2013 PGA Tour Player of the Year Award. Still, the quest for a 15th major continued to elude Woods. In 2014 he placed 69th in the Open Championship and missed the cut (failed to achieve a good enough score to continue in the second portion of the tournament) at the PGA Championship. The following year Woods tied for 17th at the Masters Tournament, while failing to make the cut at the US Open.

Meanwhile, a new generation of golfers is beginning to eclipse Woods as the most prominent representatives of the sport. According to the PGA, in "Official World Golf Ranking" (2018, https://www.pgatour.com/stats/stat.186.2017.html), the world's top-ranked golfer at the start of 2018 was Dustin Johnson (1984–), winner of the 2016 US Open as well as 17 career PGA Tour events. The world's second-ranked golfer at that time, Jordan Spieth (1993–), first achieved fame in 2015, when he won both the Master's and the US Open at the age of only 21. By early 2018 Spieth had won three major tournaments to go with 11 PGA Tour wins. Another leading figure in men's golf was Rory McIlroy (1989–), who won four major championships before the age of 25, and entered 2018 as the sixth-ranked golfer in the world.

The Champions Tour

The Champions Tour (2018, http://www.pgatour.com/champions/tournaments/schedule.html), which is run by the PGA Tour, hosts 29 events each year in the United States and Canada for golfers at least 50 years old. Many of the most successful players on the PGA Tour go on to play on the Champions Tour when they reach age 50. The tour grew out of a highly successful 1978 event called the Legends of Golf, which featured two-member teams composed of some of the game's best-known former champions. Following the success of the Legends event, the Senior PGA Tour was established in 1980. The Senior Tour proved remarkably popular, as fans flocked to golf courses and tuned in on television to see legendary competitors such as Arnold Palmer (1929–2016) and Sam Snead (1912–2002) in action. At the start of the 2003 season, the Senior Tour changed its name to the Champions Tour.

Most tournaments on the Champions Tour are played over three rounds (54 holes) rather than the customary four rounds (72 holes) of PGA tournaments. The five majors of the senior circuit are exceptions; they are played over four rounds. The major tournaments of the Champions Tour are the Senior PGA Championship, the Senior Players Championship, the Senior Open Championship (formerly the Senior British Open), the US Senior Open, and the Regions Tradition. Notable stars of the 2018 Champions Tour included Bernhard Langer (1957–), Steve Stricker (1967–), and Scott McCarron (1965–).

The Web.com Tour

The Web.com Tour is the developmental tour for the PGA Tour. Its players are professionals who have missed the criteria to get into the main tour by failing to score well enough in the PGA Tour's qualifying tournament, known as the Qualifying School, or who have made it into the main tour but failed to win enough money to stay there. The Web.com Tour gets its name from the internet services company Web.com of Jacksonville, Florida, which bought the naming rights in 2012. The tour was previously called the Nike Tour, the Buy.com Tour, and the Nationwide Tour. When the tour was first launched in its original form in 1990, it was known as the Ben Hogan Tour. In 2018 the Web.com Tour (http://www.pgatour .com/webcom/tournaments/schedule.html) consisted of 27 regular-season events.

Women's Tours

Women's professional golf, like men's golf, is organized into several regional tours. The top tour for female professional golfers is the Ladies Professional Golf Association (LPGA), which operates the LPGA Tour. Unlike the PGA Tour, the LPGA Tour and the LPGA are not distinct organizations. Both of these terms generally refer to the LPGA that is based in the United States. Internationally, there are other regional LPGAs and tours, including the LPGA of Japan, the LPGA of Korea, the Australian Ladies Professional Golf Tour, and the Ladies European Tour.

Founded in 1950 by a group of 13 golfers, the LPGA is the oldest continuing women's professional sports organization in the United States. It features the best female golfers from all over the world. The 2018 LPGA Tour (http://www.lpga.com/tournaments) consisted of 29 regular-season tournaments, as well as five majors: the US Women's Open, the KPMG Women's PGA Championship, the Ricoh Women's British Open (held jointly with the Ladies European Tour), the ANA Inspiration, and the Evian Championship.

Besides the main tour, the LPGA also coordinates a developmental tour called the Symetra Tour, once known as the Futures Tour. The Futures Tour began in Florida in 1981 as the Tampa Bay Mini Tour but is now a national tour that functions as a feeder system for the LPGA, filling the same role as the Web .com Tour does for the men. In 2001 the LPGA also created the Women's Senior Golf Tour for players over the age of 45 years. Its name was changed to the Legends Tour before the 2006 season. In 2017 the Legends Tour (http://www.thelegendstour .com/tournaments) showcased seven events.

Women in the PGA

Ever since Babe Didrikson Zaharias (1911–1956) played in the 1938 Los Angeles Open, there have been women who seek to achieve crossover success competing against men in PGA events. During the early 21st century most of the attention focused on Annika Sorenstam (1970–) and Michelle Wie (1989–). In 2003 Sorenstam was dominating women's golf almost as thoroughly as Woods was towering over his male competitors. That year, she accepted a sponsor's invitation to compete in the Bank of America Colonial tournament, where she missed the cut by four strokes. Sorenstam retired from professional golf in 2008. Between 2003 and 2008 Wie played against men in 13 PGA events, making the cut once at the 2006 SK Telecom Open. Besides Wie, top LPGA golfers in 2018 included Inbee Park (1988–), winner of the 2015 KPMG Women's PGA Championship and the world's top-ranked golfer; Shanshan Feng (1989–), winner of the 2012 LPGA Championship; Lexi Thompson (1995–), winner of the 2014 Kraft Nabisco Championship (later the ANA Inspiration); So Yeon Ryu (1990–), winner of the 2011 US Women's Open and the 2017 ANA Inspiration; Sung Hyun Park (1993–), winner of the 2017 US Women's Open; and Anna Nordqvist (1987–), winner of the 2009 McDonald's LPGA Championship (later the Women's LPGA Championship) and the 2017 Evian Championship.

TENNIS

The modern sport of tennis developed out of various games that involved hitting a ball with a racket or the hand; many of these date back to ancient times. Lawn tennis was developed in 1873 in Wales by Walter C. Wingfield (1833–1912). It is based on the older sport of real tennis (also referred to as the "Sport of Kings"), which was itself based on earlier forms of racket sports. Tennis gained popularity across England, and the first world tennis championship was held just four years later at the All England Croquet Club (which eventually became known as the All England Lawn Tennis and Croquet Club) at Wimbledon. This tournament evolved into the famous Wimbledon Championships, which remain the most prestigious tennis titles to this day. A women's championship was added at Wimbledon in 1884.

In the United States, the first National Championship for men's tennis was held in 1881 in Newport, Rhode Island. A women's championship was added six years later. The National Championship moved to Forest Hills, New York, in 1915, where it remained under various names for more than 60 years. Now known as the US Open, the event has been held at the USTA Billie Jean King National Tennis Center in Flushing, New York, since 1978.

The Development of Professional Tennis

As tennis spread throughout the British Empire during the 20th century, national federations were formed in countries where the sport caught on. These federations eventually joined forces to form the International Tennis Federation (ITF), which was the worldwide sanctioning authority for tennis. International competitions between national teams soon arose, the most important being the Davis Cup tournament, founded in 1900, and the Wightman Cup, an annual competition between women's teams from England and the United States, founded in 1923.

Most sports turned professional during the first half of the 20th century, but tennis largely remained an amateur endeavor, a pastime for wealthy country club members. By the late 1920s it became economically feasible for a top player to make a decent living on the professional tour, but it meant giving up the sport's most prestigious, amateur-only events, such as those at Wimbledon and Forest Hills. The move toward professionalism accelerated after William Tatem Tilden II (1893–1953), the best player of his time and a winner of seven US singles championships and three Wimbledon titles as an amateur, turned professional in 1931. Over the next few decades more and more top players trickled into the professional ranks, although the ITF fought hard against the professionalization of tennis. In 1968 the All England Lawn Tennis and Croquet Club decided to open Wimbledon to professional players, thus ushering in the "open era" of tennis in which professional players are allowed to compete in the sport's biggest tournaments.

About this time women players became frustrated at the gender disparity in tennis prize money. Women winning a tournament often received a mere fraction of what the men's champion in the same tournament took home. In 1971 a women-only professional tour was formed to address these inequities. This new Virginia Slims Tour was an instant hit. It made Billie Jean King (1943–) the first woman athlete in any sport to earn more than $100,000 in a single year.

The most important professional tennis tournaments for both men and women are those that consist of the Grand Slam: the Australian Open, the French Open, Wimbledon, and the US Open. (See Table 5.2.)

The total prize money for Wimbledon in 2017 was approximately $41.7 million, with the men's and women's singles champions each receiving a prize of about $2.9 million (based on 2017 exchange rates; http://www.wim

TABLE 5.2

Tennis Grand Slam events

Event	Location	Scheduled time
Australian Open	Melbourne	Last fortnight of January
French Open	Paris	May/June
Wimbledon	Wimbledon, England	June/July
US Open	Flushing Meadows, Queens, New York	August/September

SOURCE: Created by Stephen Meyer for Gale, © 2018

bledon.com/pdf/prize_money_2017.pdf). The 2017 US Open tennis tournament offered a payout of $50.5 million, with the men's and women's singles champions taking home $3.7 million each (2018, https://www.usopen.org/en_US/event_guide/prize_money.html).

Men's professional tennis is coordinated by the Association of Tennis Professionals (ATP), which organizes the ATP Tour (the principal worldwide tennis tour), and the ITF, which coordinates international play including the Davis Cup and the Grand Slam tournaments. The ATP was originally formed in 1972 as a sort of trade union to protect the interests of male professional tennis players. The organization assumed its role as the chief coordinating body of the professional tour in 1990. The top men players in 2018 included Roger Federer (1981–), Rafael Nadal (1986–), Marin Čilić (1988–), Grigor Dimitrov (1991–), Novak Djokovic (1987–), Andy Murray (1987–), and Alexander Zverev Jr. (1997–).

Women's professional tennis is coordinated by the Women's Tennis Association (WTA). The WTA was formed in 1973 as a professional organization to protect the interests of the players. By 1980 more than 250 women were playing professionally all over the world in a tour consisting of 47 global events. The tour remained under the governance of the Women's Tennis Council, an umbrella agency run by representatives from the ITF, the tournament promoters, and the players, into the 1990s. The WTA Tour in its current form was created in 1995 through the merger of the WTA Players Association and the Women's Tennis Council. The WTA runs the premier professional women's tour, which in 2005 became known as the Sony Ericsson WTA Tour. Among the world's best women tennis players in 2018 were Serena Williams (1981–), Simona Halep (1991–), Caroline Wozniacki (1990–), Garbiñe Muguruza (1993–), Elina Svitolina (1994–), Angelique Kerber (1988–), Venus Williams (1980–), and Karolína Plíšková (1991–).

Besides prize money, professional tennis players also earn large sums through endorsement deals and corporate sponsorships. Figure 5.1 shows the top-10 men and women tennis players, based on earnings, in 2017.

FIGURE 5.1

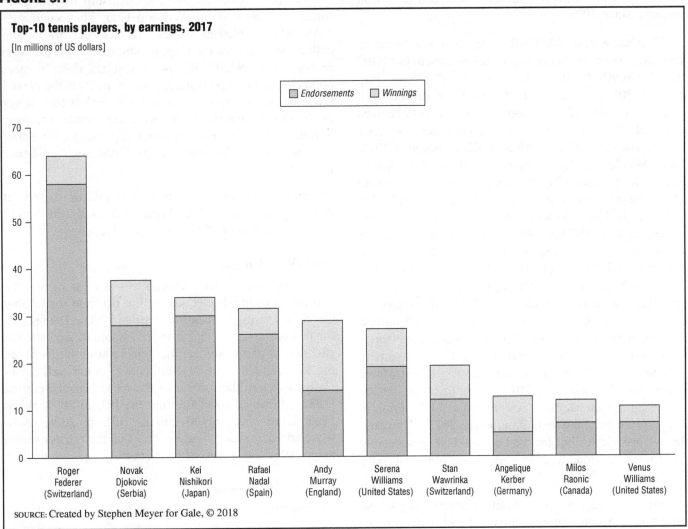

Top-10 tennis players, by earnings, 2017

[In millions of US dollars]

SOURCE: Created by Stephen Meyer for Gale, © 2018

AUTO RACING

There are several different top-level auto-racing circuits in the United States, in which different kinds of cars race. The two most popular types of race cars are stock cars and open-wheeled racers. Stock car racing is dominated by the National Association for Stock Car Auto Racing (NASCAR). Open-wheeled cars are single-seat vehicles with special aerodynamic features that allow them to travel at speeds well over 200 miles per hour (322 km/h). Open-wheeled racing was in a state of civil war between two chief circuits, the Indy Racing League (IRL) and the Champ Car Series, for several years until Champ Car was merged into the IRL in 2008. Another open-wheeled circuit, the Formula One Grand Prix, is dominant in Europe, although the Fédération Internationale de l'Automobile (FIA), the Formula One governing body, has sponsored races in the United States. Since 2012 the Formula 1 United States Grand Prix has taken place in Austin, Texas.

NASCAR

The largest sanctioning body of motor sports in the United States is NASCAR, which oversees a number of racing series, the largest among them being the NASCAR Sprint Cup, the NASCAR Nationwide Series, and the Craftsman Truck Series. Once merely a regional diversion in the South, NASCAR has exploded into a nationwide phenomenon, rivaling baseball for the number-two spot behind football for the hearts and viewing hours of US sports fans. In all, NASCAR (2018, https://www.nascar.com/content/dam/nascar/sponsorship-website/content/power-of-nascar.html) sanctions more than 1,200 races every year. Although NASCAR experienced impressive growth in popularity during the late 1990s and early 2000s, by 2005 both attendance and television viewership began to decline. David Scott and Andrew Dunn report in "NASCAR Ticket Revenue in Sharp Decline" (Heraldonline.com, July 9, 2012) that income from NASCAR ticket sales declined 38% between 2006 and 2011. In "Hendrick Motorsports Tops List of NASCAR's Most Valuable Teams" (Forbes.com, March 13, 2013), Kurt Badenhausen indicates that the sport's television ratings fell 4% between 2011 and 2012. Its popularity rebounded during the early part of 2013, as ratings for the Daytona 500, NASCAR's signature race, were up 24%

from 2012, while attracting the event's largest television audience since 2008.

That same year NASCAR signed two new lucrative television contracts. According to Badenhausen, in "NBC Nabs NASCAR TV Rights for $4.4 Billion" (Forbes.com, July 24, 2013), in July 2013 the National Broadcasting Company signed a 10-year contract to broadcast 19 Nationwide and 20 Sprint Cup races at the end of each NASCAR season. The agreement, worth $4.4 billion, began in 2015. Tripp Mickle and John Ourand report in "Fox Sports, NASCAR Finalize Rights Deal through '24 Worth $3.8B" (SportsBusinessDaily.com, August 1, 2013) that in July 2013 Fox paid $3.8 billion to extend its existing contract with NASCAR, allowing the network to air an additional three Sprint Cup and 14 Nationwide races annually through 2024. According to the article "Despite Big Increases, NASCAR Gets Off to Slow Start at Daytona" (SportingNews.com, February 27, 2015), the television audience for the Daytona 500 fell to just over 9.3 million in 2014, before surging to 13.4 million in 2015, the largest single-year increase in viewership since 1979. The article "Daytona 500 Rating Is Lowest Ever" (SportsMedia Watch.com, February 20, 2018) notes that the average viewership for the Daytona 500 slipped to 11.4 million in 2016, before climbing to 11.9 million in 2017. Thereafter, the average viewership for the Daytona 500 subsequently fell to 9.3 million in 2018, the lowest on record for the event.

Stock car racing evolved out of bootlegging in the rural South. Alcohol runners modified their cars to make them faster and more maneuverable. Eventually, these drivers began racing their souped-up cars against one another.

NASCAR was founded in 1948 by William France Sr. (1909–1992) and Edward J. Otto (1904–1996) as a way to organize, standardize, and promote racing of unmodified, or stock, cars for entertainment. The first NASCAR Strictly Stock race took place at North Carolina's Charlotte Speedway in June 1949. Over time, modifications were allowed into the sport, and by the mid-1960s only the bodies of the cars looked stock; the innards were specially built for speed.

NASCAR's rapid growth began during the 1970s, when the R. J. Reynolds Tobacco Company started sponsoring racing as a way to promote its products after they had been banned from television advertising. The top series, formerly known as the Grand National Series, became the Winston Cup. At about that time television networks began to occasionally cover stock car racing. Columbia Broadcasting System's broadcast of the 1979 Daytona 500 was the first time a stock car race had been aired nationwide from start to finish.

In 2004 Nextel assumed sponsorship of the series formerly known as the Winston Cup. That same year NASCAR established a new 10-race playoff system called the Chase for the Cup, in which the top-10 drivers (according to NASCAR's point system) after 26 races compete for the series championship. In 2008 the Nextel Cup became the Sprint Cup Series to reflect the merger of Nextel Communications with the phone company Sprint. Following another sponsorship change, the Sprint Cup became the Monster Energy NASCAR Cup Series in 2017.

Figure 5.2 shows the top-10 NASCAR drivers of 2017, by earnings, while Figure 5.3 ranks the top-10 NASCAR teams of 2017, by total value.

Open-Wheeled Cars

As millions of fans flocked to stock car racing, the two major open-wheeled series, the IRL and the Champ Car Series, struggled beginning around 2000. The reasons for this are complex, but it is reasonable to attribute the situation in part to the acrimonious relationship between the IRL and Champ Car. Neither was doing well financially, although the success of the rookie Danica Patrick (1982–) breathed some life into the IRL in 2005. When Champ Car was merged into the IRL in 2008, open-wheeled aficionados were hopeful that the merger would help restore the stature of their sport.

Indy Racing League

The IRL was formed in 1994 by a group of drivers breaking away from the Championship Auto Racing Teams (CART; later known as the Champ Car Series), which had coordinated Indy car racing since breaking away from the US Auto Club (USAC) in 1979. The IRL consists of two series: the premier IndyCar Series, which is virtually synonymous with the IRL, and the Firestone Indy Lights Series (formerly known as the Indy Pro Series), which functions as a developmental series for drivers aspiring to join the IndyCar circuit.

Before 1979 the term *IndyCar* was generically used to refer to cars racing in USAC events. By the 1980s IndyCar was a term commonly used to refer to CART, which by that time was the preeminent sanctioning body for open-wheeled racing in the United States. The name "IndyCar" became the subject of fierce legal battles during the 1990s. The Indianapolis Motor Speedway, home of the Indianapolis 500, trademarked the name in 1992 and licensed it to CART, which in turn renamed its championship the IndyCar World Series. Two years later Tony George (1959–), the president of the speedway, started his own racing series called the Indy Racing League. In 1996 CART sued to protect its right to continue using the IndyCar name. The speedway countered with its own suit. The two groups eventually reached a

FIGURE 5.2

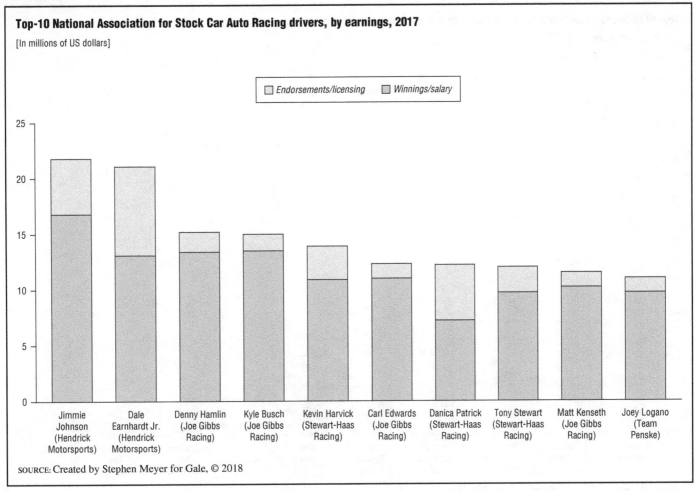

Top-10 National Association for Stock Car Auto Racing drivers, by earnings, 2017

[In millions of US dollars]

SOURCE: Created by Stephen Meyer for Gale, © 2018

settlement in which CART agreed to stop using the IndyCar name after the 1996 season, and the IRL could start using it after the 2002 season. The IRL's premier series has been called the IRL IndyCar Series since the beginning of the 2003 season. The 2018 IndyCar Series (http://www.indycar.com/schedule) featured 17 races from March to September.

Champ Car Series

The USAC was formed in 1956 to take over coordination of the national driving championship from the American Automobile Association, which had launched the championship in 1909. The USAC controlled the championship until 1979, when a group of car owners formed the Championship Auto Racing Teams that they hoped would give them power in negotiations with the USAC over media contracts, race purses, promotion, and other issues. The two entities immediately clashed, and CART soon separated from the USAC to establish its own racing series. Most of the top teams defected from the USAC, and CART quickly became the dominant open-wheeled racing circuit. The USAC held its last National Championship in 1979, before reluctantly handing the reins over to CART.

The IRL's split from CART put open-wheeled racing into a tailspin. The rivalry may have helped pave the way for NASCAR's rise, as both competing organizations struggled for control over the sport's available pot of money. In 2003 CART declared bankruptcy, and its assets were liquidated and put up for sale. A group of CART car owners bought the company and opened the 2004 season under the new name Champ Car Series. Beginning in 2005 Champ Car ran both the Champ Car World Series and the Champ Car Atlantic Championship, which functioned as a developmental circuit for drivers trying to get into Champ Car. In February 2008 the IRL and the Champ Car Series reached an agreement that unified the sport. As a result of the agreement, the Champ Car Series was discontinued.

BOXING

Boxing is unique among professional sports in that there is no nationwide commission that oversees it, no regular schedules, no seasons, and few universal rules. Every set of matches (called a card) is set up separately, usually by one of a handful of top-level boxing promoters. Each state has its own boxing commission with its own set

FIGURE 5.3

Top-10 National Association for Stock Car Auto Racing teams, by total value and revenue, 2017

[In millions of US dollars]

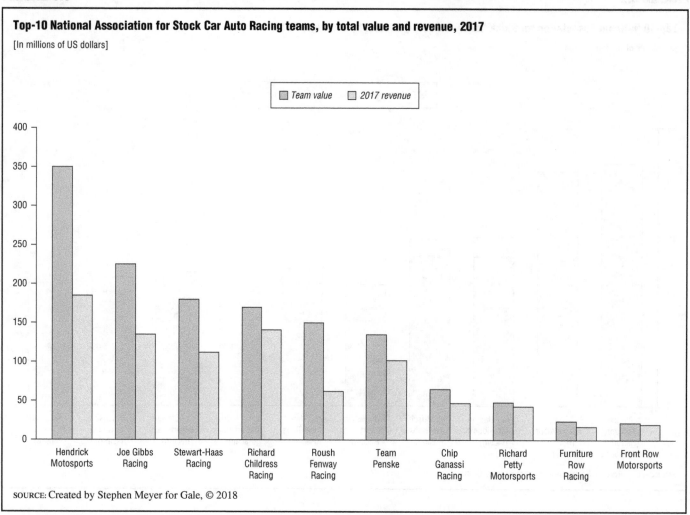

SOURCE: Created by Stephen Meyer for Gale, © 2018

of rules. In the United States and Canada, state, regional, and tribal boxing commissions are also organized into the Association of State Boxing Commissions, an umbrella organization that helps oversee and regulate professional and amateur fighting in North America.

Boxing matches in the United States consist of a maximum of 12 three-minute rounds with one minute of rest between each round. Opponents in a fight must belong to the same weight class. Table 5.3 provides a breakdown of boxing weight classes according to the sport's different sanctioning bodies. Three judges at the ringside score the fight according to a 10-point must system; that is, each judge must award 10 points to the winner of the round and fewer points to the loser of the round. Matches end in one of five ways:

- Knockout—one fighter is unable to return to his feet within 10 seconds of a knockdown

- Technical knockout—a decision is made to stop the fight because one fighter is clearly losing

- Decision—the fight ends without a knockout or technical knockout and is won based on the scoring of the three judges at the ringside

- Draw—the fight ends without a knockout or technical knockout, and the judges award each fighter the same number of points

- Disqualification—the fight is stopped because of a rule infraction on the part of one of the fighters

Unlike other professional sports, boxing does not use a playoff series or a point system to name a champion. In fact, there is not necessarily even a consensus about who is the champion of any given weight class. Different champions are recognized by several competing boxing organizations. The most prominent boxing organizations are the International Boxing Federation, the World Boxing Association, the World Boxing Council, and the World Boxing Organization. A fighter may be recognized as a champion in his weight class by more than one of these organizations at a time, or each organization may have a different champion at any given time. Some of the biggest boxing matches are unification bouts between champions who are recognized by two different sanctioning organizations, the winner walking away with both titles.

Because boxing competitions are often international in nature, it is difficult to gauge the size of the boxing

TABLE 5.3

Men's professional boxing weight classes, by sanctioning body

Weight class	Maximum weight	Sanctioning body
Minimumweight	105 pounds/47.627 kilograms	International Boxing Federation (IBF), World Boxing Association (WBA), World Boxing Council (WBC)
Mini flyweight	105 pounds/47.627 kilograms	World Boxing Organization (WBO)
Strawweight	105 pounds/47.627 kilograms	International Boxing Organization (IBO)
Light flyweight	108 pounds/48.988 kilograms	IBF, WBA, WBC
Junior flyweight	108 pounds/48.988 kilograms	WBO, IBO
Flyweight	112 pounds/50.802 kilograms	IBF, IBO, WBA, WBC, WBO
Super flyweight	115 pounds/52.163 kilograms	IBF, IBO, WBA, WBC
Junior bantamweight	115 pounds/52.163 kilograms	WBO
Bantamweight	118 pounds/53.524 kilograms	IBF, IBO, WBA, WBC, WBO
Super bantamweight	122 pounds/55.338 kilograms	IBF, IBO, WBA, WBC
Junior featherweight	122 pounds/55.338 kilograms	WBO
Featherweight	126 pounds/57.153 kilograms	IBF, IBO, WBA, WBC, WBO
Super featherweight	130 pounds/58.967 kilograms	IBF, IBO, WBA, WBC
Junior lightweight	130 pounds/58.967 kilograms	WBO
Lightweight	135 pounds/61.235 kilograms	IBF, IBO, WBA, WBC, WBO
Super lightweight	140 pounds/63.503 kilograms	IBF, WBA, WBC
Junior welterweight	140 pounds/63.503 kilograms	IBO, WBO
Welterweight	147 pounds/66.678 kilograms	IBF, IBO, WBA, WBC, WBO
Super welterweight	154 pounds/69.853 kilograms	IBF, WBA, WBC
Junior middleweight	154 pounds/69.853 kilograms	IBO, WBO
Middleweight	160 pounds/72.575 kilograms	IBF, IBO, WBA, WBC, WBO
Super middleweight	168 pounds/76.204 kilograms	IBF, IBO, WBA, WBC, WBO
Light heavyweight	175 pounds/79.379 kilograms	IBF, IBO, WBA, WBC, WBO
Cruiserweight	200 pounds/90.719 kilograms	IBF, IBO, WBA, WBC
Junior heavyweight	200 pounds/90.719 kilograms	WBO
Heavyweight	Unlimited	IBF, IBO, WBA, WBC, WBO

SOURCE: Created by Stephen Meyer for Gale, © 2018

industry in the United States. Much of the money comes from cable television, where championship fights are usually broadcast on a pay-per-view basis.

The scoring system for boxing is complex, and the overall rankings can sometimes appear arbitrary. As a result, the sport has long been a tempting target for organized crime and others seeking illicit financial gain. Even in the 21st century bribery is thought to be rampant. Mysterious judging decisions and bizarre rankings are not at all rare.

World Boxing Association

The World Boxing Association (WBA; 2018, http://www.wbanews.com) was the first sanctioning body of professional boxing. It was formed as the National Boxing Association in 1921. The first National Boxing Association–sanctioned match was a heavyweight championship fight between Jack Dempsey (1895–1983) and Georges Carpentier (1894–1975). Brilliant and colorful champions such as Joe Louis (1914–1981) carried the WBA through the World War II (1939–1945) era. The dawn of television boosted the popularity of professional boxing during the 1950s. The sport's globalization during this period led the organization to change its name in 1962 to the World Boxing Association, an entity that would usher through future legends such as Muhammad Ali (1942–2016).

World Boxing Council

The World Boxing Council (WBC; 2018, http://www.wbcboxing.com) was formed in 1963 by representatives

of 11 countries (Argentina, Brazil, Japan, Mexico, Panama, Peru, the Philippines, Spain, the United Kingdom, the United States, and Venezuela) and Puerto Rico (a territory of the United States). Its purpose, according to WBC founders, was to improve the standards of professional boxing, including the safety of fighters. Among the WBC's innovations was the shortening of world championship fights from 15 to 12 rounds in 1983, a move that was eventually adopted by the other sanctioning organizations. In 2003 the WBC filed for bankruptcy in an attempt to avoid paying $30 million in damages from a lawsuit over questionable handling of title fight eligibility. The following year the lawsuit was settled for a lesser amount, allowing the WBC to avoid having to disband and liquidate its assets.

International Boxing Federation

The International Boxing Federation (IBF; 2018, http://www.ibf-usba-boxing.com) was formed in 1983 by a group of WBA representatives who were upset with the political machinations within the WBA. Its creation was spearheaded by Robert W. Lee, the president of a smaller regional organization called the US Boxing Association (USBA). The new group was originally called the IBF-USBA. During its first year of operation the IBF remained fairly obscure. In 1984, however, the IBF decided to recognize as champions a number of high-profile fighters who were already established title holders within other organizations, including Larry Holmes (1949–) and

Marvelous Marvin Hagler (1952–). When Holmes opted to relinquish his WBC title to accept the IBF's, he lent the IBF instant credibility. Nonetheless, the IBF's reputation took a major hit in 1999, when Lee was convicted on racketeering and other charges.

World Boxing Organization

The World Boxing Organization (WBO; 2018, http://www.wboboxing.com) was formed in 1988 by a group of Puerto Rican and Dominican businessmen who were disenchanted with what they perceived as illegitimate rules and rating systems within the WBA. The WBO's first championship fight was a junior welterweight championship match between Héctor Camacho (1962–2012) and Ray Mancini (1961–). The WBO achieved a level of legitimacy comparable to that of the WBA, the WBC, and the IBF, largely thanks to its recognition as champions of many of the sport's best-known competitors. The WBO has also tended at times to provide more opportunities for non-US-based fighters than the other organizations.

Women's Boxing

Women's professional boxing began to gain in popularity during the 1990s. There are three sanctioning bodies that govern women's professional fighting: the International Women's Boxing Federation, the Women's International Boxing Association, and the Women's International Boxing Federation. Part of the sport's popularity can be attributed to the participation of Laila Ali (1977–), daughter of the boxing great Muhammad Ali. Jacqui Frazier-Lyde (1961–), daughter of the legendary boxer Joe Frazier (1944–2011), has also been prominent in the sport. Ali made her professional boxing debut in 1999. In 2001 she and Frazier squared off, with Ali emerging victorious. In August 2009 the International Olympic Committee voted unanimously to include women's boxing in the Summer Olympics, beginning with the 2012 Games in London.

Challenges to Boxing's Future

By 2018 boxing had been declining in popularity for years. A major part of the problem was the lack of big-name, attention-drawing stars, particularly in the heavyweight division. The sport thrives when it is dominated by colorful heavyweights, such as when Ali and Mike Tyson (1966–) took center stage. Ali was the public face of boxing for decades and was arguably the most recognized athlete in the world. Fans have not been as enthusiastic about plodding champions and contenders with unfamiliar names, such as the Klitschko brothers, Vitali (1971–) and Wladimir (1976–), who were at the top of the heavyweight ranks during the first decade of the 21st century.

Among the biggest names in boxing since the 1990s have been Oscar De La Hoya (1973–), Manny Pacquiao (1978–), and Floyd Mayweather Jr. (1977–). Nicknamed the "Golden Boy," De La Hoya won an Olympic gold medal in 1992 and went on to capture 10 professional titles in six different weight classes. By 2010 Pacquiao had emerged as the sport's top draw, earning fighter of the decade honors from the Boxing Writers Association of America. Meanwhile, fight promoters were eager to schedule a match between Pacquiao and Mayweather to determine the best welterweight fighter in the world.

On May 2, 2015, Pacquiao and Mayweather finally squared off at the MGM Grand Garden Arena in Las Vegas, in one of the most highly anticipated boxing matches in years. Cork Gaines notes in "The Mayweather-Pacquiao Fight Numbers Are in—They Shattered Expectations by Tens of Millions of Dollars" (Business Insider.com, May 12, 2015) that the bout broke the record for pay-per-view purchases for a single fight, with 4.4 million television viewers witnessing Mayweather's victory in a unanimous decision. The total purse for the fight was estimated at a record $350 million, with Mayweather earning roughly $210 million and Pacquiao taking home between $142 million and $143 million; indeed, the bout made Mayweather and Pacquiao the top-two highest-earning athletes of 2015.

Despite these record earnings, the bout itself left many boxing fans disappointed. For example, in "Mayweather-Pacquiao Fight: 'Fraud of the Century'" (Forbes.com, May 5, 2015), Leigh Steinberg suggests that Mayweather's conservative fighting style, combined with the fact that Pacquiao entered the match with a shoulder injury, resulted in a bout that was "inherently boring," while failing to "generate much excitement." As a result, Steinberg contends, the fight "ended up doing more damage to the image and market for boxing, and accelerated the sport's decline." According to the article "Mayweather Stripped of Title He Won in Pacquiao Fight" (Reuters.com, July 6, 2015), the legacy of the match was further tainted when Mayweather was forced to relinquish his newly won welterweight title belt after failing to comply with WBO rules.

As boxing struggled to maintain its popularity, the sport found itself competing to an increasing degree with the emerging sport of mixed martial arts (MMA), a more brutal sport that allows not only punching but also kicking, wrestling, elbowing, and choking one's opponent into submission. The top MMA circuit, the Ultimate Fighting Championship, has emerged as a serious challenger to boxing for domination of the fight game. As of April 2018, its pay-per-view events did not yet attract as many viewers as those of boxing, but viewership was increasing quickly, and the sport had a large and growing base of loyal, mostly young, fans. It has been suggested that there may also be a racial element to the rise of MMA. Profiled by Steve Cofield in "Mayweather: Whites Needed a Fight Sport, So They Invented MMA" (Yahoo.com, July 20, 2009), Mayweather opined that white fans have embraced the sport—many top Ultimate Fighting Championship contenders are white—in response to the dominance of boxing by African American and Hispanic athletes.

CHAPTER 6
COLLEGE, HIGH SCHOOL, AND YOUTH SPORTS

College athletics function as a minor, or preparatory, league for some professional sports, particularly football and basketball, but there is nothing minor about Americans' passion for them or about the sums of money that intercollegiate sports generate. Just as college sports serve as a feeder system for professional leagues, high schools fill the same role for colleges, and schools often compete for the services of elite teenage athletes. For the most part, high school and college athletes participate in sports for their own rewards. Most of them understand that the chances of striking it rich as a professional athlete are remote. For example, out of 546,428 boys who play on high school basketball teams, only about 18,684 (3.4%) will go on to play at the National Collegiate Athletic Association (NCAA) level; of these, only 1.1%, or roughly 187 players, will join the National Basketball Association (NBA). (See Table 6.1.) Regardless, the money that flows through the sports industry (an industry of which intercollegiate sports are an integral part) is so abundant that its influence can be felt in many US high schools. Even youth sports, such as Little League baseball and youth basketball leagues, have become big business, as industry insiders seek to identify the next generation of superstars at ever-younger ages.

COLLEGE SPORTS

In contrast to professional sports, where turning a profit is the motivating force behind most decisions, college sports must reconcile commercial interests, educational priorities, and a jumble of other influences ranging from alumni pride to institutional prestige. Although it may make high-minded university officials uncomfortable to admit it, college sports have become big business in the United States.

The most important governing organization of college sports in the United States is the NCAA, although there are other governing bodies as well.

National Collegiate Athletic Association

The NCAA (http://www.ncaa.org/about/resources/media-center/ncaa-101/what-ncaa) is a voluntary association whose members consisted of 1,302 institutions, conferences, organizations, and individuals in 2017. Of these, 1,102 were active member schools, meaning they had been "duly elected to active membership under the provisions of the Association bylaws" and were eligible to compete in NCAA championship sports. Schools that have applied for active membership are categorized as provisional members, candidacy members (for Division II schools), or exploratory members (for Division III schools). The NCAA's main purpose, according to its constitution (July 23, 2012, http://www.ncaa.org/about/resources/media-center/news/ncaa-constitution-references), is to maintain "intercollegiate athletics to promote the character development of participants, to enhance the integrity of higher education and to promote civility in society, student-athletes, coaches, and all others associated with these athletics programs and events should adhere to such fundamental values as respect, fairness, civility, honesty and responsibility."

Organizationally, the NCAA consists of nearly 140 committees. Several of these committees are association-wide, including the Executive Committee and committees having to do with ethics, women's opportunities, and minority opportunities. The rest are specific to one of the NCAA's three divisions (Divisions I, II, and III) which classify the schools by the number of sports they sponsor and other factors. NCAA member schools and organizations vote on the rules they will follow. It is then up to the NCAA National Office to implement and enforce the rules and bylaws dictated by the members.

The NCAA's divisions are based on factors such as the number of sports sponsored, attendance at the school's sporting events, and financial support to athletes.

TABLE 6.1

Estimated probability of competing in athletics beyond high school, 2015–16

Student-athletes	Men's basketball	Women's basketball	Football	Baseball	Men's ice hockey	Men's soccer
High school student athletes	546,428	429,380	1,083,308	488,815	35,155	440,322
NCAA student athletes	18,684	16,593	73,360	34,554	4,102	24,803
Percent high school to NCAA	3.40%	3.90%	6.80%	7.10%	11.70%	5.60%
Percent NCAA to major professional*	1.10%	0.90%	1.50%	9.10%	5.60%	1.40%

*Includes athletes competing in the National Basketball Association (NBA), the Women's National Basketball Association (WNBA), the National Football League (NFL), Major League Baseball (MLB), the National Hockey League (NHL), and Major League Soccer (MLS).

SOURCE: Created by Stephen Meyer for Gale, © 2018.

Division I is further divided into the Football Bowl Subdivision (FBS, formerly Division I-A) and the Football Championship Subdivision (FCS, formerly Division I-AA). There are also schools that do not offer football, which are sometimes referred to as Division I-AAA, although they may compete against FBS or FCS colleges in other sports. Intercollegiate sports under the auspices of the NCAA are also divided into conferences, which function like the leagues and divisions in professional sports. The most prominent conferences, often referred to collectively as the Power Five, are shown in Table 6.2.

HISTORY OF THE NCAA

Until the mid-19th century there was no governing body that oversaw intercollegiate athletics. Typically, students rather than faculty or administrators ran the programs. Even so, there was already a fair amount of commercialization and illicit professionalism in college sports. For example, James Hogan (1876–1910), the captain of the Yale University football team in 1904, was compensated with, among other things, a suite of rooms in the dorm, free University Club meals, profits from the sale of programs, and a 10-day vacation to Cuba. What ultimately led administrators to the conclusion that formal oversight was necessary was the sheer brutality of college sports, particularly football. According to *The Business of Sports* (2004), edited by Scott R. Rosner and Kenneth L. Shropshire, there were at least 18 deaths and more than 100 major injuries in intercollegiate football in 1905 alone. In response to the growing violence of college football, President Theodore Roosevelt (1858–1919) convened a White House conference of representatives from Harvard, Princeton, and Yale Universities to review the rules of the game. When the deaths and serious injuries continued, Henry Mitchell MacCracken (1840–1918), the chancellor of the University of the City of New York (now New York University), called for a national gathering of representatives from the major football schools. In early December 1905 representatives of 13 schools met with MacCracken and formed a Rules Committee. This group held another meeting in late December that was attended by representatives of more than 60 college football programs, during

TABLE 6.2

National Collegiate Athletic Association Power Five conferences, 2018

Atlantic Coast Conference (ACC)

Atlantic Division

Boston College
Clemson University
Florida State University
University of Louisville
North Carolina State University
University of Notre Dame
Syracuse University
Wake Forest University

Coastal Division

Duke University
Georgia Tech
University of Miami
University of North Carolina at Chapel Hill
University of Pittsburgh
University of Virginia
Virginia Tech

Big 10 Conference

East Division

Indiana University
University of Maryland
University of Michigan
Michigan State University
Ohio State University
Pennsylvania State University
Rutgers University

West Division

University of Illinois
University of Iowa
University of Minnesota
University of Nebraska
Northwestern University
Purdue University
University of Wisconsin

Big 12 Conference

Baylor University
Iowa State University
University of Kansas
Kansas State University
University of Oklahoma
Oklahoma State University
University of Texas
Texas Christian University
Texas Tech University
West Virginia University

Pacific 12 Conference

University of Arizona
Arizona State University
University of California, Berkeley (Cal)
University of California, Los Angeles (UCLA)
University of Colorado-Boulder
University of Oregon
Oregon State University
University of Southern California
Stanford University
University of Utah
University of Washington
Washington State University

Southeastern Conference (SEC)

Eastern Division

University of Florida
University of Georgia
University of Kentucky
University of Missouri
University of South Carolina
University of Tennessee
Vanderbilt University

Western Division

University of Alabama
University of Arkansas
Auburn University
Louisiana State University
University of Mississippi
Mississippi State University
Texas A&M University

SOURCE: Created by Stephen Meyer for Gale, © 2018.

which the Intercollegiate Athletic Association (IAA) was formed. The IAA was a national organization with 62 founding members, including schools in Minnesota, Nebraska, New Hampshire, New York, Ohio, Pennsylvania, and Texas. The IAA became the NCAA in 1910.

Initially, the NCAA's chief role was to make rules to keep sports safe and fair. The organization also served as a forum for discussion of other issues, such as the formation of athletic conferences and the transfer of oversight responsibilities from students to faculty. In 1921 the NCAA created its first national title, the National Collegiate Track and Field Championships.

By the mid-1920s college athletics had become an integral part of college life, as well as a subject of intense public interest. Along with this interest came creeping commercialism. In 1929 the Carnegie Foundation for the Advancement of Education issued a report on college sports, which stated that "a change of values is needed in a field that is sodden with the commercial and the material and the vested interests that these forces have created."

In response to the Carnegie report, schools made token attempts to reduce commercial influences on college sports; however, the trend continued. A dramatic increase in access to higher education following World War II (1939–1945) accelerated the commercialization of college athletics. In 1948, in response to a series of gambling scandals and questionable recruiting incidents, the NCAA adopted the Sanity Code, which established guidelines for recruiting and financial aid. In addition, the code set academic standards for players and defined the status of college athletes as amateurs; that is, those "to whom athletics is an avocation." The NCAA also created a Constitutional Compliance Committee to enforce the Sanity Code and investigate possible violations. The Sanity Code did not have much of an impact, however, and was repealed in 1951. The Constitutional Compliance Committee was replaced by the Committee on Infractions, which was given broader authority to sanction institutions that broke the rules. The NCAA also hired its first full-time executive director, Walter Byers (1922–2015), that same year. A national headquarters was established in Kansas City, Missouri, in 1952. The 1950s also brought the first lucrative television broadcast contracts, which provided the NCAA with the revenue it needed to become more active. Its capacity to enforce rules expanded throughout the 1950s and 1960s. Nevertheless, the influence of money on college sports continued to grow.

During the 1970s and 1980s major football colleges began to see that they could make more money from broadcast revenue by negotiating their own deals. A group of schools, led by the University of Georgia and the University of Oklahoma, began to challenge the NCAA's monopoly on the negotiation of lucrative television contracts. In 1984 the US Supreme Court ruled in *NCAA v. Board of Regents of the University of Oklahoma* (468 US 85) that the NCAA had violated antitrust laws. This ruling allowed colleges to start negotiating broadcast deals directly. Meanwhile, the relationship between sports and the academic performance of athletes remained a matter of intense debate. In 1986 the NCAA implemented Proposition 48, later modified by Proposition 16 (1995), which set minimum academic standards for athletes entering college. Among the requirements, student-athletes needed to maintain a 2.0 grade point average (GPA) in academic courses and have a Scholastic Assessment Test (SAT) score of 1010 or a combined American College Test (ACT) score of 86. Over time these minimums were revised, and by 2018 they varied by division as detailed later in this chapter.

Scandals and Sanctions in NCAA Sports Programs

There have been several cases of institutions and their boosters making illicit payments to players. For example, during the early 1980s Southern Methodist University (SMU) became a football powerhouse through a highly organized system of player payments, in blatant violation of NCAA rules. According to Chris DuFresne, in "Life after 'Death'" (LATimes.com, December 28, 2005), the payoff system, which had been in place for several years, began to unravel in November 1986, when the SMU linebacker David Stanley admitted that he had accepted $25,000 from boosters. After an investigation revealed widespread corruption that went as high as the Texas governor's office, the NCAA hit the university with what became known in college sports as the "death penalty." The sanctions included cancellation of SMU's entire 1987 football season and restriction of the following season to eight games.

The NCAA has not wielded the death penalty again since the SMU scandal, but its threat has not halted corrupt practices in college sports. Another high-profile case involved the NBA star Chris Webber (1973–). In July 2003 Webber pleaded guilty to criminal contempt related to charges that he had received tens of thousands of dollars from the booster Ed Martin (1933?–2003) while a member of the University of Michigan basketball team in 1994. Martin pleaded guilty to money laundering in May 2002. Webber's sentence, a fine of $100,000, was announced in August 2005.

ACADEMIC IMPROPRIETY. Special treatment of student-athletes does not always involve money. In 1999 a University of Minnesota employee told the *St. Paul Pioneer Press* that she had completed course work for at least 20 members of the school's basketball program. Academics also figured prominently in a scandal that resulted in the NCAA stripping the University of Memphis of its entire 2007–08 basketball season, which included an impressive 38 victories and a trip to the Final Four. The university's star player, Derrick Rose (1988–), now a point guard for the NBA's Minnesota Timberwolves, allegedly paid another student to take the SAT exams for him, after he failed the ACT three times.

Sara Ganim reports in "UNC Fake Class Scandal and NCAA's Response Wind Their Way to Washington" (CNN.com, April 8, 2014) that in 2012 the University of North Carolina came under investigation by the NCAA for allowing student-athletes to enroll in independent study classes that enabled them to receive high grades without completing any course work. According to Ganim, some athletes were coerced into taking these so-called paper classes by coaches and other school administrators to ensure they remained eligible for intercollegiate competition. Ultimately, the NCAA declined to sanction the university on the grounds that the issue did not specifically involve athletic competition.

Academic impropriety also played a central role in a major scandal that hit Syracuse University in 2015. In "Everything You Need to Know about Syracuse's NCAA Scandal" (SBNation.com, March 9, 2015), Ricky O'Donnell indicates that an eight-year investigation conducted by the NCAA uncovered a range of violations perpetrated by the university between 2001 and 2012, including academic fraud, providing improper benefits to student-athletes, and drug policy violations. Solomon explains in "What Syracuse's NCAA Case Revealed about Academic Fraud" (CBSSports.com, March 7, 2015) that the NCAA's report on the violations revealed that Stan Kissel, the school's director of basketball operations, had helped Syracuse basketball players obtain term papers written by other students, which were subsequently submitted to teachers under their own name. Furthermore, in 2012 members of the Syracuse athletic department negotiated with academic officials to reinstate Fab Melo (1990–), the team's star center, after poor grades had rendered him ineligible. As a result of the infractions, the Syracuse basketball team was forced to vacate (forfeit) 108 wins under the longtime head coach Jim Boeheim (1944–), while also surrendering three basketball scholarships annually over a four-year span.

RECRUITING VIOLATIONS. During this time, a series of high-profile scandals effectively ended the career of University of Louisville head basketball coach Rick Pitino (1952–). The first controversy emerged in October 2015, when former sex worker Katina Powell revealed that Louisville assistant coach Andre McGee (1987–) had procured prostitutes and strippers for high school basketball recruits. In June 2017 the NCAA placed Louisville on probation for four years and ordered the school to repay money earned through the Atlantic Coast Conference (ACC) revenue sharing program during the period in question. More significantly, the NCAA announced that Louisville would be required to vacate up to 123 victories that involved players implicated in the scandal, including its 2013 title win. The school promptly appealed the ruling.

A more far-reaching scandal came to light in September 2017, when the Federal Bureau of Investigation (FBI) arrested 10 people in connection with bribes paid to college basketball recruits. Among those arrested were four coaches working for Division I programs, as well as adidas executive James Gatto, who allegedly paid $100,000 to the family of high school basketball star Brian Bowen (1998–) in exchange for his commitment to play at the University of Louisville. In the aftermath of the revelations, Pitino was fired as Louisville's head coach. In February 2018 the NCAA officially nullified Louisville's 2013 national championship, making it the first school in history to have a title vacated. Meanwhile, by early 2018 the University of Southern California and the University of Arizona were under investigation for allegedly making illegal payments to basketball recruits and their families. Nathan Fenno writes in "Big Names at USC and Arizona Linked to College Basketball Bribery and Corruption Case" (LATimes.com, February 23, 2018) that in one instance FBI wiretaps allegedly revealed that Arizona head coach Sean Miller (1968–) had offered top recruit Deandre Ayton (1998–) $100,000 in exchange for his commitment to play for the school. Miller subsequently denied the allegations, and he remained the head coach of the Wildcats as of April 2018.

SEXUAL MISCONDUCT. Among the worst scandals in NCAA history emerged in November 2011, when Jerry Sandusky (1944–), an assistant football coach for Pennsylvania State University (Penn State, or PSU), was indicted on multiple charges of child molestation. As details of the case became public, Sandusky was implicated in the sexual abuse of 10 boys over a 14-year period, with many of the incidents occurring on university property. The scandal shook the historic Penn State football program to its foundation. The legendary head coach Joe Paterno (1926–2012) was fired in the wake of the allegations, after it was revealed that he had known about Sandusky's actions for years; shortly thereafter a commemorative statue of Paterno was removed from the Penn State campus. The university's president Graham Spanier (1948–) and the athletic director Tim Curley (1954–) resigned. In June 2012 Sandusky was convicted on 45 counts of unlawful sexual intercourse, endangering the welfare of children, and other criminal charges and sentenced to 30 to 60 years in prison. Teri Thompson and Christian Red report in "NCAA Hammers Penn State with 4-Year Postseason Ban, Vacates Wins from 1998–2011, Imposes $60M Fine and Slashes Scholarships" (NYDailyNews.com, July 23, 2012) that in the aftermath of the scandal the NCAA punished Penn State with severe sanctions, including a $60 million fine, banning the team from postseason play for four years, and reducing its football scholarships from 25 to 15. Arguably most bitter for Penn State fans, all of the team's wins between

1998 and 2011 were vacated. As a result, Paterno was no longer the "winningest" coach in NCAA football history.

In another notable episode, players on the Baylor University football team were accused of sexually assaulting female students between 2012 and 2016. An investigation revealed that university officials had known about at least one instance of sexual assault in 2013 but failed to disclose the information to legal authorities. Head football coach Art Briles (1955–) was fired and the university president, Ken Starr (1946–), resigned.

As of 2018 dozens of colleges and universities were under investigation for mishandling sexual assault cases against athletes, athletic department staff members, or coaches. Among the most notable cases was Michigan State University (MSU), which came under fire in 2017 during the trial of Larry Nassar (1963–), the former team doctor of USA Gymnastics and an MSU physician and professor who was found guilty of molesting hundreds of female athletes, many of them underage, over a span of several decades. Following an investigation into MSU's handling of sexual assault allegations against athletes and coaches, in "OTL: Michigan State Secrets Extend Far beyond Larry Nassar Case" (ESPN.com, February 1, 2018), Paula Lavigne and Nicole Noren describe "a pattern of widespread denial, inaction and information suppression" on the part of the university. As investigations into the school's handling of sexual misconduct cases continued, both the athletic director and university president resigned in early 2018. Lavigne and Noren report that criminal sexual assault charges were pending against former members of the football team who had been dismissed from the university and the team; in several other cases from the period 2009–17, including police reports of rape and domestic violence, no charges were filed. Lauren Allswede, a former sexual assault counselor at MSU, told Lavigne and Noren, "As a Big Ten university with high-profile football, basketball and hockey programs, they want to protect the integrity of the programs—don't want scandal, don't want sexual assault allegations, or domestic violence allegations." She continued, "None of it was transparent. It was very insulated, and people were a lot of times discouraged from seeking resources outside of the athletic department."

COLLEGE SPORTS PARTICIPATION

Table 6.3 shows participation in women's sports at NCAA schools during the 2016–17 school year. Overall, 13,477 women participated on NCAA Division I outdoor track and field teams that year, the highest total of any women's sport; nearly as many women (13,181) participated during the indoor track season. NCAA women's Division I soccer teams had a total of 9,209 participants in 2016–17. Including all sports, both championship (sports in which schools compete for a championship

title) and emerging (nonchampionship sports offered as a way of providing additional athletic opportunities to female students), 84,468 women participated in Division I sports that year. Another 51,357 women played at the Division II level, and 79,492 women competed at the Division III level.

Table 6.4 shows participation in men's collegiate sports during the 2016–17 school year. Overall, 94,682 student-athletes participated on 2,948 Division I men's teams that year. The sport with the greatest number of Division I teams was basketball, with 347. Basketball teams, however, were relatively small, averaging 15.8 members per squad in Division I. By comparison, 28,141 men played football at the Division I level in 2016–17, with an average of 112.1 members per squad. Outdoor track was second, with 11,033 participants, followed by baseball, with 10,453 participants. Division II men's sports included 70,522 participants, and Division III had 111,409 participants.

Table 6.5 puts college sports participation in historical perspective. During the 1981–82 school year there were 231,445 student-athletes competing in NCAA championship sports in all divisions; 167,055 of them were men. By the 1994–95 school year the total number of student-athletes had grown to 294,212. About twice as much of this growth was on the women's side as on the men's. The total number of student-athletes had grown to 491,930 by the 2016–17 school year. It is important to note, however, a change in the way the total is calculated: provisional NCAA members were included in the count beginning in the 1995–96 school year. In addition, the numbers for 1995–96 and 1996–97 were adjusted to comply with the Equity in Athletics Disclosure Act, making it difficult to compare current participation numbers with data from before 1995.

Table 6.6 and Table 6.7 provide a breakdown of championship sports teams sponsored by NCAA member schools for both women and men. During the 2016–17 school year there were 1,103 women's basketball teams, the most of any women's sport. Women's cross-country was second with 1,071 teams, followed by volleyball with 1,069 squads. Between 1995–96, when women's water polo was introduced as a competitive sport, and 2016–17 the number of NCAA women's water polo teams more than tripled, from 20 to 61. Basketball was also the leading sport for men, with 1,089 teams in Divisions I, II, and III. Cross-country was second, with 990 teams, and baseball was third, with 950 teams.

Table 6.8 illustrates trends in the average number of sports teams per school. As the table shows, the gender balance shifted considerably between 1981–82 and 2016–17. For example, in 1981–82 the average number of teams across all divisions was 9.1 for men and 6.4 for women; by 2016–17 the average number of men's teams

TABLE 6.3

National Collegiate Athletic Association participation in women's sports, by division, 2016–17

Sport	Division I			Division II			Division III			Overall		
	Teams	Athletes	Avg. squad	Teams	Athletes	Avg. squad	Teams	Athletes	Avg. squad	Teams	Athletes	Avg. squad
Championship sports												
Basketball	345	5,000	14.5	319	4,866	15.3	439	6,666	15.2	1,103	16,532	15.0
Bowling	34	306	9.0	30	272	9.1	12	101	8.4	76	679	8.9
Cross country	344	5,985	17.4	307	3,959	12.9	420	6,022	14.3	1,071	15,966	14.9
Fencing	26	420	16.2	4	51	12.8	15	237	15.8	45	708	15.7
Field hockey	79	1,802	22.8	33	795	24.1	164	3,469	21.2	276	6,066	22.0
Golf	263	2,181	8.3	192	1,560	8.1	212	1,631	7.7	667	5,372	8.1
Gymnastics	61	1,083	17.8	7	131	18.7	15	309	20.6	83	1,523	18.3
Ice hockey	36	846	23.5	5	117	23.4	59	1,392	23.6	100	2,355	23.6
Lacrosse	111	3,424	30.8	107	2,494	23.3	280	5,834	20.8	498	11,752	23.6
Rifle	24	163	6.8	3	17	5.7	3	9	3.0	30	189	6.3
Rowing	89	5,600	62.9	16	500	31.3	41	1,345	32.8	146	7,445	51.0
Sand volleyball	52	878	16.9	9	150	16.7	3	42	14.0	64	1,070	16.7
Skiing	12	163	13.6	7	72	10.3	16	179	11.2	35	414	11.8
Soccer	329	9,209	28.0	268	7,462	27.8	438	10,967	25.0	1,035	27,638	26.7
Softball	291	6,229	21.4	296	6,031	20.4	414	7,739	18.7	1,001	19,999	20.0
Swimming/diving	194	5,592	28.8	104	2,057	19.8	250	5,035	20.1	548	12,684	23.1
Tennis	315	2,872	9.1	226	2,013	8.9	372	3,851	10.4	913	8,736	9.6
Track, indoor	325	13,181	40.6	195	6,161	31.6	283	8,394	29.7	803	27,736	34.5
Track, outdoor	334	13,477	40.4	246	7,453	30.3	318	8,977	28.2	898	29,907	33.3
Volleyball	330	5,356	16.2	306	5,001	16.3	433	7,030	16.2	1,069	17,387	16.3
Water polo	34	701	20.6	10	195	19.5	17	263	15.5	61	1,159	19.0
Subtotal	**3,628**	**84,468**		**2,690**	**51,357**		**4,204**	**79,492**		**10,522**	**215,317**	
Emerging sports												
Archery			0.0			0.0			0.0	0	0	0.0
Badminton			0.0			0.0			0.0	0	0	0.0
Equestrian	18	683	37.9	5	120	24.0	21	530	25.2	44	1,333	30.3
Rugby	7	200	28.6	3	96	32.0	4	134	33.5	14	430	30.7
Squash	11	149	13.5	0		N/A	19	249	13.1	30	398	13.3
Sync. swimming	2	47	23.5	0		0.0	1	8	8.0	3	55	18.3
Team handball			N/A			N/A			N/A	0	0	N/A
Triathlon	2	13	6.5	3	17	5.7	4	21	5.3	9	51	5.7
Subtotal	**40**	**1,092**		**11**	**233**		**49**	**942**		**100**	**2,267**	
Total	**3,668**	**85,560**		**2,701**	**51,590**		**4,253**	**80,434**		**10,622**	**217,584**	

N/A = Not applicable.

Notes:
1. Participation totals are adjusted to reflect all institutions sponsoring each sport.
2. Provisional members are included in these numbers.
3. Coed sport teams from the sports sponsorship database were added to both the men's and women's team data. The following sports had coed teams: a) cross country, b) equestrian, c) fencing, d) golf, e) rifle, f) skiing, g) swimming and driving, h) indoor track and field and i) outdoor track and field.
4. The total row contains data from the emerging sports subtotal row added to the championship sports subtotal row.

SOURCE: Erin Irick, "2016–17 Participation Study—Women's Sports," in *1981–82—2016–17 NCAA Sports Sponsorship and Participation Rates Report*, National Collegiate Athletic Association, October 2017, http://www.ncaa.org/sites/default/files/2016-17NCAA-0472_ParticRatesReport-FINAL_20171120.pdf (accessed February 12, 2018)

declined to 8.3, whereas the women's teams increased to 9.5. This is likely because of the smaller number of team members on many women's sports teams when compared with men's teams. (See Table 6.3 and Table 6.4.) For example, the average football team over all divisions had 108.9 team members in 2016–17, whereas the largest average among the women's teams over all divisions was in rowing (51 athletes). To provide opportunities for women athletes to participate at the collegiate level schools have increased the number of teams available to them.

Women's Sports and Gender Equity

Table 6.9 illustrates what has happened to the gender gap in college sports since the 1981–82 school year.

The average number of male student-athletes per college across all divisions increased modestly from 225.8 in 1981–82 to 250.9 in 2016–17, whereas the average number of female student-athletes per college nearly doubled, from 98.7 in 1981–82 to 195 in 2016–17. The difference is most pronounced in Division I sports. Overall, the average number of women athletes per Division I institution grew by 118.3 between 1990–91 and 2016–17, whereas the average number of male athletes stayed roughly the same.

In *Women in Intercollegiate Sport: A Longitudinal, National Study—Thirty-Seven Year Update, 1977–2014* (2014, http://www.acostacarpenter.org), R. Vivian Acosta and Linda Jean Carpenter of Brooklyn College examine

TABLE 6.4

National Collegiate Athletic Association participation in men's sports, by division, 2016–17

Sport	Division I			Division II			Division III			Overall		
	Teams	Athletes	Avg. squad	Teams	Athletes	Avg. squad	Teams	Athletes	Avg. squad	Teams	Athletes	Avg. squad
Championship sports												
Baseball	295	10,453	35.4	270	10,752	39.8	385	13,775	35.8	950	34,980	36.8
Basketball	347	5,484	15.8	318	5,395	17.0	424	7,833	18.5	1,089	18,712	17.2
Cross country	311	4,797	15.4	280	3,665	13.1	399	5,888	14.8	990	14,350	14.5
Fencing	21	379	18.0	2	30	15.0	12	230	19.2	35	639	18.3
Football	251	28,141	112.1	172	19,252	111.9	248	25,670	103.5	671	73,063	108.9
FBS	128	15,291	119.5			N/A			N/A	N/A	N/A	N/A
FCS	123	12,850	104.5			N/A			N/A	N/A	N/A	N/A
Golf	297	2,918	9.8	233	2,427	10.4	299	3,182	10.6	829	8,527	10.3
Gymnastics	15	298	19.9	0		0.0	1	20	20.0	16	318	19.9
Ice hockey	60	1,690	28.2	7	203	29.0	77	2,306	29.9	144	4,199	29.2
Lacrosse	70	3,276	46.8	67	2,628	39.2	234	7,995	34.2	371	13,899	37.5
Rifle	18	122	6.8	3	24	8.0	3	26	8.7	24	172	7.2
Skiing	11	151	13.7	6	69	11.5	16	219	13.7	33	439	13.3
Soccer	203	5,897	29.0	217	6,784	31.3	415	12,305	29.7	835	24,986	29.9
Swimming/Diving	133	3,802	28.6	75	1,534	20.5	223	4,355	19.5	431	9,691	22.5
Tennis	253	2,572	10.2	169	1,681	9.9	328	3,704	11.3	750	7,957	10.6
Track, indoor	260	10,168	39.1	173	6,174	35.7	276	9,549	34.6	709	25,891	36.5
Track, outdoor	281	11,033	39.3	215	7,410	34.5	311	10,152	32.6	807	28,595	35.4
Volleyball	21	420	20.0	25	428	17.1	82	1,159	14.1	128	2,007	15.7
Water polo	25	581	23.2	7	150	21.4	15	282	18.8	47	1,013	21.6
Wrestling	76	2,500	32.9	61	1,916	31.4	101	2,759	27.3	238	7,175	30.1
Subtotal	**2,948**	**94,682**		**2,300**	**70,522**		**3,849**	**111,409**		**9,097**	**276,613**	
Non-championship sports												
Archery			N/A			N/A			N/A	0	0	N/A
Badminton			N/A			N/A			N/A	0	0	N/A
Bowling			N/A	1	12	12.0	1	5	5.0	2	17	8.5
Equestrian	0	0	N/A			N/A	7	14	2.0	7	14	2.0
Rowing	29	1,407	48.5	2	43	21.5	25	879	35.2	56	2,329	41.6
Rugby	1	62	62.0	1	37	37.0	1	55	55.0	3	154	51.3
Sailing	11	246	22.4	1	18	18.0	10	149	14.9	22	413	18.8
Squash	12	195	16.3			N/A	20	281	14.1	32	476	14.9
Subtotal	**53**	**1,910**		**5**	**110**		**64**	**1,383**		**122**	**3,403**	
Total	**3,001**	**96,592**		**2,305**	**70,632**		**3,913**	**112,792**		**9,219**	**280,016**	

N/A = Not applicable.
FBS = Football bowl subdivision.
FCS = Football championship subdivision.
Notes:
1. Participation totals are adjusted to reflect all institutions sponsoring each sport.
2. Provisional members are included in these numbers.
3. Coed sport teams from the sports sponsorship database were added to both the men's and women's team data. The following sports had coed teams: a) cross country, b) equestrian, c) fencing, d) golf, e) rifle, f) sailing, g) skiing, h) swimming and diving, i) indoor track and field and j) outdoor track and field.
4. The total row contains data from the non-championship sports subtotal row added to the championship sports subtotal row.

SOURCE: Erin Irick, "2016–17 Participation Study—Men's Sports," in *1981–82—2016–17 NCAA Sports Sponsorship and Participation Rates Report*, National Collegiate Athletic Association, October 2017, http://www.ncaa.org/sites/default/files/2016-17NCAA-0472_ParticRatesReport-FINAL_20171120.pdf (accessed February 12, 2018)

the status of women's college athletics between 1977 and 2014. The researchers find that nationwide college women have more athletic teams available to them than ever before. Since 1978 (the mandatory compliance date for Title IX, which is explained later in this chapter) the number of women's athletic teams per school rose from 5.6 to 8.8 in 2012. There were 9,581 varsity women's intercollegiate teams in the NCAA in 2014.

According to Acosta and Carpenter, the sport most frequently found in women's intercollegiate athletic programs was basketball, which was offered by 99.1% of NCAA schools in 2014. Three other sports (volleyball, soccer, and cross-country) were offered for women at more than 90% of colleges in 2014. Basketball was the most popular sport throughout the period covered during the study. It ranked number one in 1977, when it was offered at 90.4% of colleges. Like basketball, volleyball has maintained its ranking since 1977, when it was offered at 80.1% of schools.

Title IX

No piece of legislation has had a greater impact on gender equity in sports participation than Title IX of the Education Amendments of 1972 of the Civil Rights Act of 1964, which is usually referred to simply as Title IX. Title IX was based on the notion that unequal federal funding between genders was an illegal form of

TABLE 6.5

National Collegiate Athletic Association men's and women's championship sports participation, 1981–2017

Year	Men	Percent change men	Women	Percent change women	Total	Percent change total
1981–82	167,055	N/A	64,390	N/A	231,445	N/A
1982–83	176,822	5.85	78,027	21.18	254,849	10.11
1983–84	186,008	5.20	82,452	5.67	268,460	5.34
1984–85	197,446	6.15	89,072	8.03	286,518	6.73
1985–86	196,437	−0.51	92,192	3.50	288,629	0.74
1986–87	187,561	−4.52	89,640	−2.77	277,201	−3.96
1987–88	176,396	−5.95	88,266	−1.53	264,662	−4.52
1988–89	178,521	1.20	90,180	2.17	268,701	1.53
1989–90	175,539	−1.67	88,206	−2.19	263,745	−1.84
1990–91	182,836	4.16	92,473	4.84	275,309	4.38
1991–92	183,675	0.46	94,922	2.65	278,597	1.19
1992–93	184,732	0.58	97,978	3.22	282,710	1.48
1993–94	186,939	1.19	102,994	5.12	289,933	2.55
1994–95	186,607	−0.18	107,605	4.48	294,212	1.48
1995–96	206,385	10.60	125,250	16.40	331,635	12.72
1996–97	199,391	−3.39	129,289	3.22	328,680	−0.89
1997–98	200,030	0.32	133,445	3.21	333,475	1.46
1998–99	207,685	3.83	145,873	9.31	353,558	6.02
1999–00	208,481	0.38	146,617	0.51	355,098	0.44
2000–01	214,154	2.72	155,698	6.19	369,852	4.15
2001–02	209,890	−1.99	153,601	−1.35	363,491	−1.72
2002–03	214,464	2.18	158,469	3.17	372,933	2.60
2003–04	214,854	0.18	160,997	1.60	375,851	0.78
2004–05	219,744	2.28	164,998	2.49	384,742	2.37
2005–06	224,926	2.36	168,583	2.17	393,509	2.28
2006–07	230,259	2.37	172,534	2.34	402,793	2.36
2007–08	236,774	2.83	175,994	2.01	412,768	2.48
2008–09	240,822	1.71	180,347	2.47	421,169	2.04
2009–10	245,875	2.10	184,426	2.26	430,301	2.17
2010–11	252,946	2.88	191,131	3.64	444,077	3.20
2011–12	257,690	1.88	195,657	2.37	453,347	2.09
2012–13	262,249	1.77	200,953	2.71	463,202	2.17
2013–14	267,604	2.04	205,021	2.02	472,625	2.03
2014–15	273,061	2.04	209,472	2.17	482,533	2.10
2015–16	274,973	0.70	211,886	1.15	486,859	0.90
2016–17	276,613	0.60	215,317	1.62	491,930	1.04

N/A = not available.

Note: Data for the academic years 1995–96 and 1996–97 have been adjusted using data from the Equity in Athletics Disclosure Act (EADA) form. As a result, the data published in this report for the academic years 1995–96 and 1996–97 will not necessarily match the data for the corresponding years in previous publications.

SOURCE: Adapted from Erin Irick, "Divisions I, II, and III Overall 1981–82—1996–97," and "Divisions I, II, and III Overall 1988–89—2016–17," in *1981–82—2016–17 NCAA Sports Sponsorship and Participation Rates Report*, National Collegiate Athletic Association, October 2017, http://www.ncaa.org/sites/default/files/2016-17NCAA-0472_ParticRatesReport-FINAL_20171120.pdf (accessed February 12, 2018)

discrimination. Title IX requires institutions receiving federal funding (including both secondary schools and colleges) to provide resources equally to male and female students. Critics of Title IX have been dismayed by the fact that compliance has sometimes meant cuts in men's sports programs, but the biggest impact has been an explosion in the prevalence and popularity of women's sports. In 2002 President George W. Bush (1946–) officially renamed Title IX the Patsy T. Mink Equal Opportunity in Education Act, after the legislation's author, a congresswoman from Hawaii. It is still, however, generally referred to as Title IX.

In 1972 the gender disparity in sports participation was overwhelming. Amy S. Wilson of the NCAA reports in *45 Years of Title IX: The Status of Women in Intercollegiate Athletics* (June 5, 2017, http://www.ncaa.org/sites/default/files/TitleIX45-295-FINAL_WEB.pdf) that 294,015 girls were participating in interscholastic high school sports programs that year, compared with 3.7 million boys. By 2016 the number of girls participating in high school sports rose to more than 3.3 million. (See Figure 6.1.) Participation levels in collegiate sports saw a similar rise. As Figure 6.2 shows, in 1982 there were 73,351 female athletes participating in NCAA sports, which accounted for 30.4% of all student athletes that year. By 2016 there were 211,886 female athletes, accounting for 43.5% of all NCAA athletes. At the same time, as noted in Figure 6.2, women comprised 54% of undergraduate enrollment across all NCAA divisions.

Women Coaches in College

One ironic consequence of the increase in the number of women's sports offered in college is a decrease in the percentage of teams that are coached by women. Acosta and Carpenter note that in 1972 women coached more than 90% of women's college sports teams. By 1978 the percentage had dropped to 58.2%. Acosta and Carpenter suggest that this drop was because of the rapid increase in the number of women's sports teams, which was not accompanied by a comparable growth in the number of qualified female coaches. The percentage, however, has continued to fall since 1978; by 2016 it stood at 40.2%. (See Figure 6.3.) In their report, Acosta and Carpenter argue that the continued decline in women's representation in college coaching is due in part to discrimination and differences in the way men and women coaches are recruited. The percentage varies substantially from sport to sport. According to Acosta and Carpenter, 59.2% of women's college basketball teams had female coaches in 2014. Notable female basketball coaches of major NCAA programs during this time included Tara VanDerveer (1953–) of Stanford University, C. Vivian Stringer (1948–) of Rutgers University, and Sylvia Hatchell (1952–) of the University of North Carolina, Chapel Hill. Other women's sports that were predominantly led by female coaches in 2014 included field hockey (92.4%), lacrosse (86%), and softball (66.3%). Men, however, dominated the coaching ranks of women's track and field (where only 17.9% of coaches were female), cross-country (22.8%), and swimming and diving (23.9%).

As Figure 6.4 shows, the percentage of female athletic directors remained roughly the same between 1996 and 2016. In 2016, 19.6% of the nation's collegiate athletic directors were women. Women, however, were far more likely to be athletic directors of Division III schools than Division I schools in 2016. (See Figure 6.5.)

TABLE 6.6

National Collegiate Athletic Association women's sports teams, by sport, 1981–2017

Year	Archery[a]	Badminton[a]	Basketball	Bowling[a]	Cross country	Equestrian[a]	Fencing	Field hockey	Golf	Gymnastics	Ice hockey[a]	Lacrosse	Rifle[b]	Rowing
1981–82		11	705	11	417		76	268	125	179	17	105	16	43
1982–83			747		464		68	262	119	170	17	113		45
1983–84			746		500		65	257	120	160	15	114		48
1984–85			751		541		62	251	123	150	15	114		51
1985–86			759		611		58	245	141	143	14	113		48
1986–87			757		633		55	233	139	125		114		38
1987–88			756		638		52	231	133	121		114		45
1988–89			764		638		48	225	132	112		118		39
1989–90			761		648		49	219	143	108		119		39
1990–91			786		666		48	217	145	103		118		12
1991–92			810		677		47	213	162	96		122		56
1992–93			827		700		42	211	177	91		126		51
1993–94			855		727		43	214	206	92		133		67
1994–95			869		747		41	221	216	90		144		74
1995–96[c]			952		842		51	231	288	96	21	164	10	90
1996–97[c]			956		834		43	228	303	91	22	183	12	98
1997–98[c]			956		843		44	234	329	91	30	201	11	111
1998–99[c]	6	10	1,001	5	891	41	45	240	364	90	40	213	44	122
1999–00[c]	3	3	1,011	23	882	30	45	239	382	90	50	225	43	129
2000–01[c]	3	3	1,020	25	923	47	46	248	437	90	63	238	45	138
2001–02[c]	3	4	1,017	39	928	46	46	252	451	89	69	249	46	140
2002–03[c]	3	4	1,016	43	930	44	45	253	456	86	70	256	43	141
2003–04[c]	3	3	1,022	42	942	41	44	255	477	86	72	258	39	143
2004–05[c]	3	3	1,025	45	940	39	45	257	483	85	74	264	36	141
2005–06[c]	2	3	1,039	44	958	45	44	258	504	86	75	271	37	142
2006–07[c]	2	2	1,050	49	967	48	45	259	512	86	79	286	36	144
2007–08[c]	1	2	1,057	52	988	45	43	258	516	85	81	301	36	144
2008–09[c]	1	2	1,054	55	996	46	41	260	543	84	84	319	35	146
2009–10[c]	0	0	1,059	57	1,005	47	41	262	557	83	84	334	36	143
2010–11[c]	0	0	1,072	62	1,026	46	41	264	575	83	87	357	34	142
2011–12[c]	0	0	1,084	63	1,035	49	42	266	596	83	86	376	34	145
2012–13[c]	0	0	1,090	60	1,049	50	42	266	617	82	89	416	31	147
2013–14[c]	0	0	1,101	61	1,061	49	42	270	631	82	90	443	34	145
2014–15[c]	0	0	1,107	64	1,072	47	43	271	651	82	91	470	32	146
2015–16[c]	0	0	1,107	68	1,071	44	44	273	656	83	98	483	30	146
2016–17[c]	0	0	1,103	76	1,071	44	45	276	667	83	100	498	30	146

Year	Rugby[a]	Beach volleyball[a]	Skiing	Soccer	Softball	Squash[a]	Synchronized swimming[a]	Swimming/diving	Team handball[a]	Tennis	Track, indoor	Track, outdoor	Triathlon	Volleyball	Water polo[a]
1981–82			33	80	416	16		348		610	239	427		603	
1982–83			35	103	441	16		361		652	280	462		638	
1983–84			36	133	451	17		370		657	327	472		645	
1984–85			37	165	493	17		374		667	358	482		649	
1985–86			38	201	528	17		390		687	385	520		685	
1986–87			41	230	543			392		690	391	526		701	
1987–88			43	259	543			397		690	416	537		705	
1988–89			39	270	549			397		691	419	540		719	
1989–90			40	294	557			396		694	421	537		722	
1990–91			41	318	580			396		711	447	553		741	
1991–92			44	350	605			394		723	466	561		762	
1992–93			37	387	618	23		391		732	479	574		784	
1993–94			35	446	646	23		393		759	489	582		810	
1994–95			37	515	656	23		400		774	496	593		828	
1995–96[c]			53	631	735	27	7	443		859	533	656		903	20
1996–97[c]			43	694	760	27	6	433		855	529	641		915	23
1997–98[c]			42	724	778	26	6	444		852	540	649		915	32
1998–99[c]			44	790	831	27	7	458	0	877	560	671		960	37
1999–00[c]			42	811	857	28	8	458	0	870	558	662		967	40
2000–01[c]			48	851	877	30	9	470	0	891	593	696		975	50
2001–02[c]			45	868	895	27	9	478	0	898	595	697		974	55
2002–03[c]	2		42	879	899	29	8	481	0	891	611	703		973	56

Spending on College Sports

Even in hard economic times, athletic departments demand a substantial share of college budgets. Frank Fear reports in "Subsidies Are the Name of the Game in D-1 College Sports" (SportsColumn.com, June 7, 2015) that Division I public universities devoted roughly $2.5 billion in subsidies to athletic departments in 2014. Fear notes that only seven (3%) out of 230 publicly funded Division I schools generated enough income to pay for their athletic programs that year.

In *Revenues & Expenses: 2004–15 NCAA Division I Intercollegiate Athletics Program Report* (July 2016,

TABLE 6.6

National Collegiate Athletic Association women's sports teams, by sport, 1981–2017 [CONTINUED]

Year	Rugby[a]	Beach volleyball[a]	Skiing	Soccer	Softball	Squash[a]	Synchronized swimming[a]	Swimming/ diving	Team handball[a]	Tennis	Track, indoor	Track, outdoor	Triathlon	Volleyball	Water polo[a]
2003–04[c]	2		42	895	908	27	8	488	0	880	617	701		978	59
2004–05[c]	3		39	913	911	27	8	489	0	876	621	704		982	61
2005–06[c]	4		40	930	932	26	8	497	0	888	630	722		992	61
2006–07[c]	5		44	941	942	27	8	504	0	895	641	732		1,007	61
2007–08[c]	5		42	956	950	28	8	509	0	898	645	745		1,014	60
2008–09[c]	5		41	959	949	28	8	510	0	900	661	758		1,015	60
2009–10[c]	4		38	967	957	28	0	512	0	912	673	767		1,025	59
2010–11[c]	5		35	984	969	29	1	523	0	921	694	778		1,039	60
2011–12[c]	5	14	34	996	976	30	1	527	0	934	711	801		1,047	64
2012–13[c]	5	29	34	1,011	988	30	2	530	0	939	733	816		1,056	61
2013–14[c]	6	39	34	1,022	997	29	2	539	0	931	754	835		1,064	61
2014–15[c]	7	46	32	1,030	1,003	31	2	548	0	930	772	861		1,071	60
2015–16[c]	12	56	33	1,034	1,004	30	2	541	0	929	784	880	4	1,070	59
2016–17[c]	14	64	35	1,035	1,001	30	3	548	0	913	803	898	9	1,069	61

[a]Empty cells for these sports indicate that the data were not tracked for that year.
[b]Prior to the 1995–96 academic year, women's rifle data were included with the men's rifle data. Rifle is a co-ed championship sport.
[c]Provisional members are included in these numbers.

SOURCE: Erin Irick, "NCAA Sports Sponsorship, 1981–82—2016–17: Divisions I, II, and III Overall Number of Women's Teams," in *1981–82—2016–17 NCAA Sports Sponsorship and Participation Rates Report*, National Collegiate Athletic Association, October 2017, http://www.ncaa.org/sites/default/files/2016-17NCAA-0472_ParticRatesReport-FINAL_20171120.pdf (accessed February 12, 2018)

http://www.ncaapublications.com/productdownloads/D1REVEXP2015.pdf), Daniel L. Fulks indicates that in 2004 the median (half were higher and half were lower) Division I-FBS athletic program generated revenues of $22.9 million and expenses of just under $29 million. By 2015 the median-generated revenues had increased to $47.9 million, whereas the median expenses had grown to $66.3 million.

In fiscal year (FY) 2015 football and men's basketball accounted for a huge share of both the median revenues and expenses in Division I-FBS college sports. (See Table 6.10.) That year football programs generated $21.6 million in median revenues and $16.4 million in median expenses, and men's basketball programs generated $5.7 million in median revenues and $5.8 million in median expenses. Table 6.11 details where Division I-FBS schools' athletics revenues came from in FY 2015. Ticket sales were the biggest source, accounting for a median of just under $9 million of the total revenue.

Academic Eligibility

Incoming student-athletes must meet a set of academic standards to participate in NCAA-sanctioned sports programs. These standards vary according to the division in which a school competes. According to the NCAA, in *2017–18 Guide for the College-Bound Student-Athlete* (2017, http://www.ncaapublications.com/productdownloads/CBSA18.pdf), Division I academic eligibility rules for the 2017–18 school year require that student-athletes:

- Graduate from high school

- Complete 16 core courses: four years of English; three years of math; two years of natural or physical science; one extra year of English, math, or natural

or physical science; two years of social science; and four extra core courses of English, math, or science, or foreign language, nondoctrinal religion, or philosophy

- Achieve a minimum required GPA in core courses

- Achieve a combined SAT or ACT score that matches the student's GPA on a special NCAA chart

The requirements for Divisions II and III are similar to those for Division I, although less stringent. For example, as the NCAA outlines in "Test Scores" (2018, http://www.ncaa.org/student-athletes/future/test-scores), Division II athletes had to maintain a 2.0 GPA and achieve minimum scores of 820 on the SAT and 68 on the ACT, whereas the eligibility of Division I athletes was determined using a sliding scale that raised test score requirements as GPA declined. A student athlete with a GPA of 3.5 would need an SAT score of 430 or an ACT score of 39 to gain eligibility in Division I, whereas a student athlete with a GPA of 2.5 would need an SAT score of 900 or an ACT score of 68 to be eligible to compete.

In *Guide for the College-Bound Student-Athlete*, the NCAA also outlines the rules for recruiting high school athletes, which vary somewhat by sport as well as by division. The recruiting rules for Division I are summarized in Table 6.12 and include regulations that pertain to phone contact, campus visits, and other forms of communication between coaches and prospective college athletes.

HIGH SCHOOL SPORTS

Participation

According to Laura Kann et al., in "Youth Risk Behavior Surveillance—United States, 2015" (*Morbidity*

TABLE 6.7

National Collegiate Athletic Association men's sports teams, by sport, 1981–2017

Year	Archery[a]	Badminton[a]	Baseball	Basketball	Bowling[a]	Cross country	Equestrian[a]	Fencing	Football	Golf	Gymnastics	Ice hockey	Lacrosse	Rifle[b]
1981–82			642	741	13	650		79	497	590	79	130	138	83
1982–83			650	754		672		72	509	598	71	123	138	92
1983–84			650	749		683		71	507	591	71	122	141	88
1984–85			652	752		694		67	503	595	65	124	144	88
1985–86			657	759	10	682		65	509	591	61	125	144	84
1986–87			662	760		681		58	510	577	56	126	150	65
1987–88			666	759		682		55	510	583	50	128	149	66
1988–89			667	768		670		48	522	570	47	126	150	61
1989–90			672	768		674		48	524	569	45	123	152	55
1990–91			692	795		695		49	534	603	43	123	157	50
1991–92			713	814		706		49	546	610	40	123	160	47
1992–93			730	831		723		47	553	619	40	121	168	50
1993–94			751	854		730		45	561	637	33	123	170	46
1994–95			763	868		736		42	566	652	29	122	172	43
1995–96[c]			827	938		815		47	600	726	39	123	177	59
1996–97[c]			820	941		786		38	600	695	28	127	183	42
1997–98[c]			817	938		790		37	599	696	27	129	186	40
1998–99[c]	6	4	844	980	10	827	33	37	605	716	26	131	197	41
1999–00[c]	1	0	857	989	3	811	0	37	610	719	24	126	203	38
2000–01[c]	1	0	860	991	1	860	10	52	624	750	24	132	208	45
2001–02[c]	1	0	866	990	2	858	8	38	617	754	23	134	211	43
2002–03[c]	1	0	861	987	0	859	5	39	619	748	20	135	214	42
2003–04[c]	1	0	864	994	1	871	4	37	617	758	20	133	211	35
2004–05[c]	1	0	873	1,000	1	865	3	36	614	762	19	133	214	35
2005–06[c]	1	0	890	1,013	2	879	8	36	618	777	19	133	222	36
2006–07[c]	1	0	897	1,022	2	898	8	36	625	782	19	136	226	29
2007–08[c]	0	0	906	1,031	0	912	2	35	629	795	18	138	239	29
2008–09[c]	0	0	905	1,030	1	916	3	34	633	792	18	139	247	30
2009–10[c]	0	0	910	1,038	1	928	5	34	633	798	17	136	262	31
2010–11[c]	0	0	922	1,051	1	952	7	34	644	811	17	135	280	28
2011–12[c]	0	0	927	1,060	1	960	8	35	651	812	17	135	295	27
2012–13[c]	0	0	936	1,071	0	972	11	34	655	819	17	138	319	26
2013–14[c]	0	0	943	1,081	0	982	9	34	664	824	17	138	339	27
2014–15[c]	0	0	951	1,089	0	989	9	34	670	831	16	139	350	25
2015–16[c]	0	0	948	1,090	1	994	7	35	672	835	16	142	362	23
2016–17[c]	0	0	950	1,089	2	990	7	35	671	829	16	144	371	24

Year	Rowing	Rugby[a]	Sailing[a]	Skiing	Soccer	Squash	Swimming/diving	Tennis	Track, indoor	Track, outdoor	Volleyball	Water polo	Wrestling
1981–82	48		15	55	521	21	377	690	422	577	63	49	363
1982–83	50		18	50	523	25	380	696	435	587	55	51	351
1983–84	48			46	533	21	378	700	446	580	58	52	342
1984–85	53		20	50	544	22	381	694	453	581	62	52	325
1985–86	46		22	47	550	21	375	691	447	572	58	53	317
1986–87	41		15	47	548	16	375	686	439	569	50	56	300
1987–88	40		19	50	546	17	383	687	446	564	50	58	289
1988–89	35			39	543	18	368	673	440	557	51	58	286
1989–90	36			40	547	18	361	675	434	554	54	55	278
1990–91	43			45	567	23	365	692	456	566	58	54	280
1991–92	51			46	581	24	367	701	476	580	58	48	275
1992–93	51			37	591	22	369	705	489	582	59	47	265
1993–94	60			35	609	24	368	720	493	588	61	39	264
1994–95	59			35	618	25	368	726	490	588	60	37	257
1995–96[c]	55			50	678	25	400	805	527	651	74	44	277
1996–97[c]	90			40	678	31	371	767	509	622	71	42	248
1997–98[c]	90			39	682	31	371	757	512	625	68	43	246
1998–99[c]	70		22	40	717	21	381	769	526	637	79	43	242
1999–00[c]	55		21	38	715	25	374	758	518	635	75	42	234
2000–01[c]	60		25	44	730	26	385	774	553	659	83	46	235
2001–02[c]	57		24	41	734	22	388	770	553	657	81	48	231
2002–03[c]	58	1	29	38	732	25	383	754	557	662	84	46	222
2003–04[c]	55	2	26	39	729	23	387	744	563	657	81	46	223
2004–05[c]	59	1	33	35	737	21	381	742	565	656	79	46	224
2005–06[c]	60	2	24	36	752	25	381	754	567	670	82	45	228
2006–07[c]	63	3	26	40	763	27	390	745	575	678	80	41	229

and Mortality Weekly Report, vol. 65, no. 6, June 10, 2016), 48.6% of US high school students were physically active for 60 minutes or more per day for five or more days a week in 2015. (See Table 6.13.) High school boys (57.8%) were considerably more likely than high school girls (39.1%) to engage in that level of physical activity that year. Slightly more than a quarter (27.1%) of all students were physically active for 60 minutes or more

TABLE 6.7

National Collegiate Athletic Association men's sports teams, by sport, 1981–2017 [CONTINUED]

Year	Rowing	Rugby[a]	Sailing[a]	Skiing	Soccer	Squash	Swimming/diving	Tennis	Track, indoor	Track, outdoor	Volleyball	Water polo	Wrestling
2007–08[c]	87	2	24	39	775	31	389	754	575	687	82	42	227
2008–09[c]	63	1	25	38	777	28	393	749	593	701	83	42	224
2009–10[c]	61	1	24	34	782	29	399	752	601	706	90	41	217
2010–11[c]	60	1	23	32	794	30	410	758	616	722	95	43	224
2011–12[c]	60	1	22	32	803	31	413	765	634	735	98	43	219
2012–13[c]	60	1	24	32	815	31	416	767	651	742	105	43	220
2013–14[c]	58	1	24	32	818	31	421	766	670	754	109	44	226
2014–15[c]	58	2	24	30	827	32	427	765	681	780	113	44	229
2015–16[c]	57	3	23	32	832	32	426	766	690	795	122	45	232
2016–17[c]	56	3	22	33	835	32	431	750	709	807	128	47	238

[a]Empty cells for these sports indicate that the data were not tracked for that year.
[b]Prior to the 1995–96 academic year, women's rifle data were included with the men's rifle data. Rifle is a co-ed championship sport.
[c]Provisional members are included in these numbers.

SOURCE: Erin Irick, "NCAA Sports Sponsorship, 1981–82—2016–17: Divisions I, II, and III Overall Number of Men's Teams," in *1981–82—2016–17 NCAA Sports Sponsorship and Participation Rates Report*, National Collegiate Athletic Association, October 2017, http://www.ncaa.org/sites/default/files/2016-17NCAA-0472_ParticRatesReport-FINAL_20171120.pdf (accessed February 12, 2018)

TABLE 6.8

Average number of men's and women's sports teams, per college, 1981–2017

Year	Division I			Division II			Division III			Overall		
	Men's	Women's	Overall	Men's	Women's	Overall	Men's	Women's	Overall	Men's	Women's	Overall
1981–82	10.3	7.3	17.5	7.9	5.5	13.4	8.8	6.1	14.8	9.1	6.4	15.5
1982–83	10.2	6.9	17.1	7.4	5.7	13.1	8.3	6.2	14.6	8.8	6.3	15.1
1983–84	10.2	7.1	17.3	7.5	5.9	13.4	8.2	6.3	14.6	8.7	6.5	15.3
1984–85	10.2	7.3	17.4	7.5	6.1	13.6	8.2	6.6	14.8	8.7	6.7	15.5
1985–86	10.1	7.7	17.9	7.3	6.3	13.6	8.2	6.8	15.0	8.7	7.0	15.7
1986–87	9.7	7.8	17.5	7.1	6.2	13.3	8.4	7.0	15.4	8.6	7.1	15.7
1987–88	9.6	7.8	17.4	7.1	6.2	13.3	8.4	7.1	15.6	8.6	7.2	15.7
1988–89	9.4	7.7	17.2	6.9	6.1	13.0	8.3	7.2	15.4	8.4	7.1	15.5
1989–90	9.4	7.8	17.2	6.9	6.2	13.1	8.2	7.2	15.4	8.3	7.2	15.5
1990–91	9.5	7.8	17.3	6.8	6.0	12.8	8.3	7.2	15.4	8.3	7.1	15.4
1991–92	9.6	8.1	17.6	6.7	5.9	12.6	8.2	7.2	15.4	8.3	7.2	15.5
1992–93	9.5	8.2	17.7	6.7	5.9	12.6	8.1	7.3	15.3	8.2	7.2	15.4
1993–94	9.6	8.4	18.0	6.5	5.9	12.4	7.9	7.4	15.3	8.1	7.3	15.4
1994–95	9.5	8.5	18.0	6.1	5.6	11.7	7.3	7.0	14.3	7.7	7.1	14.8
1995–96*	9.6	9.0	18.6	6.5	6.1	12.5	7.8	7.7	15.5	8.0	7.6	15.6
1996–97*	9.4	9.1	18.5	6.3	6.1	12.4	7.6	7.8	15.5	7.8	7.7	15.5
1997–98*	9.3	9.3	18.7	6.4	6.4	12.8	7.7	8.0	15.7	7.8	8.0	15.8
1998–99*	9.4	9.6	19.0	6.3	6.5	12.8	7.6	8.1	15.7	7.8	8.1	15.9
1999–00*	9.1	9.7	18.8	6.1	6.4	12.4	7.5	8.2	15.7	7.8	8.1	15.7
2000–01*	9.2	10.0	19.2	6.4	6.8	13.2	7.9	8.5	16.4	7.9	8.5	16.3
2001–02*	9.2	10.1	19.2	6.5	7.0	13.4	7.9	8.6	16.5	7.9	8.6	16.5
2002–03*	9.0	10.1	19.1	6.4	7.1	13.5	7.9	8.7	16.6	7.9	8.7	16.5
2003–04*	8.9	10.1	19.1	6.5	7.2	13.7	7.8	8.6	16.4	7.8	8.7	16.5
2004–05*	8.9	10.2	19.0	6.4	7.1	13.6	7.8	8.6	16.4	7.8	8.7	16.5
2005–06*	8.9	10.2	19.1	6.5	7.2	13.7	7.8	8.5	16.3	7.8	8.7	16.4
2006–07*	8.8	10.2	19.0	6.6	7.5	14.1	7.9	8.7	16.6	7.8	8.8	16.6
2007–08*	8.6	10.2	18.8	6.8	7.6	14.5	8.6	8.9	17.5	8.1	9.0	17.0
2008–09*	8.8	10.3	19.0	6.6	7.5	14.2	8.1	8.9	17.0	7.9	8.9	16.9
2009–10*	8.8	10.3	19.0	6.7	7.6	14.3	8.2	8.9	17.1	7.9	9.0	16.9
2010–11*	8.7	10.3	19.0	6.8	7.8	14.6	8.3	9.0	17.2	8.0	9.0	17.0
2011–12*	8.7	10.3	19.0	6.8	7.9	14.7	8.3	9.1	17.4	8.0	9.1	17.1
2012–13*	8.7	10.4	19.0	6.9	7.9	14.8	8.4	9.2	17.6	8.1	9.2	17.2
2013–14*	8.7	10.4	19.1	6.9	8.0	15.0	8.5	9.2	17.7	8.1	9.3	17.4
2014–15*	8.7	10.5	19.1	7.1	8.2	15.3	8.5	9.3	17.8	8.1	9.4	17.5
2015–16*	8.7	10.5	19.2	7.1	8.3	15.4	8.6	9.4	18.0	8.2	9.4	17.6
2016–17*	8.6	10.6	19.2	7.2	8.4	15.6	8.7	9.5	18.2	8.3	9.5	17.8

*Provisional members are included in these numbers.

SOURCE: Erin Irick, "NCAA Sports Sponsorship, 1981–82—2016–17: Average Number of Teams per Institution," in *1981–82—2016–17 NCAA Sports Sponsorship and Participation Rates Report*, National Collegiate Athletic Association, October 2017, http://www.ncaa.org/sites/default/files/2016-17NCAA-0472_ParticRatesReport-FINAL_20171120.pdf (accessed February 12, 2018)

TABLE 6.9

Average number of student-athletes per college, by gender and division, 1981– 2017

	Division I			Division II			Division III			Overall		
Year	Men's	Women's	Overall	Men's	Women's	Overall	Men's	Women's	Overall	Men's	Women's	Overall
1981–82	273.5	114.8	388.3	185.8	81.6	267.4	206.5	94.7	301.1	225.8	98.7	324.5
1982–83	293.3	120.3	413.6	180.2	78.1	258.3	202.8	100.3	303.1	228.7	101.6	330.3
1983–84	301.8	120.3	422.1	194.1	91.2	285.3	213.8	107.5	321.3	239.9	107.9	347.8
1984–85	318.2	127.2	445.4	203.6	97.8	301.4	227.1	116.6	343.7	254.2	115.9	370.1
1985–86	315.2	133.0	448.2	199.5	103.8	303.3	227.0	118.3	345.3	251.9	120.1	372.0
1986–87	290.8	128.7	419.5	186.7	95.3	282.0	224.2	114.0	338.2	239.9	115.0	354.9
1987–88	275.6	125.9	401.5	177.1	94.3	271.4	207.5	112.5	320.0	225.7	113.3	338.9
1988–89	277.9	127.8	405.7	172.2	92.7	264.9	208.2	114.7	322.9	225.2	114.3	339.4
1989–90	275.8	126.0	401.7	168.4	90.1	258.5	202.2	110.5	312.7	220.9	111.2	332.1
1990–91	277.7	128.3	405.9	171.2	87.3	258.6	206.3	113.2	319.4	222.9	112.1	335.0
1991–92	278.7	132.9	411.6	168.6	87.6	256.2	200.1	114.2	314.3	219.7	113.9	333.5
1992–93	277.5	137.8	415.3	164.5	86.2	250.7	197.2	115.4	312.7	216.5	115.6	332.1
1993–94	286.5	147.4	433.8	159.1	85.8	244.9	186.2	116.1	302.3	212.6	118.3	330.9
1994–95	278.8	153.1	431.8	146.6	81.3	227.9	173.7	112.4	286.0	199.7	116.7	316.4
1995–96*	284.9	169.4	454.3	157.3	90.7	248.0	189.5	129.2	318.7	209.4	130.3	339.7
1996–97*	276.8	172.3	449.1	154.3	90.6	244.9	185.0	129.7	314.7	204.4	131.5	335.9
1997–98*	277.7	180.4	458.1	157.4	96.6	254.0	186.6	132.4	319.0	206.8	137.2	344.0
1998–99*	274.1	194.1	468.3	160.0	103.0	263.0	185.6	136.7	322.3	205.0	144.4	349.4
1999–00*	267.3	195.6	463.0	152.5	99.4	251.9	188.9	136.8	325.7	202.7	144.3	346.9
2000–01*	272.3	203.2	473.6	159.4	107.6	266.4	195.5	143.6	338.5	209.0	151.8	359.8
2001–02*	263.9	203.2	467.2	156.6	104.6	261.2	192.4	140.6	333.1	204.8	150.1	354.9
2002–03*	266.1	210.0	476.1	163.4	108.9	272.2	197.9	144.5	342.4	210.0	155.5	365.6
2003–04*	265.5	213.4	478.9	165.5	112.5	278.0	194.9	142.5	337.4	209.2	156.6	365.8
2004–05*	268.5	216.8	485.2	166.8	114.4	281.2	202.0	146.1	348.1	213.2	159.5	372.8
2005–06*	269.3	218.1	487.4	171.0	117.1	288.1	202.7	146.4	349.1	214.4	160.3	374.6
2006–07*	270.6	221.5	492.0	177.6	122.6	300.2	210.5	149.4	359.9	219.8	164.0	383.8
2007–08*	269.4	222.9	492.3	188.1	126.1	314.1	234.0	153.8	387.8	232.3	167.6	399.8
2008–09*	274.2	227.0	501.3	184.7	127.1	311.8	223.0	157.2	380.2	228.5	170.7	399.2
2009–10*	276.2	230.2	506.5	189.9	131.3	321.2	227.2	159.2	386.4	232.3	173.8	406.1
2010–11*	274.0	233.6	507.6	199.3	135.9	335.3	231.9	164.1	396.0	235.8	177.8	413.6
2011–12*	273.8	234.7	508.4	202.8	140.9	343.8	236.1	167.6	403.7	238.3	180.8	419.0
2012–13*	274.0	236.5	510.5	203.5	142.7	346.3	239.8	172.5	412.4	240.2	184.1	424.2
2013–14*	277.9	240.1	518.0	207.1	147.1	354.2	242.9	173.6	416.5	243.5	186.7	430.3
2014–15*	278.7	242.2	520.8	215.0	153.6	368.6	246.1	175.9	422.0	247.2	189.9	437.1
2015–16*	279.1	243.2	522.3	217.1	155.8	372.9	248.4	177.0	425.3	248.8	191.3	440.2
2016–17*	278.4	246.6	524.9	220.0	160.7	380.8	251.8	179.5	431.3	250.9	195.0	445.9

*Provisional members are included in these numbers.

SOURCE: Erin Irick, "NCAA Sports Participation 1981–82—2016–17: Average Number of Student-Athletes per Institution," in *1981–82—2016–17 NCAA Sports Sponsorship and Participation Rates Report*, National Collegiate Athletic Association, October 2017, http://www.ncaa.org/sites/default/files/2016-17NCAA-0472_ParticRatesReport-FINAL_20171120.pdf (accessed February 12, 2018)

per day all seven days a week, and more than half (53.4%) of students said they engaged in strengthening activities three or more times a week. (See Table 6.14.) As Table 6.15 shows, high school students in Montana (54%) and Oklahoma (54%) were the most physically active in 2015, whereas Mississippi high school students (34.2%) were the least likely to engage in 60 minutes or more of physical activity at least five days a week. Over half (51.6%) of all high school students attended a physical education class at least once a week in 2015, while 29.8% took physical education every day. (See Table 6.16.) As shown in Table 6.17, 57.6% of all high school students played on a sports team in 2015. Team sports participation peaked in ninth grade, with 63% of all high school freshmen playing a team sport that year. By comparison, roughly half (50.8%) of high school seniors played on a sports team in 2015.

Since 1971 the National Federation of State High School Associations (NFHS) has compiled data on sports participation from its member associations. The most recent data are published in *2016–17 High School Athletics Participation Survey* (2017, http://www.nfhs.org/ParticipationStatistics/PDF/2016-17_Participation_Survey_Results.pdf). Table 6.18 summarizes these NFHS data between 1971 and 2017. During the 2016–17 school year the number of participants in high school sports reached nearly 8 million. At 3.4 million, participation among girls reached an all-time high in 2016–17. The total for boys that year was almost 4.6 million, roughly the same as the totals for the previous six years.

Table 6.19 shows the most popular high school sports for boys in 2016–17. Nearly 1.1 million boys participated in football during the 2016–17 school year. Boys' track and field had 600,136 participants, about half as many participants as football. Basketball (550,305), baseball (491,790), and soccer (450,234) were the third-, fourth-, and fifth-most popular boys'

FIGURE 6.1

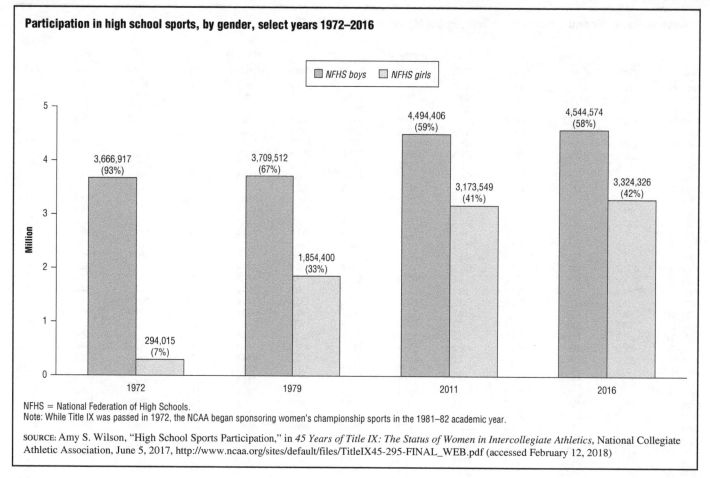

Participation in high school sports, by gender, select years 1972–2016

■ NFHS boys ☐ NFHS girls

NFHS = National Federation of High Schools.
Note: While Title IX was passed in 1972, the NCAA began sponsoring women's championship sports in the 1981–82 academic year.

SOURCE: Amy S. Wilson, "High School Sports Participation," in *45 Years of Title IX: The Status of Women in Intercollegiate Athletics*, National Collegiate Athletic Association, June 5, 2017, http://www.ncaa.org/sites/default/files/TitleIX45-295-FINAL_WEB.pdf (accessed February 12, 2018)

sports, respectively. Nationwide, 18,214 schools supported boys' basketball programs, the most of any team sport. Among high school girls, outdoor track and field was the most popular sport, with 494,477 participants, followed by volleyball (444,779), basketball (430,368), soccer (388,339), and fast-pitch softball (367,405). (See Table 6.20.) As with boys' basketball, girls' basketball was the most prevalent high school athletic program in the United States, with 17,934 schools supporting girls' basketball programs in 2016–17.

According to the NFHS, in *2016–17 High School Athletics Participation Survey*, the state with the largest number of high school athletes during the 2016–17 school year was Texas, with 834,558. Other leading states included California (800,364), New York (367,849), Illinois (341,387), and Ohio (340,146).

FIGURE 6.2

Participation in intercollegiate sports, by gender, select years 1982–2016

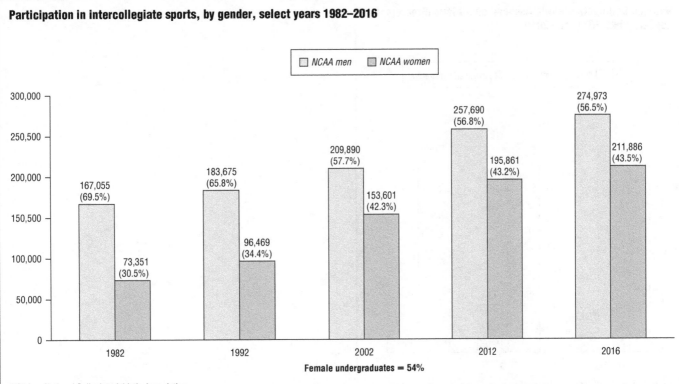

NCAA = National Collegiate Athletic Association.
Note: In this report, graphics comparing men's and women's sport participation numbers begin with 1982, the year the NCAA began sponsoring women's championship sports.

SOURCE: Amy S. Wilson, "Championship Sports Participation: All Divisions," in *45 Years of Title IX: The Status of Women in Intercollegiate Athletics*, National Collegiate Athletic Association, June 5, 2017, http://www.ncaa.org/sites/default/files/TitleIX45-295-FINAL_WEB.pdf (accessed February 12, 2018)

FIGURE 6.3

Head coaches of National Collegiate Athletic Association sports teams, by gender, 1996, 2011, and 2016

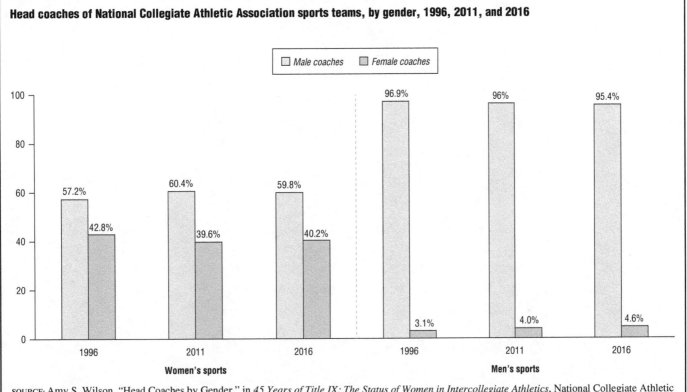

SOURCE: Amy S. Wilson, "Head Coaches by Gender," in *45 Years of Title IX: The Status of Women in Intercollegiate Athletics*, National Collegiate Athletic Association, June 5, 2017, http://www.ncaa.org/sites/default/files/TitleIX45-295-FINAL_WEB.pdf (accessed February 12, 2018)

FIGURE 6.4

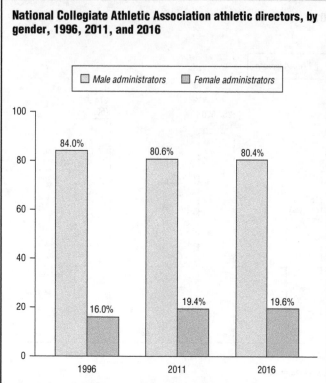

National Collegiate Athletic Association athletic directors, by gender, 1996, 2011, and 2016

☐ Male administrators   ■ Female administrators

	1996	2011	2016
Male	84.0%	80.6%	80.4%
Female	16.0%	19.4%	19.6%

SOURCE: Amy S. Wilson, "Administrators by Gender: Directors of Athletics," in *45 Years of Title IX: The Status of Women in Intercollegiate Athletics*, National Collegiate Athletic Association, June 5, 2017, http://www.ncaa.org/sites/default/files/TitleIX45-295-FINAL_WEB.pdf (accessed February 12, 2018).

FIGURE 6.5

National Collegiate Athletic Association athletic directors, by gender and division, 1996 and 2016

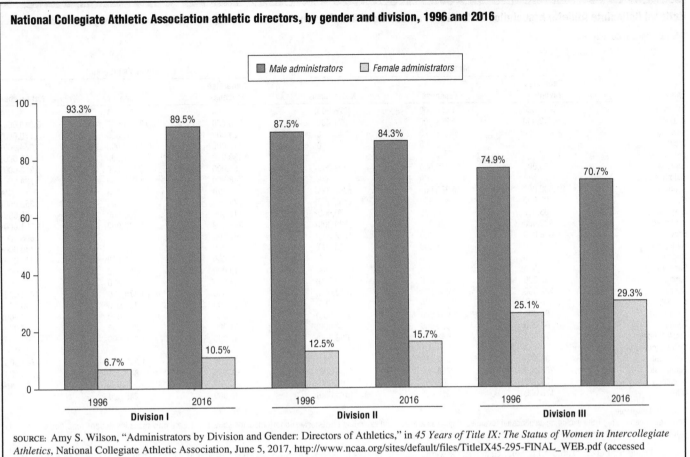

SOURCE: Amy S. Wilson, "Administrators by Division and Gender: Directors of Athletics," in *45 Years of Title IX: The Status of Women in Intercollegiate Athletics*, National Collegiate Athletic Association, June 5, 2017, http://www.ncaa.org/sites/default/files/TitleIX45-295-FINAL_WEB.pdf (accessed February 12, 2018)

TABLE 6.10

National Collegiate Athletic Association Division I—Football Bowl Subdivision revenues and expenses, by sport, fiscal year 2015

[Median value; in dollars]

Sport	Men's programs			Women's programs		
	Generated revenues	Expenses	Net revenue	Generated revenues	Expenses	Net revenue
Baseball	440,000	1,664,000	(926,000)	N/A	N/A	N/A
Basketball	5,712,000	5,808,000	271,000	328,000	2,861,000	(2,010,000)
Bowling	0	0	0	24,000	359,000	(170,000)
Crew	0	0	0	116,000	1,557,000	(1,064,000)
Equestrian	0	0	0	139,000	1,772,000	(1,130,000)
Fencing	30,000	256,000	(207,000)	51,000	424,000	(213,000)
Field hockey	N/A	N/A	N/A	48,000	1,092,000	(734,000)
Football	21,602,000	16,385,000	5,231,000	N/A	N/A	N/A
Golf	90,000	576,000	(332,000)	73,000	564,000	(353,000)
Gymnastics	93,000	776,000	(670,000)	116,000	1,206,000	(890,000)
Ice hockey	882,000	2,496,000	(629,000)	224,000	1,913,000	(1,504,000)
Lacrosse	668,000	1,711,000	(748,000)	167,000	1,264,000	(685,000)
Rifle	0	43,000	(43,000)	29,000	72,000	(40,000)
Rugby	0	0	0	71,000	219,000	(88,000)
Sand volleyball	N/A	N/A	N/A	16,000	202,000	(108,000)
Skiing	53,000	528,000	(437,000)	54,000	580,000	(414,000)
Soccer	122,000	1,001,000	(612,000)	101,000	1,175,000	(758,000)
Softball	N/A	N/A	N/A	114,000	1,155,000	(749,000)
Swimming	85,000	1,002,000	(677,000)	70,000	1,048,000	(722,000)
Tennis	67,000	630,000	(444,000)	54,000	688,000	(437,000)
Track & field/ Cross country	70,000	1,043,000	(636,000)	87,000	1,279,000	(792,000)
Volleyball	138,000	824,000	(621,000)	106,000	1,229,000	(743,000)
Water polo	204,000	708,000	(356,000)	61,000	844,000	(638,000)
Wrestling	127,000	1,007,000	(590,000)	N/A	N/A	N/A
Other	176,000	619,000	(375,000)	36,000	245,000	(87,000)

N/A = Not available.
Note: Revenues are reported excluding all allocated revenues. Expenses are reported excluding third-party support. Medians shown represent only those institutions reporting some amount for revenues or expenses.

SOURCE: Daniel L. Fulks, "Table 3.11. Total Generated Revenues and Expenses by Sport, Division I—FBS, Fiscal Year 2015—Median Values," in *Revenues and Expenses: 2004–15 NCAA Division I Intercollegiate Athletics Program Report*, National Collegiate Athletic Association, July 2016, http://www.ncaapublications.com/productdownloads/D1REVEXP2015.pdf (accessed February 13, 2018)

TABLE 6.11

Sources of revenue, National Collegiate Athletic Association Division I—Football Bowl Subdivision, fiscal year 2015

[Median value; in dollars]

	Public	Private	Total
Total ticket sales	**7,401,000**	**10,573,000**	**8,992,000**
NCAA and conference distributions	5,244,000	8,592,000	6,080,000
Guarantees and options	912,000	316,000	878,000
Cash contributions from alumni and others	8,701,000	11,659,000	9,531,000
Third-party support	—	—	—
Other:			
Concessions/programs/novelties	988,000	1,094,000	1,071,000
Broadcast rights	1,538,000	15,339,000	2,568,000
Royalties/advertising/sponsorship	3,264,000	4,223,000	3,290,000
Sports camps	143,000	33,000	110,000
Endowment/investment income	214,000	1,979,000	307,000
Miscellaneous	778,000	736,000	765,000
Total generated revenues	**31,430,000**	**60,357,000**	**47,962,000**
Allocated revenues:			
Direct institutional support	3,016,000	13,819,000	3,816,000
Indirect institutional support	225,000	52,000	144,000
Student fees	3,168,000	—	2,299,000
Direct government support	0	—	0
Total allocated revenues	**11,248,000**	**16,847,000**	**12,670,000**
Total all revenues	**51,456,000**	**77,725,000**	**63,659,000**

NCAA = National Collegiate Athletic Association.
Note: There were 111 public and 17 private institutions reporting.

SOURCE: Daniel L. Fulks, "Table 3.7. Sources of Revenues, Division I—FBS, Fiscal Year 2015—Median Values," in *Revenues and Expenses: 2004–15 NCAA Division I Intercollegiate Athletics Program Report*, National Collegiate Athletic Association, July 2016, http://www.ncaapublications.com/productdownloads/D1REVEXP2015.pdf (accessed February 13, 2018)

TABLE 6.12

Summary of National Collegiate Athletic Association Division I, II, and III recruiting rules, 2017–18

Recruiting method	Men's basketball	Women's basketball	Football	Other sports
		Sophomore year—Division I		
Recruiting materials	• You may receive brochures for camps, questionnaires, NCAA materials, and nonathletics recruiting publications. • You may begin receiving recruiting materials June 15 after your sophomore year.	• You may receive brochures for camps, questionnaires, NCAA materials, and nonathletics recruiting publications.	• You may receive brochures for camps, questionnaires, NCAA materials, and nonathletics recruiting publications.	• You may receive brochures for camps, questionnaires, NCAA materials, and nonathletics recruiting publications. • Men's ice hockey—You may begin receiving recruiting materials January 1 of your sophomore year.
Telephone calls	• You may make calls to the coach at your expense only. • College coach can make unlimited calls beginning June 15 after your sophomore year.	• You may make calls to the coach at your expense only. • College coach cannot call you.	• You may make calls to the coach at your expense only. • College coach cannot call you.	• Sports other than Lacrosse may make calls to the coach at your expense only. • College coach cannot call you. • Women's ice hockey—A college coach may call international college-bound student-athletes once on or after July 7 through July 31 after sophomore year. • Men's ice hockey—May not be made before January 1 of sophomore year.
Off-campus contact	• None allowed.	• None allowed.	• None allowed.	• None allowed. • Men's ice hockey—May not be made before June 15 after sophomore year.
Official visit	• None allowed.	• None allowed.	• None allowed.	• None allowed.
Unofficial visit	• You may make an unlimited number of unofficial visits, except during a dead period.	• You may make an unlimited number of unofficial visits, except during a dead period.	• You may make an unlimited number of unofficial visits, except during a dead period.	• You may make an unlimited number of unofficial visits, except during a dead period. • Lacrosse, women's gymnastics, wrestling—not permitted.
		Junior year—Division I		
Electronic correspondence (e.g., text messaging, instant messenger, email)	• You may begin receiving electronic correspondence June 15 after your sophomore year. • Correspondence must be private between you and the coach until you provide a written commitment to the NCAA school.	• You may begin receiving electronic correspondence September 1 of your junior year. • Correspondence must be private between you and the coach until you provide a written commitment to the NCAA school.	• You may begin receiving electronic correspondence September 1 of your junior year. • Correspondence must be private between you and the coach until you provide a written commitment to the NCAA school.	• All forms of electronic correspondence permissible September 1 of your junior year. • Correspondence must be private until you provide a written commitment to the NCAA school.
Recruiting materials	• Allowed. • You may begin receiving recruiting materials June 15 after your sophomore year.	• You may begin receiving September 1 of your junior year.	• You may begin receiving September 1 of your junior year.	• You may begin receiving September 1 of your junior year. • Men's ice hockey—You may begin receiving recruiting materials January 1 after your sophomore year.
Telephone calls	• You may make calls to the coach at your expense.	• You may make calls to the coach at your expense.	• You may make calls to the coach at your expense.	• You may make calls to the coach at your expense. • Lacrosse—You may not call a coach before September 1 of your junior year.
College coaches may call you	• Unlimited.	• Unlimited beginning September 1 of your junior year.	• One call from April 15 to May 31 of your junior year. Additional calls may not be made before September 1 of your senior year.	• May not be made before September 1 at the beginning of your junior year. • Swimming & diving—May not be made before July 1 following completion of junior year, or the opening day of classes of your senior year, whichever is earlier.
Off-campus contact	• Allowed beginning opening day of classes. Contacts other than April period may only occur at your school. Contacts in April may occur at your school or residence. • No contact on the day of a competition. • Contacts may not occur during the time of day when classes are in session.	• Allowed beginning March 1 of your junior year only at the student's school or residence. • No contact on the day of a competition. • Contacts may not occur during the time of day when classes are in session.	• None allowed.	• Women's gymnastics—Allowed after your junior year beginning July 15. • Women's ice hockey—Allowed after your junior year beginning July 7. • Fencing—Allowed after completion of participation in the USA Fencing National Championship and July Challenge and after completion of junior year.

TABLE 6.12

Summary of National Collegiate Athletic Association Division I, II, and III recruiting rules, 2017–18 (CONTINUED)

Recruiting method	Men's basketball	Women's basketball	Football	Other sports
Official visit	• Allowed January 1 of your junior year. • You may make only one official visit per college and up to a maximum of five official visits to Division I colleges. There is no limit to official visits to Division II colleges.	• Allowed April of your junior year beginning Thursday following the Women's Final Four.®	• Allowed April 1 of your junior year through the Sunday before the last Wednesday in June, provided the official visit is not in conjunction with participation in an institutional camp or clinic.	• Wrestling—Allowed beginning your junior year after September 1 only at the student's school or residence. • Lacrosse—Allowed beginning your junior year after September 1 only at the student's school or residence. • All other sports—Allowed beginning July 1 after your junior year. • None allowed.
Unofficial visit	• You may make an unlimited number of unofficial visits, except during a dead period.	• You may make an unlimited number of unofficial visits, except during a dead period.	• You may make an unlimited number of unofficial visits, except during a dead period.	• You may make an unlimited number of unofficial visits, except during a dead period. • Wrestling, Lacrosse and Women's gymnastics—Not allowed before September 1 of your junior year.
Senior year—Division I				
Electronic correspondence (e.g., text messaging, instant messenger, email)	• You may begin receiving electronic correspondence June 15 after your sophomore year. • Correspondence must be private between you and the coach until you provide a written commitment to the NCAA school.	• You may begin receiving electronic correspondence September 1 of your junior year. • Correspondence must be private between you and the coach until you provide a written commitment to the NCAA school.	• You may begin receiving electronic correspondence September 1 of your junior year. • Correspondence must be private between you and the coach until you provide a written commitment to the NCAA school.	• All forms of electronic correspondence permissible September 1 of your junior year. • Correspondence must be private until you provide a written commitment to the NCAA school.
Recruiting materials	• Allowed.	• Allowed.	• Allowed.	• Allowed.
Telephone calls	• You may make calls to the coach at your expense.	• You may make calls to the coach at your expense.	• You may make calls to the coach at your expense.	You may make calls to the coach at your expense.
College coaches may call you	• Unlimited.	• Unlimited.	• Once per week beginning September 1 outside contact period. • Unlimited calls after you sign an NLI, written offer of admission and/or financial aid; OR after the college receives a financial deposit from you. • Unlimited during contact period.	• Unlimited calls after you sign an NLI, written offer of admission and/or financial aid; OR after the college receives a financial deposit from you.
Off-campus contact	• Allowed.	• Allowed.	• Allowed beginning July 1 prior to your senior year.	• Allowed.
Official visit	• You may make only one official visit per college and up to a maximum of five official visits to Division I colleges. There is no limit to official visits to Division II colleges.	• You may make only one official visit per college and up to a maximum of five official visits to Division I colleges. There is no limit to official visits to Division II colleges.	• Allowed beginning opening day of classes your senior year. • You may make only one official visit per college and up to a maximum of five official visits to Division I colleges. There is no limit to official visits to Division II colleges.	• Allowed beginning opening day of classes your senior year. • You may make only one official visit per college and up to a maximum of five official visits to Division I colleges. There is no limit to official visits to Division II colleges.
Unofficial visit	• You may make an unlimited number of unofficial visits, except during a dead period.	• You may make an unlimited number of unofficial visits, except during a dead period.	• You may make an unlimited number of unofficial visits, except during a dead period.	• You may make an unlimited number of unofficial visits, except during a dead period.

TABLE 6.12

Summary of National Collegiate Athletic Association Division I, II, and III recruiting rules, 2017–18 [CONTINUED]

Recruiting method	Men's basketball	Women's basketball	Football	Other sports
How often can a coach see me or talk to me off the college's campus?	• A college coach may contact you or your parents/legal guardians (including evaluating you off the college's campus) seven times. • Unlimited number of contacts and evaluation after you sign an NLI, written offer of admission and/or financial aid; OR after the college receives a financial deposit from you.	• A college coach may contact you or your parents/legal guardians (including evaluating you off the college's campus) seven times. • Unlimited number of contacts and evaluation after you sign an NLI, written offer of admission and/or financial aid; OR after the college receives a financial deposit from you.	• A college coach may contact you or your parents/legal guardians (including evaluating you off the college's campus) six times. • One evaluation during September, October and November. • Two evaluations—April 15 through May 31 (once to evaluate athletics ability and once to evaluate academic qualifications). • Unlimited number of contacts and evaluation after you sign an NLI, written offer of admission and/or financial aid; OR after the college receives a financial deposit from you.	• A college coach may contact you or your parents/legal guardians not more than three times. • Unlimited number of contacts and evaluation after you sign an NLI, written offer of admission and/or financial aid; OR after the college receives a financial deposit from you.

NLI = National Letter of Intent.
NCAA = National Collegiate Athletic Association.

SOURCE: "Recruiting Calendars," in *2017–18 Guide for the College-Bound Student-Athlete*, National Collegiate Athletic Association, 2017, http://www.ncaapublications.com/productdownloads/CBSA18.pdf (accessed February 13, 2018)

TABLE 6.13

Participation in physical activity among high school students, by sex, grade, and race and ethnicity, 2015

Category	Did not participate in at least 60 minutes of physical activity on at least 1 day			Physically active at least 60 minutes/day on 5 or more days		
	Female	Male	Total	Female	Male	Total
	%	%	%	%	%	%
Race/ethnicity						
White*	14.3	8.8	11.6	43.5	62.0	52.7
Black*	25.2	16.2	20.4	33.4	52.2	43.5
Hispanic	19.2	11.9	15.6	33.1	53.5	43.4
Grade						
9	14.7	9.5	12.0	43.9	62.3	53.7
10	15.8	10.4	13.1	41.9	58.7	50.2
11	18.2	12.4	15.5	36.6	56.3	46.5
12	21.4	12.4	16.9	33.4	53.3	43.5
Total	**17.5**	**11.1**	**14.3**	**39.1**	**57.8**	**48.6**

*Non-Hispanic.
Note: Because of changes in question context starting in 2011, national Youth Risk Behavior Survey (YRBS) prevalence estimates derived from the 60 minutes of physical activity question in 2011, 2013, and 2015 are not comparable to those reported in 2009 or earlier. On the 2005–2009 national YRBS questionnaire, physical activity was assessed with three questions (in the following order) that asked the number of days students participated in 1) at least 20 minutes of vigorous physical activity; 2) at least 30 minutes of moderate physical activity; and 3) at least 60 minutes of aerobic (moderate and vigorous) physical activity. On the 2011, 2013, and 2015 national YRBS questionnaires, only the 60 minutes of aerobic physical activity question was included. Physical activity refers to doing any kind of physical activity that increased the student's heart rate and made them breathe hard some of the time during the 7 days before the survey.

SOURCE: Laura Kann et al., "Table 105. Percentage of High School Students Who Did not Participate in at Least 60 Minutes of Physical Activity on at Least 1 Day and Who Were Physically Active at Least 60 Minutes/Day on 5 or More Days, by Sex, Race/Ethnicity, and Grade—United States, Youth Risk Behavior Survey, 2015," in "Youth Risk Behavior Surveillance—United States, 2015," *Morbidity and Mortality Weekly Report*, vol. 65, no. 6, June 10, 2016, https://www.cdc.gov/healthyyouth/data/yrbs/pdf/2015/ss6506_updated.pdf (accessed February 13, 2018)

TABLE 6.14

Participation in vigorous physical activity among high school students, by sex, grade, and race and ethnicity, 2015

Category	Physically active at least 60 minutes/day on all 7 days			Participated in muscle strengthening activities		
	Female	Male	Total	Female	Male	Total
	%	%	%	%	%	%
Race/ethnicity						
White*	19.5	38.5	29.0	46.1	63.0	54.5
Black*	16.6	30.8	24.2	34.5	69.8	52.3
Hispanic	14.7	34.2	24.6	39.9	64.4	52.4
Grade						
9	20.9	40.1	31.0	48.2	64.9	56.9
10	19.0	36.7	27.8	43.0	67.3	54.9
11	16.0	34.3	25.3	39.3	62.5	51.1
12	14.3	32.6	23.5	39.9	59.9	50.0
Total	**17.7**	**36.0**	**27.1**	**42.7**	**63.7**	**53.4**

*Non-Hispanic.
Note: Because of changes in question context starting in 2011, national YRBS prevalence estimates derived from the 60 minutes of physical activity question in 2011, 2013, and 2015 are not comparable to those reported in 2009 or earlier. On the 2005–2009 national YRBS questionnaire, physical activity was assessed with three questions (in the following order) that asked the number of days students participated in 1) at least 20 minutes of vigorous physical activity; 2) at least 30 minutes of moderate physical activity; and 3) at least 60 minutes of aerobic (moderate and vigorous) physical activity. On the 2011, 2013, and 2015 national YRBS questionnaires, only the 60 minutes of aerobic physical activity question was included. Physical activity refers to doing any kind of physical activity that increased students' heart rate and made them breathe hard some of the time during the 7 days before the survey. Muscle-strengthening activities include push-ups, sit-ups, or weight lifting, during the 7 days before the survey.

SOURCE: Laura Kann et al., "Table 107. Percentage of High School Students Who Were Physically Active at Least 60 Minutes/Day on All 7 Days and Who Participated in Muscle Strengthening Activities on 3 or More Days, by Sex, Race/Ethnicity, and Grade—United States, Youth Risk Behavior Survey, 2015," in "Youth Risk Behavior Surveillance—United States, 2015," *Morbidity and Mortality Weekly Report*, vol. 65, no. 6, June 10, 2016, https://www.cdc.gov/healthyyouth/data/yrbs/pdf/2015/ss6506_updated.pdf (accessed February 13, 2018)

TABLE 6.15

Participation in physical activity among high school students, by state, 2015

Site	Did not participate in at least 60 minutes of physical activity on at least 1 day			Physically active at least 60 minutes/day on 5 or more days		
	Female	Male	Total	Female	Male	Total
	%	%	%	%	%	%
State surveys						
Alabama	21.0	14.4	17.5	31.1	51.6	41.3
Alaska	18.4	14.0	16.1	38.8	49.3	44.2
Arizona	17.3	14.5	15.9	40.0	52.7	46.4
Arkansas	24.9	15.1	20.0	35.0	51.9	43.3
California	14.7	11.5	13.1	41.4	55.0	48.1
Connecticut	16.9	11.7	14.3	39.9	50.8	45.3
Delaware	22.9	14.1	18.5	33.3	53.1	43.3
Florida	24.7	15.1	19.9	30.6	53.1	41.9
Hawaii	21.4	14.5	18.0	30.7	45.8	38.1
Idaho	14.7	9.0	11.7	43.6	62.3	53.1
Illinois	14.3	13.6	13.9	42.5	56.7	49.6
Indiana	17.8	12.9	15.4	38.5	54.5	46.5
Kentucky	18.8	13.9	16.5	29.9	44.1	37.0
Maine	18.1	13.6	15.9	34.9	47.4	41.2
Maryland	22.8	16.6	19.8	30.1	44.0	36.9
Massachusetts	18.0	12.0	15.1	37.4	52.9	45.2
Michigan	18.5	13.4	15.9	42.0	50.1	46.0
Mississippi	26.6	19.0	22.9	23.5	45.1	34.2
Missouri	18.8	13.5	16.4	40.1	51.9	45.7
Montana	12.3	9.2	10.7	47.6	60.1	54.0
Nebraska	15.7	12.7	14.1	46.3	59.0	52.8
Nevada	16.4	9.4	13.0	42.4	58.9	50.6
New Hampshire	15.1	12.2	13.6	40.7	52.9	46.9
New Mexico	18.1	11.0	14.6	44.3	60.1	52.2
New York	19.8	17.6	18.8	37.3	46.8	41.8
North Carolina	21.6	13.5	17.6	33.7	53.1	43.4
North Dakota	13.5	10.9	12.1	42.9	59.3	51.3
Oklahoma	17.1	7.7	12.4	43.9	64.2	54.0
Pennsylvania	18.5	12.5	15.5	37.4	53.8	45.6
Rhode Island	17.5	14.4	16.0	35.0	52.2	43.7
South Carolina	26.8	14.3	20.6	31.4	53.7	42.3
South Dakota	16.4	12.9	14.7	37.8	56.4	47.4
Tennessee	21.2	15.2	18.2	33.8	51.3	42.7
Vermont	16.9	11.8	14.4	38.3	53.3	45.8
Virginia	21.6	12.5	16.9	35.6	54.2	45.2
West Virginia	18.8	15.5	17.2	39.2	50.4	44.9
Wyoming	14.3	11.9	13.0	43.7	57.4	50.7
Median	18.1	13.5	15.9	38.3	53.1	45.3
Range	(12.3–26.8)	(7.7–19.0)	(10.7–22.9)	(23.5–47.6)	(44.0–64.2)	(34.2–54.0)

Note: Physical activity refers to doing any kind of physical activity that increased their heart rate and made them breathe hard some of the time during the 7 days before the survey.

SOURCE: Adapted from Laura Kann et al., "Table 106. Percentage of High School Students Who Did not Participate in at Least 60 Minutes of Physical Activity on at Least 1 Day and Who Were Physically Active at Least 60 Minutes/Day on 5 or More Days, by Sex—Selected US Sites, Youth Risk Behavior Survey, 2015," in "Youth Risk Behavior Surveillance—United States, 2015," *Morbidity and Mortality Weekly Report*, vol. 65, no. 6, June 10, 2016, https://www.cdc.gov/healthyyouth/data/yrbs/pdf/2015/ss6506_updated.pdf (accessed February 13, 2018)

TABLE 6.16

Attendance in physical education classes among high school students, by sex, grade, and race and ethnicity, 2015

| | Attended PE classes | | | Attended PE classes daily | | |
| | Female | Male | Total | Female | Male | Total |
Category	%	%	%	%	%	%
Race/ethnicity						
White*	45.9	51.0	48.4	21.1	29.6	25.4
Black*	52.2	65.4	59.2	32.2	38.9	35.8
Hispanic	50.1	60.5	55.4	33.0	42.4	37.7
Grade						
9	70.4	72.2	71.4	39.5	44.6	42.2
10	53.9	61.3	57.5	27.0	36.1	31.5
11	34.6	42.2	38.5	18.1	25.2	21.8
12	29.1	42.9	36.1	16.0	27.9	21.9
Total	**47.8**	**55.3**	**51.6**	**25.5**	**33.8**	**29.8**

PE = physical education.
*Non-Hispanic.
Note: Attendance is in an average week when the student was in school.

SOURCE: Laura Kann et al., "Table 111. Percentage of High School Students Who Attended Physical Education (PE) Classes on ≥ 1 Days and Who Attended PE Classes on All 5 Days, by Sex, Race/Ethnicity, and Grade—United States, Youth Risk Behavior Survey, 2015," in "Youth Risk Behavior Surveillance—United States, 2015," *Morbidity and Mortality Weekly Report*, vol. 65, no. 6, June 10, 2016, https://www.cdc.gov/healthyyouth/data/yrbs/pdf/2015/ss6506_updated.pdf (accessed February 13, 2018)

TABLE 6.17

Team sports participation among high school students, by sex, grade, and race and ethnicity, 2015

| | Female | Male | Total |
Category	%	%	%
Race/Ethnicity			
White*	60.7	64.4	62.4
Black*	47.7	66.5	57.6
Hispanic	40.7	56.3	48.5
Grade			
9	57.6	68.1	63.0
10	55.1	63.5	59.2
11	51.7	62.3	57.0
12	46.9	54.6	50.8
Total	**53.0**	**62.2**	**57.6**

*Non-Hispanic.
Note: Team sports participation refers to programs run by their school or community groups during the 12 months before the survey.

SOURCE: Laura Kann et al., "Table 113. Percentage of High School Students Who Played on at Least One Sprots Team, by Sex, Race/Ethnicity, and Grade—United States, Youth Risk Behavior Survey, 2015," in "Youth Risk Behavior Surveillance—United States, 2015," *Morbidity and Mortality Weekly Report*, vol. 65, no. 6, June 10, 2016, https://www.cdc.gov/healthyyouth/data/yrbs/pdf/2015/ss6506_updated.pdf (accessed February 13, 2018)

TABLE 6.18

Participation in high school athletics programs, by sex, 1971–2017

Year	Boys participants	Girls participants	Total
1971–72	3,666,917	294,015	3,960,932
1972–73	3,770,621	817,073	4,587,694
1973–74	4,070,125	1,300,169	5,370,294
1975–76	4,109,021	1,645,039	5,754,060
1977–78	4,367,442	2,083,040	6,450,482
1978–79	3,709,512	1,854,400	5,563,912
1979–80	3,517,829	1,750,264	5,268,093
1980–81	3,503,124	1,853,789	5,356,913
1981–82	3,409,081	1,810,671	5,219,752
1982–83	3,355,558	1,779,972	5,135,530
1983–84	3,303,599	1,747,346	5,050,945
1984–85	3,354,284	1,757,884	5,112,168
1985–86	3,344,275	1,807,121	5,151,396
1986–87	3,364,082	1,836,356	5,200,438
1987–88	3,425,777	1,849,684	5,275,461
1988–89	3,416,844	1,839,352	5,256,196
1989–90	3,398,192	1,858,659	5,256,851
1990–91	3,406,355	1,892,316	5,298,671
1991–92	3,429,853	1,940,801	5,370,654
1992–93	3,416,389	1,997,489	5,413,878
1993–94	3,472,967	2,130,315	5,603,282
1994–95	3,536,359	2,240,461	5,776,820
1995–96	3,634,052	2,367,936	6,001,988
1996–97	3,706,225	2,474,043	6,180,268
1997–98	3,763,120	2,570,333	6,333,453
1998–99	3,832,352	2,652,726	6,485,078
1999–00	3,861,749	2,675,874	6,537,623
2000–01	3,921,069	2,784,154	6,705,223
2001–02	3,960,517	2,806,998	6,767,515
2002–03	3,988,738	2,856,358	6,845,096
2003–04	4,038,253	2,865,299	6,903,552
2004–05	4,110,319	2,908,390	7,018,709
2005–06	4,206,549	2,953,355	7,159,904
2006–07	4,321,103	3,021,807	7,342,910
2007–08	4,372,115	3,057,266	7,429,381
2008–09	4,422,662	3,114,091	7,536,753
2009–10	4,455,740	3,172,637	7,628,377
2010–11	4,494,406	3,173,549	7,667,955
2011–12	4,484,987	3,207,533	7,692,520
2012–13	4,490,854	3,222,723	7,713,577
2013–14	4,527,994	3,267,664	7,795,658
2014–15	4,519,312	3,287,735	7,807,047
2015–16	4,541,959	3,324,306	7,866,265
2016–17	4,563,238	3,400,297	7,963,535

SOURCE: "Athletics Participation Survey Totals," in *2016–17 High School Athletics Participation Survey*, National Federation of State High School Associations, 2017, http://www.nfhs.org/ParticipationStatistics/PDF/2016-17_Participation_Survey_Results.pdf (accessed February 13, 2018)

TABLE 6.19

Most popular high school sports for boys, by number of schools and number of participants, 2016–17

Schools		Participants	
1. Basketball	18,214	1. Football—11-player	1,057,382
2. Track and field—outdoor	16,699	2. Track and field—outdoor	600,136
3. Baseball	15,979	3. Basketball	550,305
4. Cross country	15,087	4. Baseball	491,790
5. Football—11-player	14,099	5. Soccer	450,234
6. Golf	13,223	6. Cross country	266,271
7. Soccer	12,188	7. Wrestling	244,804
8. Wrestling	10,629	8. Tennis	158,171
9. Tennis	9,725	9. Golf	141,466
10. Swimming & diving	7,342	10. Swimming & diving	138,364

SOURCE: "Ten Most Popular Boys Programs," in *2016–17 High School Athletics Participation Survey*, National Federation of State High School Associations, 2017, http://www.nfhs.org/ParticipationStatistics/PDF/2016-17_Participation_Survey_Results.pdf (accessed February 13, 2018)

TABLE 6.20

Most popular high school sports for girls, by number of schools and number of participants, 2016–17

Schools		Participants	
1. Basketball	17,934	1. Track and field—outdoor	494,477
2. Track and field—outdoor	16,658	2. Volleyball	444,779
3. Volleyball	15,992	3. Basketball	430,368
4. Softball—fast pitch	15,440	4. Soccer	388,339
5. Cross country	14,880	5. Softball—fast pitch	367,405
6. Soccer	11,823	6. Cross country	226,039
7. Tennis	10,121	7. Tennis	187,519
8. Golf	10,076	8. Swimming & diving	170,797
9. Swimming & diving	7,721	9. Competitive spirit squads	144,243
10. Competitive spirit squads	6,541	10. Lacrosse	93,473

SOURCE: "Ten Most Popular Girls Programs," in *2016–17 High School Athletics Participation Survey*, National Federation of State High School Associations, 2017, http://www.nfhs.org/ParticipationStatistics/PDF/2016-17_Participation_Survey_Results.pdf (accessed February 13, 2018)

CHAPTER 7
THE OLYMPICS

If professional team sports in the United States epitomize the corporatization of athletics, the Olympics, at least in theory, exemplify the opposite: global goodwill and the pursuit of athletic excellence for its own sake. The rhetoric of the Olympics reflects this ideal. The official motto of the Olympics, *Citius, Altius, Fortius*, is Latin for "Faster, Higher, Stronger," while the Olympic creed states that "the most important thing in the Olympic Games is not to win but to take part, just as the most important thing in life is not the triumph but the struggle." The imagery associated with the Olympic Games is also rich in symbolism. The five interconnected rings on the Olympic flag, representing the five major continents, are an emblem of international unity. The Olympic flame, for its part, traces its origins to the games in ancient Greece and is believed to have been first inspired by the story of Prometheus, the Greek titan who stole fire from the gods. Over the years, the Olympic mascot has also become an important symbol of the games, one intended to convey the unique national character of the host nation. For example, Soohorang, the white tiger who served as mascot for the 2018 winter games in PyeongChang, South Korea, derived its name from the Korean words for "protection" and "tiger." The white tiger is traditionally considered a guardian animal in Korean culture.

This spirit of goodwill does not, however, diminish the fact that vast sums of money change hands via the Olympics. Nor does it prevent the pursuit of these vast sums, or political grandstanding, from sometimes overshadowing the Olympic ideal.

The Olympics are divided into the Summer and Winter Olympiads. Table 7.1 lists the sports that were included in the 2016 summer games in Rio de Janeiro, Brazil. The winter Olympic Games are much smaller than the summer games. Table 7.2 shows the list of winter sports that were featured in the 2018 winter games in PyeongChang, South Korea.

The International Olympic Committee (IOC) regularly reviews which sports are to be included in the Olympic Games. The Olympic Charter limits the number of sports that can take place at the Olympics; therefore, sports must be cut to accommodate the addition of new ones. A number of factors are taken into consideration, most prominently popularity and cost. For example, beach volleyball made its Olympic debut in 1996, and snowboarding was added to the winter games program in 1998. In contrast, baseball and softball were eliminated following the 2008 games. Baseball and softball, however, are slated to return in 2020. As reported in "Five Additional Sports Unanimously Approved by the IOC for Tokyo 2020" (August 4, 2016, https://tokyo2020.org/en/news/notice/20160804-01.html), the IOC selected baseball/softball, karate, skateboarding, sport climbing, and surfing to be added to the 2020 summer games in Tokyo, Japan.

Throughout the history of the Olympic Games, US athletes have excelled on the world stage. Table 7.3 lists the top US Olympic medal winners of all time. The swimmer Michael Phelps (1985–) is the Olympic record holder for both total medals won (28) and gold medals won (23). Since the launch of the modern Olympics in 1896, the United States has won more medals than any other country. As Table 7.4 shows, between 1896 and 2016 the United States won 1,132 gold, 904 silver, and 792 bronze medals, for a total of 2,828. The country with the second-highest medal total, the Soviet Union, collected 1,204 medals between 1952 and 1988.

HISTORY OF THE OLYMPICS

In *The Olympic Games in Antiquity* (2018, https://stillmed.olympic.org/media/Document%20Library/Museum/Visit/TOM_Schools/Teaching_Resources/The_Olympic_Games_in_Antiquity/The_Olympic_Games_in_Antiquity_EN.pdf), the IOC explains that the roots of the Olympic Games are in ancient Greece. Exactly when the ancient

TABLE 7.1

Sports at the 2016 Summer Olympics in Rio de Janeiro, Brazil

Archery	Handball
Athletics	Hockey
Badminton	Judo
Basketball	Marathon swimming
Beach volleyball	Modern pentathlon
Boxing	Rowing
Canoe slalom	Rugby
Canoe sprint	Sailing
Cycling BMX	Shooting
Cycling mountain bike	Swimming
Cycling road	Synchronized swimming
Cycling track	Table tennis
Diving	Taekwondo
Equestrian dressage	Tennis
Equestrian eventing	Trampoline
Equestrian jumping	Triathlon
Fencing	Volleyball
Football (soccer)	Water polo
Golf	Weightlifting
Gymnastics artistic	Wrestling freestyle
Gymnastics rhythmic	Wrestling Greco-Roman

SOURCE: Created by Stephen Meyer for Gale, © 2018

TABLE 7.2

Sports at the 2018 Winter Olympics in PyeongChang, South Korea

Alpine skiing	Luge
Biathlon	Nordic combined
Bobsleigh	Short track speed skating
Cross country skiing	Skeleton
Curling	Ski jumping
Figure skating	Snowboard
Freestyle skiing	Speed skating
Ice hockey	

SOURCE: Created by Stephen Meyer for Gale, © 2018

Olympics started is unknown, but the first recorded games took place in the city of Olympia in 776 BC. The games grew in importance over the next few centuries, reaching their peak during the sixth and fifth centuries BC. By that time they had grown from a single event—a 200-yard (183-m) foot race called the stadion—to 20 events that were spread over several days. The Greek Olympic Games were held every four years.

As the Roman Empire rose to power in the region and subsequently adopted Christianity as its official religion, the Olympic Games declined in stature. The games, which had always been a religious as much as an athletic celebration, were eventually outlawed in AD 393 by the emperor Theodosius I (347–395).

Interest in the Olympics was revived during the mid-19th century, when modern archaeologists began unearthing the ruins of ancient Olympia. In 1890 the French historian and educator Pierre de Coubertin (1862–1937) developed the idea of holding an international competition of young athletes as a way to promote peace and cooperation among nations. He presented his ideas at Sorbonne University in Paris, France, in 1894, and two years later the first modern Olympic Games were held in Athens, Greece.

According to the IOC, in "Athens 1896" (2018, https://www.olympic.org/athens-1896), the inaugural Olympic Games of 1896 featured 241 athletes from 14 countries competing in 43 events, which was the largest international sporting event ever held up to that time. The event was repeated in Paris in 1900 and again in St. Louis, Missouri, in 1904. Other summer Olympic Game sites over the years are shown in Table 7.5.

Winter Olympics History

By 1908 movement toward establishing a winter version of the Olympics had begun. That year, figure skating was introduced during the summer games in London. A cluster of winter events was scheduled to be added for 1916, but the games were canceled because of the outbreak of World War I (1914–1918). In 1924 several nations participated in the International Winter Sports Week in Chamonix, France. Two years later the IOC retroactively renamed the event the first Olympic winter games, according to the IOC, in "Factsheet: The Olympic Winter Games" (September 2014, https://stillmed.olympic.org/Documents/Reference_documents_Factsheets/The_Olympic_Winter_Games.pdf). The winter games took place during regular Olympic years until 1992. Beginning with the 1994 games in Lillehammer, Norway, the winter games have been held every four years, alternating with the summer games. Table 7.6 shows the sites at which all the Winter Olympics have been held or are scheduled to be held.

Politics and the Olympics

Wars and other political complications affected the Olympic movement at several points during the 20th century. The 1916 games were a casualty of World War I, and World War II (1939–1945) caused the cancellation of the 1940 and 1944 Olympics.

TERRORIST ATTACKS. Twice the Olympics have been the scene of violent acts of terrorism. At the 1972 summer games in Munich, West Germany, the Palestinian terrorist group Black September took members of the Israeli team hostage on September 5. A rescue attempt was unsuccessful, and by the end of the 20-hour ordeal the militants had killed 11 Israeli athletes and coaches, as well as a West German police officer. During the crisis Mark Spitz (1950–), a Jewish American swimmer who had finished his events after winning a then-record seven gold medals, was evacuated out of fear that he was a target for the terrorists. In the aftermath of the attack, the games were temporarily suspended, and

TABLE 7.3

Top US Olympic medal winners, all time

Rank	Athlete	Sport	Dates	Gold	Silver	Bronze	Total
1	Michael Phelps	Swimming	2004–2016	23	3	2	28
2	Natalie Coughlin	Swimming	2004–2012	3	4	5	12
	Ryan Lochte	Swimming	2004–2016	6	3	3	12
	Jenny Thompson	Swimming	1992–2004	8	3	1	12
	Dara Torres	Swimming	1984–2008	4	4	4	12
6	Matt Biondi	Swimming	1984–1992	8	2	1	11
	Mark Spitz	Swimming	1968–1972	9	1	1	11
	Carl Osborn	Shooting	1912–1924	5	4	2	11
9	Gary Hall, Jr.	Swimming	1996–2004	5	3	2	10
	Carl Lewis	Athletics	1984–1996	9	1	0	10
	Ray Ewry	Athletics	1900–1908	10	0	0	10
12	Allyson Felix	Athletics	2004–2016	6	3	0	9
	Shirley Babashoff	Swimming	1972–1976	3	6	0	9
	Martin Sheridan	Athletics	1904–1908	5	3	1	9
15	Nathan Adrian	Swimming	2008–2016	5	1	2	8
	Allison Schmidt	Swimming	2008–2016	4	2	2	8
	Apolo Anton Ohno	Short track speed skating	2002–2010	2	2	4	8
	Jason Lezak	Swimming	2000–2012	4	2	2	8
	Don Shollander	Swimming	1964–1968	7	1	0	8
	Charlie Daniels	Swimming	1904–1908	5	1	2	8

SOURCE: Created by Stephen Meyer for Gale, © 2018

TABLE 7.4

Top Olympic medal–winning countries, all time

	Country	Dates	Gold	Silver	Bronze	Total
1	United States	1896–2016	1,132	904	792	2,828
2	Soviet Union	1952–1988	473	376	355	1,204
3	Germany	1896–2016	318	345	341	1,004
4	Great Britain	1896–2016	283	316	307	906
5	France	1896–2016	263	282	332	877
6	Italy	1900–2016	256	225	241	722
7	Sweden	1900–2016	199	215	242	656
8	China	1984–2016	239	184	173	596
9	Russia	1908–2016	202	183	200	585
10	East Germany	1968–1988	192	165	162	519

SOURCE: Created by Stephen Meyer for Gale, © 2018

TABLE 7.5

Locations of the summer Olympic Games

1896—Athens, Greece
1900—Paris, France
1904—St. Louis, United States
1908—London, United Kingdom
1912—Stockholm, Sweden
1916—Games not held due to World War I
1920—Antwerp, Belgium
1924—Paris, France
1928—Amsterdam, Netherlands
1932—Los Angeles, United States
1936—Berlin, Germany
1940—Games not held due to World War II
1944—Games not held due to World War II
1948—London, United Kingdom
1952—Helsinki, Finland
1956—Melbourne, Australia
1960—Rome, Italy
1964—Tokyo, Japan
1968—Mexico City, Mexico
1972—Munich, West Germany
1976—Montreal, Canada
1980—Moscow, U.S.S.R.
1984—Los Angeles, United States
1988—Seoul, South Korea
1992—Barcelona, Spain
1996—Atlanta, United States
2000—Sydney, Australia
2004—Athens, Greece
2008—Beijing, China
2012—London, United Kingdom
2016—Rio de Janeiro, Brazil
2020—Tokyo, Japan
2024—Paris, France
2028—Los Angeles, United States

SOURCE: Created by Stephen Meyer for Gale, © 2018

a large memorial ceremony was held in the Olympic stadium.

On July 27, 1996, one person was killed, another died of a heart attack running to the scene, and 111 were injured when a bomb exploded in the Centennial Olympic Park at the 1996 summer games in Atlanta, Georgia. The perpetrator, Eric Robert Rudolph (1966–)—a member of a radical Christian group violently opposed to abortion and homosexuality—was not arrested until 2003. In 2005 he pleaded guilty to the Olympic bombing, as well as to a string of other bombings that occurred between 1996 and 1998, and was sentenced to four consecutive life sentences without parole.

RIGHTS ISSUES. At times, the Olympics can draw international attention to contentious political issues affecting the host country. Kathy Lally notes in "Russia Antigay Law Casts a Shadow over Sochi's 2014 Olympics"

(WashingtonPost.com, September 29, 2013) that Russia's passage of a law banning the promotion of nontraditional sexual relationships sparked controversy on the eve of the

TABLE 7.6

Locations of the winter Olympic Games

1924—Chamonix, France
1928—St. Moritz, Switzerland
1932—Lake Placid, United States
1936—Garmisch-Partenkirchen, Germany
1940—Games not held due to World War II
1944—Games not held due to World War II
1948—St. Moritz, Switzerland
1952—Oslo, Norway
1956—Cortina d'Ampezzo, Italy
1960—Squaw Valley, United States
1964—Innsbruck, Austria
1968—Grenoble, France
1972—Sapporo, Japan
1976—Innsbruck, Austria
1980—Lake Placid, United States
1984—Sarajevo, Yugoslavia
1988—Calgary, Canada
1992—Albertville, France
1994—Lillehammer, Norway
1998—Nagano, Japan
2002—Salt Lake City, United States
2006—Torino (Turin), Italy
2010—Vancouver, Canada
2014—Sochi, Russia
2018—PyeongChang, South Korea
2022—Beijing, China

SOURCE: Created by Stephen Meyer for Gale, © 2018

2014 Winter Olympics in Sochi, leading gay and lesbian athletes from around the world to express concern about possible harassment during the games. The location of the 2014 Winter Olympics also prompted a reevaluation of a disturbing chapter from Russian history, as members of the Circassian ethnic group staged worldwide demonstrations protesting the mass killing of their ancestors by the Russian Empire at Sochi 150 years earlier. According to Gabriele Barbati, in "Circassians Protest Winter Olympics Being Held at Sochi Genocide Site" (IBTimes.com, February 6, 2014), an estimated 650,000 to 2 million Circassians were killed during the 1864 Sochi genocide, while millions more were forcibly expelled from their homeland in the surrounding region.

NUCLEAR TENSION. On the eve of the 2018 winter games in South Korea, escalating tensions between North Korea and the United States appeared to pose a threat to the overall stability of the Korean Peninsula. The conflict revolved around a series of missile tests conducted by North Korea in 2017. The tests prompted a barrage of hostile rhetoric between North Korean leader Kim Jong-un (1984?–) and President Donald Trump (1946–), raising fears about a possible military standoff. An opportunity to alleviate tensions emerged in January 2018, when South Korea invited North Korea to participate in the PyeongChang games under the Korean Unification Flag. Zeeshan Aleem notes in "North and South Korea Marched Together under One Flag at the Olympics" (Vox.com, February 9, 2018) that the overture was viewed as a gesture of reconciliation amid the long-standing conflict between the two nations. According to Aleem, North and South Korea also agreed to form a combined women's hockey team for the PyeongChang games, marking the first time that athletes from the two countries competed alongside each other in the Olympics.

BOYCOTTS. The Olympics have also been used to make political statements. In "Long History of Olympics Protests" (BBC.co.uk, April 7, 2008), Paul Reynolds provides an overview of notable boycotts throughout Olympic history. The first boycott occurred in 1908, when Irish athletes refused to participate in the London games, in protest against British political oppression. The 1956 games in Melbourne, Australia, were the scene of two different boycotts: by the Netherlands, Spain, and Switzerland in response to the Soviet Union's brutal handling of the Hungarian uprising that year; and by Egypt, Iraq, and Lebanon in protest of British and French involvement in the Suez crisis in the Middle East. Several African nations threatened to boycott the Olympics in 1968, 1972, and 1976 in protest of South African and Rhodesian racial policies; the IOC ultimately banned South Africa and Rhodesia from participating in the 1968 and 1972 Olympics. In 1980 and 1984 the two major Cold War powers traded boycotts: the United States and 61 other Western nations stayed home from the 1980 Olympics in Moscow in protest of the Soviet invasion of Afghanistan; four years later the Soviet Union and 14 of its allied nations retaliated by boycotting the Los Angeles games on the grounds that the American hosts could not guarantee their safety. In 1988 North Korea boycotted the Olympics in South Korea, arguing that the two countries should have been named cohosts.

SCANDAL. In 1998 it emerged that several members of the IOC had accepted gifts from the 2002 Salt Lake City Winter Olympics organizing committee in exchange for their site selection votes. Ten IOC members were forced off the committee, and the process for selecting host cities subsequently underwent a dramatic transformation.

More controversy occurred during the 2002 winter games, when Russia's Elena Berezhnaya (1977–) and Anton Sikharulidze (1976–) received high marks in the pairs figure skating competition, in spite of committing a noticeable error. Meanwhile, the Canadian skaters Jamie Salé (1977–) and David Pelletier (1974–) delivered a seemingly flawless performance, convincing the event's announcers that they had earned the gold medal. When the scores were revealed, however, the Russians had been awarded the top prize. In the subsequent investigation, the French judge said she was pressured to vote for the Russians. The scandal resulted in a second gold medal being awarded to the Canadian pair, and the IOC and the International Skating Union decided to declare both pairs as Olympic cochampions. New scoring rules, including anonymous judging, were adopted afterward.

A different controversy emerged six years later during the 2008 summer games, when questions arose regarding the ages of some members of the Chinese women's gymnastics team. Allegations surfaced that some of the Chinese athletes were younger than 16, the minimum age that is dictated by Olympic rules for the sport. At the 2012 London Olympics, eight women badminton players from China, Indonesia, and South Korea were expelled from the games after it was determined that they had intentionally attempted to lose doubles matches to gain more favorable draws during the medal round of competition.

STRUCTURE OF THE OLYMPIC MOVEMENT
International Olympic Committee

The Olympics are run by a complex array of organizations that are known primarily by their initials. At the center of the structure is the IOC (2018, https://www.olympic.org). Based in Lausanne, Switzerland, the IOC was created by the International Athletic Congress of Paris in 1894 to oversee the control and development of the modern Olympic Games. Membership in the IOC is limited to one representative from most countries, and two representatives from the largest and most active member countries, or countries that have hosted the Olympics. Members must speak French or English and be citizens and residents of a country with a recognized national Olympic committee (NOC). The IOC runs the Olympic movement according to the terms of the Olympic Charter (September 15, 2017, https://stillmed.olympic.org/media/Document%20Library/OlympicOrg/General/EN-Olympic-Charter.pdf#_ga=2.89144281.355293387.1521049579-821051481.1518554830).

The next level of Olympic oversight, the international federations (IFs), coordinate international competition within a particular sport. These federations make all the rules that pertain to their sport and run the world championships and other international competitions within their realm. Each country that competes in a sport at the international level has a national governing body (NGB), which coordinates the sport domestically.

US Olympic Committee

In the United States, building a team to represent the nation at the Olympics is the responsibility of the US Olympic Committee (USOC). The USOC consists of 72 member organizations. Thirty-nine of them are NGBs (such as USA Gymnastics and USA Track and Field) each of which supports a particular sport. In the United States the NGBs are responsible for selecting the athletes who will represent their country in their sport at the Olympics. Other USOC members include community- and education-based multisport organizations, US Armed Forces sports, and organizations that are involved in sports for people with disabilities.

Besides its role in developing the US Olympic team, the USOC is instrumental in US cities' bids to host the Winter or Summer Olympics or the Pan American Games. The USOC may vote on and endorse a particular city's bid to serve as host. All US Olympic Trial site selections also go through the USOC.

Among the world's major Olympic governing bodies, the USOC is the only one that receives no government funding. A substantial portion of its money comes from the IOC. Although it does not receive direct financial support from the government, it nevertheless manages to provide millions of dollars per year in direct support to athletes, as well as assistance to NGBs. Ben Fischer reports in "USOC Benefits from Rio TV, Sponsorship Boosts to Post $78.5m Surplus in '16" (SportsBusiness Daily.com, May 16, 2017) that the USOC generated $336 million in revenues during the 2016 summer games in Rio de Janeiro.

THE FLOW OF OLYMPIC MONEY

All the symbols, images, phrases, and other intellectual property that are associated with the Olympics belong to the IOC. In *Olympic Marketing Fact File: 2018 Edition* (2018, https://stillmed.olympic.org/media/Document%20Library/OlympicOrg/Documents/IOC-Marketing-and-Broadcasting-General-Files/Olympic-Marketing-Fact-File-2018.pdf), the IOC indicates that it generates marketing revenue through six major channels: broadcasting, The Olympic Partners international sponsorships, IOC licensing, host-country licensing, ticketing, and domestic sponsorships. The IOC manages the first three; the others are managed by the Organizing Committees for the Olympic Games (OCOGs) within the host country, under the IOC's direction.

As with the major professional sports in the United States, the biggest financial driver of the Olympics is broadcasting. Since the 1990s television broadcasts of the Olympics have brought in a tremendous amount of revenue to the IOC. According to the IOC, in *IOC Marketing: Media Guide—Olympic Winter Games PyeongChang 2018* (2018, https://stillmed.olympic.org/media/Document%20Library/OlympicOrg/Games/Winter-Games/Games-PyeongChang-2018-Winter-Olympic-Games/IOC-Marketing/Media-Guide.pdf), of the $5.7 billion in revenues generated during the 2013–16 Olympic cycle, 73% ($4.2 billion) derived from broadcast rights.

The IOC explains in *Olympic Marketing Fact File: 2018 Edition* that the 2016 summer games in Rio de Janeiro aired in 220 countries and territories worldwide and attracted a global television audience of 3.2 billion. This figure marked a decline from the 2012 summer games in London, England, which attracted 3.6 billion television viewers, as well as the 2008 summer games in Beijing, China, which drew 3.5 billion viewers. Digital viewership, however, was growing during the same period, with 1.3 billion unique digital users accounting for 4.4 billion online video views in 2016 far surpassing the 700 million video views and 400 million digital viewers watching Olympic events online during the Beijing games in 2008. The IOC reports that social media platforms provided an additional means of accessing Olympic broadcasts during the 2016 games in Rio de Janeiro, with 7.2 billion video views on official pages or profiles.

A second key revenue source is the IOC's corporate sponsorship program, known officially as the Olympic Partners (TOP) program. The IOC notes in *Olympic Marketing Fact File: 2018 Edition* that for the 2013–16 cycle the TOP program consisted of 12 international corporations, which in return for their money were ensured exclusive sponsorship in their business category. As with broadcast rights, the United States dominated the TOP program; five of the TOP sponsors were US based.

Ticket sales represent another major source of revenue for the IOC. In *Olympic Marketing Fact File: 2018 Edition*, the IOC indicates that of the 6.8 million tickets that were available during the Rio games 6.2 million (91%) were sold. To make the Rio games as accessible as possible to the public, organizers stressed affordability when determining ticket prices. The IOC reports in *International Olympic Committee Marketing Report: Rio 2016* (2016, https://stillmed.olympic.org/media/Document%20 Library/OlympicOrg/Games/Summer-Games/Games-Rio-2016-Olympic-Games/Media-Guide-for-Rio-2016/IOC-Marketing-Report-Rio-2016.pdf) that more than half of the tickets made available for the games sold for about $20, with some tickets selling for only $13.

Slightly more than 90% of the IOC's revenue is subsequently distributed to the other organizations that collectively make up the Olympic movement, including the OCOGs, which are the committees that run the Olympics within the country that has been selected to host the games; the NOCs, whose main role within each of the approximately 200 countries in the Olympic family is to field their country's Olympic team; and the IFs, which coordinate and monitor international competition within their specific sport or family of sports. The IOC retains just under 10% of its overall revenue. These funds are used to cover the organization's operating and administrative costs.

The vast commercial activity that fuels the Olympic flame would seem to conflict with the philosophical groundings of the Olympic movement, which value the noble spirit of competition above financial matters. Nowhere is the commercialization of the games more apparent than in the presence of paid athletes at the games. Besides allowing professional athletes to compete at the Olympics, the United States and other nations also provide financial compensation based on performance. Sean Cunningham reports in "How Much Do Countries Pay Their Gold Medalists?" (RealClearLife.com, February 2018) that the US government pays its athletes $37,500 for each gold medal won at the Olympics. This sum is relatively modest compared with other countries. For example, Australian gold medalists received the equivalent of $126,000 from the government, while gold medalists from Singapore are awarded $1 million, the most of any country. By contrast, Olympic medalists from the United Kingdom receive no monetary compensation.

The Olympic Charter acknowledges this apparent contradiction, and the IOC has implemented policies designed to address it. No advertising is allowed in the venues where events take place or on the uniforms of athletes, coaches, or officials. The TOP program is designed to generate the maximum amount of support with a minimum number of corporate sponsors, and images of Olympic events are not allowed to be used for commercial purposes.

SELECTION OF OLYMPIC SITES

One of the IOC's chief responsibilities is to select the cities that will host the Olympics. Olympic site selection is a two-phase procedure. The first phase is called the invitation phase. Applicant cities must be proposed to the IOC by their NOC. They must then complete a questionnaire that outlines how they plan to carry out the monumental task of hosting the games. The IOC assesses the applications with regard to the cities' ability to organize the games. Criteria include technical capacity, government support, public opinion, general infrastructure, security, venues, accommodations, and transportation. The IOC then accepts a handful of these applicants for the next step, called the candidate phase.

In the second phase, candidate cities must provide the IOC with a candidature file. These files are analyzed by the IOC Evaluation Commission, which consists of IOC members, representatives of the IFs, the NOCs, the IOC Athletes' Commission, the International Paralympic Committee, and other experts. The Evaluation Commission also physically inspects the candidate cities. It then issues a report, on whose basis the IOC Executive Board prepares a list of final candidates. This list is submitted to the IOC session for a vote.

By the 21st century, the financial burdens associated with hosting the Olympics, such as construction and infrastructure costs, began to discourage otherwise strong candidate cities from entering bids to host the games. In response to these concerns, the IOC issued a new set of application guidelines, *Olympic Agenda 2020: 20 + 20 Recommendations* (2014, https://stillmed.olympic.org/Documents/Olympic_Agenda_2020/Olympic_Agenda_2020-20-20_Recommendations-ENG.pdf), in December 2014. The new guidelines included measures designed to reduce the costs associated with the application process, by limiting the number of presentations allowed by candidate cities and offering substantial financial assistance from the IOC. At the same time, Olympic Agenda 2020 aimed to mitigate the potential negative impact of hosting the games by encouraging proposals that addressed the long-term economic and social needs of host cities. Despite these changes, the IOC continued to face a shortage of candidate cities. According to the article "IOC Pledges Changes to Bid Process after Budapest Exit" (Reuters.com, February 24, 2017), in 2015 several major cities, among them Oslo, Norway, Krakow, Poland, and Stockholm, Sweden, withdrew bids to host the 2022 winter games. Meanwhile, over the next two years Hamburg, Germany, Rome, Italy, Budapest, Hungary, and US candidate Boston, Massachusetts, all dropped bids to host the 2024 summer games, leaving only Paris and Los Angeles as candidates.

In July 2017 the IOC introduced further changes to the host city application process as reported in "IOC Approves New Candidature Process for Olympic Winter Games 2026" (July 11, 2017, https://www.olympic.org/news/ioc-approves-new-candidature-process-for-olympic-winter-games-2026). On the one hand, the invitation phase was expanded to one year, giving prospective host cities and their national Olympic committees additional time to formulate their proposals. At the same time, the candidate phase was reduced from two years to one, with the aim of reducing the costs associated with preparing bids. Meanwhile, in September 2017 the IOC named Paris as the host of the 2024 summer games and Los Angeles as the host of the 2028 summer games. It marked the first time the IOC named host cities for two separate Olympics at the same time.

DOPING

Almost from the beginning, the use of performance-enhancing substances, known as doping, has plagued the Olympics. An early example was Thomas J. Hicks (1875–1963), winner of the 1904 marathon, who was given strychnine and brandy. Doping methods improved over time, sometimes with disastrous results. The Danish cyclist Knut Jensen (1936–1960) died after falling from his bicycle during the 1960 games. He was found to have taken amphetamines. The international sports federations and the IOC banned doping during the 1960s, but for most of the time since then officials have lacked the tools to adequately police the use of illicit substances. The highest-profile Olympic athlete to be disqualified for doping in the 20th century was the Canadian sprinter Ben Johnson (1961–), winner of the 100-meter race in 1988. A few years later, it was reported that East German sports officials had doped female athletes for years without the IOC's knowledge. Described in the PBS documentary *Doping for Gold* (May 7, 2008, http://www

.pbs.org/wnet/secrets/doping-for-gold-2/42/), it was the largest state-sponsored doping program in history. As the problem of doping grew out of control during the 1990s, the international sports community responded by forming the World Anti-Doping Agency (WADA) in 1999. WADA oversees the monitoring and enforcing of doping regulations at the Olympics.

WADA's creation did not, however, solve the problem entirely. Olympic athletes from every era have been found to be in violation of anti-doping rules. For the 2008 summer games, new methods were put in place that allowed blood samples to be stored for up to eight years in case new tests were developed in that time. In "Backup Samples Positive for 5 Olympians" (Associated Press, July 8, 2009), Stephen Wilson reports that 15 athletes tested positive for drug-related violations during the Beijing Olympics. Six of the cases were detected months after the close of the Olympics. The only US athlete on the list did not actually use a substance herself; rather, one was given to the horse she rode in an equestrian event. The last US competitors to test positive for banned substances in their own bodies during competition at the Olympics were the shot-putter Bonnie Dasse (1959–) and the hammer thrower Jud Logan (1959–), both in 1992.

Since that time, however, it was discovered after the fact that several Americans had been doping during the Olympics and were stripped of their medals or barred from the Olympics. Others, who appeared headed for the Olympics, fell under a cloud of suspicion and were also barred. In the wake of the BALCO scandal (see Chapter 9 for more information), the sprinter Kelli White (1977–) received a two-year ban that kept her out of the 2004 Olympics. The sprinter Tim Montgomery (1975–), who was also implicated in the BALCO affair, failed to qualify for the 2004 games, but in 2005 he received a two-year ban from competing and was stripped of a number of his past medals and results, including a former world-record performance in the 100-meter dash. Perhaps the highest-profile Olympic athlete embroiled in BALCO was the sprinter Marion Jones (1975–). Jones proclaimed her innocence through several years of investigation, but in October 2007 she admitted to having used illegal performance-enhancing drugs during the 2000 Olympics in Sydney, Australia, in which she won three gold medals and two bronze. Facing pressure from the USOC, she surrendered her Olympic medals and was retroactively disqualified from all events dating back to September 1, 2000. The IOC also banned her from the Beijing Olympics. In 2008 the sprinter Antonio Pettigrew (1967–2010) admitted to using performance-enhancing drugs between 1997 and 2003, a span that included the 2000 Sydney Olympics in which he won a gold medal in the 4x400 relay event. In August 2008 the IOC decided to strip the medals from all the members of Pettigrew's relay team. Like Montgomery and Jones, Pettigrew also received a ban from competing and was stripped of a number of his past awards and results. In January 2013 the IOC stripped Lance Armstrong (1971–) of the bronze medal he won at the 2000 Summer Olympics in Sydney, after the US Anti-Doping Agency revealed that the cyclist had used banned substances throughout his career.

One of the most extensive doping rings in Olympic history emerged in November 2015, when WADA published a report accusing the Russian Anti-Doping Agency (Rusada) of mishandling drug-testing results involving Russian athletes. According to "WADA Statement: Independent Investigation Confirms Russian State Manipulation of the Doping Control Process" (July 18, 2016, https://www.wada-ama.org/en/media/news/2016-07/wada-statement-independent-investigation-confirms-russian-state-manipulation-of), in July 2016 a follow-up report revealed that Rusada officials had manipulated anti-doping procedures at both the 2013 International Association of Athletic Federations World Championships in Moscow and the 2014 Winter Olympics in Sochi. Alex Hall reports in "119 Russian Athletes Are Banned from the Rio Olympics Due to Ongoing Doping Scandal" (SBNation.com, August 3, 2016) that 119 Russian athletes, including every weightlifter and all but one athlete on the track and field team, were barred from competing at the 2016 summer games in Rio de Janeiro as a result of WADA's findings.

Despite its efforts to introduce strong anti-doping measures, the IOC struggled to implement effective drug-testing protocols at the Olympics. According to the article "WADA Reveals up to 50% of Drug Tests at 2016 Olympic Games Had to Be Aborted" (Guardian.com, October 27, 2016), an investigation conducted by WADA following the 2016 summer games in Rio de Janeiro showed that a failure of anti-doping officials to coordinate testing efforts, combined with funding shortages, resulted in canceling half of all athlete drug tests over the course of the games. Meanwhile, in December 2017 the IOC banned Russia from officially participating in the 2018 winter games in PyeongChang. Will Hobson reports in "Russia Is Banned from Winter Olympics for Doping Program" (WashingtonPost.com, December 6, 2017) that Russian athletes found in compliance with anti-doping rules were allowed to participate under the designation "Olympic Athlete from Russia (OAR)."

OTHER OLYMPIC GAMES
Special Olympics

Special Olympics is a global nonprofit organization that provides opportunities for athletic training and competition for people with developmental disabilities.

The organization reports in "History of Special Olympics" (2018, https://www.specialolympics.org/history.aspx) that as of 2016 there were 5.3 million Special Olympic athletes worldwide. The 2015 Special Olympics World Summer Games in Los Angeles, California, included more than 6,200 athletes from 165 countries, while the 2017 World Winter Games in Austria hosted nearly 2,700 athletes who represented over 100 countries. The 2019 World Summer Games were scheduled to take place in Abu Dhabi, United Arab Emirates.

The roots of the Special Olympics go back to 1962, when Eunice Kennedy Shriver (1921–2009), the sister of President John F. Kennedy (1917–1963), started a day camp for developmentally disabled children. In June of that year Shriver invited 35 boys and girls to Camp Shriver at Timberlawn, her home in Rockville, Maryland. Her idea was that children who were cognitively impaired were capable of accomplishing much more than was generally believed at the time, if they were given opportunities to do so. Building on Camp Shriver, Shriver began to actively promote the notion of involving people with disabilities in physical activities and competition. Through the Kennedy Foundation, she targeted grants to universities, community centers, and recreation departments that created such opportunities. The foundation helped fund 11 camps similar to Camp Shriver across the country in 1963. By 1969, 32 camps serving 10,000 children were being supported by the foundation.

In 1967 the Kennedy Foundation worked with the Chicago Park District to organize a citywide track meet for mentally disabled people that was modeled on the Olympics. According to "History of Special Olympics," the first Special Olympics at Soldier Field attracted 1,000 athletes from 26 states and Canada, who competed in track and field, floor hockey, and aquatics. Three years later the Special Olympics were granted special status by the USOC, becoming one of only two national organizations (along with the US Olympic Committee) with the right to use the "Olympics" name. In February 1977 the first Special Olympics winter games were held, with about 500 athletes competing in skating and skiing events at Steamboat Springs, Colorado.

The Special Olympics movement grew substantially during the 1980s and 1990s. In 1981 the organization launched the Law Enforcement Torch Run, a fund-raiser that was aimed at increasing awareness of the Special Olympics throughout the United States. The movement truly became international in scope in 1988, when the IOC officially sanctioned the Special Olympics. By 2006 the Special Olympics had grown to 2.5 million competitors, representing 165 nations worldwide. Within two years, the number of athletes had grown to 3 million and the number of participating countries had increased to 180.

Paralympics

While the Special Olympics serves people with mental disabilities, athletes with physical disabilities, including mobility limitations, amputees, and people with visual disabilities and cerebral palsy, may compete in the Paralympics. The International Paralympic Committee (IPC) explains in "Paralympics—History of the Movement" (2018, https://www.paralympic.org/the-ipc/history-of-the-movement) that the concept for the Paralympics grew out of a 1948 event in Stoke Mandeville, England, a competition for World War II veterans with spinal cord injuries. The first Olympic-style competition for people with physical disabilities took place in 1960 in Rome, Italy. These became the Paralympic Games. The Winter Paralympics were added in 1976.

Unlike the Special Olympics, the Paralympics have always been held during the same year as the Olympic Games. Since the 1988 summer games in Seoul, South Korea, and the 1992 winter games in Albertville, France, the Paralympics have been held using the same venues as well. Paralympic athletes live in the same Olympic village as their Olympic counterparts, and the ticketing, technology, and transportation systems are shared. More than 4,300 athletes from 159 countries competed in 528 events at the 2016 summer games in Rio de Janeiro. The 2018 winter Paralympics took place in PyeongChang, South Korea in March 2018, with more than 560 athletes competing in alpine skiing, biathlon, cross-country skiing, Para ice hockey, snowboarding, and wheelchair curling.

The IPC oversees the Paralympics, performing much the same role as the IOC does for the Olympics. The national Paralympics organization for the United States is US Paralympics, which is a division of the USOC.

Deaflympics

Besides the Special Olympics and the Paralympics, the IOC also sanctions the Deaflympics, which have existed since 1924. The first Deaflympics, which were organized by the International Committee of Sports for the Deaf (2018, http://www.deaflympics.com), were held in Paris that year. The winter games were added in 1949.

The International Committee of Sports for the Deaf (2018, http://www.deaflympics.com/athletes.asp) explains that athletes must have a hearing loss of at least 55 decibels in their better ear to qualify for the Deaflympics. To ensure a level playing field, hearing aids, cochlear implants, and other devices that augment hearing are not used during the competition. According to the International Committee of Sports for the Deaf, in "Samsun 2017" (2017, http://www.deaflympics.com/games/2017-s), 2,859 deaf athletes from 86 countries competed in the 23rd Summer Deaflympics in Samsun, Turkey, in July 2017.

CHAPTER 8
SPORTS AND HEALTH

Sport is a preserver of health.

—Hippocrates

The truth of Hippocrates's assertion has been nearly universally accepted for centuries, but only since the 20th century have researchers worked to quantify the impact of physical activity, or the lack thereof, on physical and mental well-being. In 1990 the US Department of Health and Human Services (HHS) created the Healthy People initiative, a program aimed at providing Americans with guidance and resources to help them lead longer, healthier lives. The HHS launches a new Healthy People project every 10 years. According to Healthy People 2020 (2018, https://www.healthypeople.gov/2020/topics-objectives/topic/physical-activity), the initiative's exercise goals "reflect the strong state of the science supporting the health benefits of regular physical activity among youth and adults." At the core of the project's objectives is the promotion of "regular physical activity" among Americans, which by definition "includes participation in moderate and vigorous physical activities and muscle-strengthening activities."

Hippocrates may not have appreciated as fully the other side of the sports–health nexus. As sports become a bigger business and as the pressure to perform becomes increasingly intense, greater attention is being given to the potential negative health impact of sports participation, especially on children and youth.

BENEFITS OF PHYSICAL ACTIVITY

In October 2008 the HHS released *2008 Physical Activity Guidelines for Americans* (https://health.gov/PAGuidelines/pdf/paguide.pdf), the first comprehensive attempt to provide a standardized set of guidelines for physical exercise. The report provides a list of basic health benefits that are associated with physical activity. For children, these benefits include improved cardiovascular, bone, and muscle fitness. At the same time, the report's findings suggest that there is some evidence that physical activity has the potential to reduce depression in adolescents. The health benefits for adults who engage in physical activity are numerous and include lowering the risk of heart disease, stroke, breast and colon cancer, and early death, while also alleviating depression and promoting improved cognitive functioning. Four years later, the HHS published *Physical Activity Guidelines for Americans Midcourse Report: Strategies to Increase Physical Activity among Youth* (December 2012, http://www.health.gov/paguidelines/midcourse/pag-mid-course-report-final.pdf), a follow-up study aimed at assessing the health benefits of physical activity for young people. In February 2018 the HHS published the *2018 Physical Activity Guidelines Advisory Committee Scientific Report* (2018, https://health.gov/paguidelines/second-edition/report/pdf/PAG_Advisory_Committee_Report.pdf), a comprehensive summary of physical activity recommendations based on 10 years of scientific research. These new findings were designed to serve as the foundation for an updated edition of *Physical Activity Guidelines for Americans.*

The specific health benefits of sports participation depend on the sport. Speed walking, jogging, cycling, swimming, and skiing have been shown to build cardiovascular endurance. Sports that involve gentle bending or stretching, including bowling, golf, and tai chi, are identified as promoting flexibility, which in turn may reduce the risk of injury. Other sports, such as those involving weightlifting or throwing, build strength. One important result of building strong muscles and, especially, bones is that it helps stave off osteoporosis by increasing the mineral content of bones.

Coronary heart disease, diabetes, colon cancer, and high blood pressure can all be prevented or improved through regular physical activity. Obesity is recognized as a key factor in these chronic health problems.

According to the Centers for Disease Control and Prevention (CDC), in "Overweight and Obesity: Data and Statistics" (August 29, 2017, https://www.cdc.gov/obesity/data/index.html), the obesity rate for adults in the United States reached 36.5% in 2011–14, and childhood obesity rates topped 17% during the same period. Furthermore, obesity-related health problems cost Americans an estimated $147 billion in 2008 (about $167.1 billion in 2018 dollars). Jeffrey Levi et al. estimate in *F as in Fat: How Obesity Threatens America's Future, 2012* (September 2012, https://www.rwjf.org/content/dam/farm/reports/reports/2012/rwjf401318) that by 2030 the nationwide obesity rate is expected to average 44% throughout all 50 states.

Sports participation helps control weight by burning calories that would otherwise be stored as fat. The more vigorous the sport and the more frequent the participation, the more calories are burned. Table 8.1 shows the approximate number of calories that a 154-pound (70-k) individual would burn in various moderate and vigorous physical activities in 30 minutes and in one hour. A dietary calorie, also known as a large calorie or kilocalorie, measures the energy required to increase the temperature of a kilogram of water by a single Celsius degree. By contrast, a small calorie measures the energy needed to increase the temperature of a gram of water by a single Celsius degree. When discussing diet and weight loss, the word *calorie* always refers to the kilocalorie.

TABLE 8.1

Calories burned through selected sports and other physical activities

	Approximate calories used (burned) by a 154-pound man	
	In 1 hour	In 30 minutes
Moderate physical activities:		
Hiking	370	185
Light gardening/yard work	330	165
Dancing	330	165
Golf (walking and carrying clubs)	330	165
Bicycling (less than 10 mph)	290	145
Walking (3.5 mph)	280	140
Weight training (general light workout)	220	110
Stretching	180	90
Vigorous physical activities:		
Running/jogging (5 mph)	590	295
Bicycling (more than 10 mph)	590	295
Swimming (slow freestyle laps)	510	255
Aerobics	480	240
Walking (4.5 mph)	460	230
Heavy yard work (chopping wood)	440	220
Weight lifting (vigorous effort)	440	220
Basketball (vigorous)	440	220

SOURCE: "How many calories does physical activity use (burn)?" in *ChooseMyPlate.gov: Physical Activity*, US Department of Agriculture, 2018, https://www.choosemyplate.gov/physical-activity-calories-burn (accessed February 13, 2018)

Sports Participation and Mental Health

Besides the obvious physical benefits of sports participation, there are psychological benefits as well. Anna Campbell and Heather A. Hausenblas of the University of Florida find in "Effects of Exercise Interventions on Body Image: A Meta-analysis" (*Journal of Health Psychology*, vol. 14, no. 6, September 2009) that physical exercise has a noticeably positive effect on an individual's body image. In the article "Exercise Improves Body Image for Fit and Unfit Alike" (ScienceDaily.com, October 9, 2009), Hausenblas explains that even less-athletic individuals develop improved perceptions of their body through sports participation, suggesting that the mental health benefits of physical exercise are distinct from the physiological benefits of exercise. Hausenblas states, "It may be that the requirements to receive the psychological benefits of exercise, including those relating to body image, differ substantially from the physical benefits." Conversely, body image has been shown to have an impact on how frequently people exercise. In "An Investigation of the Links between Body Image and Exercise Participation" (*Sport and Exercise Psychology Review*, vol. 10, no. 3, September 2014), Charalampos Fountoulakis and Sarah Grogan report that individuals who enjoy positive body images are more likely than those who are unsatisfied with their body to engage in physical exercise.

The idea that sports participation can help improve one's mood is well supported by other scientific research. The Mayo Clinic indicates in "Depression and Anxiety: Exercise Eases Symptoms" (September 27, 2017, https://www.mayoclinic.org/diseases-conditions/depression/in-depth/depression-and-exercise/art-20046495) that physical exercise releases endorphins and neurotransmitters, chemicals in the brain that have the potential to alleviate anxiety and depression. At the same time, exercise promotes self-confidence and social interaction, while also providing a distraction from stress that is related to daily life. In "Adolescent Women's Sports Involvement and Sexual Behavior/Health: A Process-Level Investigation" (*Journal of Youth and Adolescence*, vol. 33, no. 5, October 2004), Stephanie Jacobs Lehman and Susan Silverberg Koerner find evidence of a link between girls' involvement in organized sports and positive sexual health and behavior. This study links participation in organized sports with positive behavior that is related to sexual risk-taking, sexual/reproductive health, and sexual/reproductive health–seeking behavior. This effect is connected to self-empowerment and a positive view of one's own body. According to the Women's Sports Foundation, in *Her Life Depends on It III: Sport, Physical Activity, and the Health and Well-Being of American Girls and Women* (May 12, 2015, https://www.womenssportsfoundation.org/wp-content/uploads/2015/05/hldoi-iii_full-report.pdf), sports participation among girls plays a role in reducing the risk of unwanted pregnancy and depression, while improving academic performance and boosting self-esteem.

HEALTH RISKS OF SPORTS PARTICIPATION
Injuries

TYPES OF INJURIES. The National Institute of Arthritis and Musculoskeletal and Skin Diseases (NIAMS) details in *Health Topics: Sports Injuries* (February 28, 2016, https://www.niams.nih.gov/health-topics/sports-injuries#tab-types) the kinds of injuries that athletes are likely to sustain and the activities in which they sustain them. The NIAMS lists muscle sprains and strains, injuries to the knee and Achilles tendon, pain in the shin bone area, bone fractures, and dislocated joints as the most common types of sports injuries. (See Table 8.2.)

The NIAMS divides all sports injuries into two broad categories: acute and chronic. Acute injuries are those that occur suddenly during an activity. They are characterized by severe pain, swelling, and inability to use the injured body part. Chronic injuries typically occur through overuse over a long period. They generally result in pain when engaging in the activity, and a dull ache when at rest. There may also be swelling. After suffering an injury, the human body immediately begins the healing process. Treatments and stages of recovery that occur after a sports injury are shown in Table 8.3. Among the best ways to prevent sports injuries include stretching, wearing appropriate footwear, and avoiding exercises or movements that place undue strain on the body. (See Table 8.4.)

According to Maureen Haggerty, Teresa G. Odle, and Rebecca J. Frey, in "Sports Injuries" (Jacqueline L. Longe, ed., *Gale Encyclopedia of Medicine*, 2015), the vast majority (95%) of sports injuries are minor soft-tissue traumas. Bruises (or contusions) occur when blood collects at the point of the injury, causing a discoloration of the skin. Sprains involve a partial or complete tear of a ligament and account for about one-third of sports injuries. Strains are similar to sprains, except that a strain involves a tear in a muscle or tendon rather than in a ligament. Other soft-tissue sports injuries include tendinitis (inflammation of a tendon) and bursitis (inflammation of the fluid-filled sacs that allow tendons to glide over bones). These two injuries usually result from repeated stress on the tissue, rather than from a single traumatic event.

Injuries related to excessive training, also known as overuse injuries, have become increasingly common in the 21st century. John P. DiFiori et al. note in "Overuse Injuries and Burnout in Youth Sports: A Position Statement from the American Medical Society for Sports Medicine" (*Clinical Journal of Sports Medicine*, vol. 24, no. 1, January 2014) that overuse injuries account for between 45.9% and 54%, or roughly half, of all sports-related injuries. Young athletes are particularly vulnerable to overuse injuries. Rapid physical development among children, particularly

TABLE 8.2

Common types of sports injuries

- Muscle sprains and strains
- Knee injuries
- Achilles tendon injuries
- Pain along the shin bone
- Fractures
- Dislocations

SOURCE: "What are the types?" in *Health Topics: Sports Injuries*, US Department of Health and Human Services, National Institutes of Health, National Institute of Arthritis and Musculoskeletal and Skin Diseases, February 28, 2016, https://www.niams.nih.gov/health-topics/sports-injuries#tab-types (accessed February 13, 2018)

TABLE 8.3

How to treat sports injuries

Doctors first treat sports injuries with R-I-C-E (Rest, Ice, Compression, and Elevation).

- Rest. Decrease your regular activities and rest the injured area.
- Ice. Put an ice pack on the injury for 20 minutes, four to eight times per day. You can use a:
  - Cold pack.
  - Ice bag.
  - Plastic bag filled with crushed ice and wrapped in a towel.
- Compression. Put even pressure on the painful area to help reduce the swelling.
- Elevation. Put the injured area on a pillow at a level above your heart.

Your doctor may recommend other things to treat your sports injury.

- Nonsteroidal anti-inflammatory drugs (NSAIDs), such as aspirin or ibuprofen, can help decrease swelling and pain.
- Immobilization is a common treatment for sports injuries. It keeps you from moving the injured area and prevents more damage. To limit movement of your injured area, your doctor may recommend using a:
  - Sling.
  - Splint.
  - Cast.
  - Leg immobilizer.
- Surgery, in some cases, is needed to fix sports injuries. Surgery can fix torn tendons and ligaments or put broken bones back in place. Most sports injuries don't need surgery.
- Rehabilitation is a key part of treatment. It involves step-by-step exercises that get the injured area back to normal. Rehabilitation may include the following tips:
  - Moving the injured area helps it to heal. The sooner this is done, the better. Exercises start by gently moving the injured body part through a range of motions.
  - The next step is to stretch. After a while, weights may be used to strengthen the injured area.
  - As injury heals, scar tissue forms. After a while, the scar tissue shrinks. This shrinking brings the injured tissues back together. When this happens, the injured area becomes tight or stiff. This is when you are at greatest risk of injuring the area again. You should stretch the muscles every day. You should always stretch as a warmup before you play or exercise.
  - Don't play your sport until you are sure you can stretch the injured area without pain, swelling, or stiffness. When you start playing again, start slowly. Build up slowly to full speed.
- Rest after an injury is an important part of the healing process. Your doctor can guide you on the proper balance between rest and rehabilitation.
- Other therapies your doctor may recommend include:
  - Electrostimulation, which gives you mild electric shocks.
  - Cold packs.
  - Heat packs.
  - Ultrasound or sound waves.
  - Massage.

SOURCE: "How are they treated?" in *Health Topics: Sports Injuries*, US Department of Health and Human Services, National Institutes of Health, National Institute of Arthritis and Musculoskeletal and Skin Diseases, February 28, 2016, https://www.niams.nih.gov/health-topics/sports-injuries#tab-treatment (accessed February 13, 2018)

TABLE 8.4

How to prevent sports injuries

These tips can help you avoid sports injuries:

- Don't bend your knees more than halfway when doing knee bends.
- Don't twist your knees when you stretch. Keep your feet as flat as you can.
- When jumping, land with your knees bent.
- Do warmup exercises before you play any sport.
- Always stretch before you play or exercise.
- Don't overdo it.
- Cool down after hard sports or workouts.
- Wear shoes that fit properly, are stable, and absorb shock.
- Use the softest exercise surface you can find; don't run on asphalt or concrete.
- Run on flat surfaces.

For adults:

- Don't be a "weekend warrior." Don't try to do a week's worth of activity in a day or two.
- Learn to do your sport right. Use proper form to reduce your risk of "overuse" injuries.
- Use safety gear.
- Know your body's limits.
- Build up your exercise level gradually.
- Strive for a total body workout of cardiovascular, strength training, and flexibility exercises.

For parents and coaches:

- Group children by their skill level and body size, not by their age, especially for contact sports.
- Match the child to the sport. Don't push the child too hard to play a sport that she or he may not like or be able to do.
- Try to find sports programs that have certified athletic trainers.
- See that all children get a physical exam before playing.
- Don't play a child who is injured.
- Get the child to a doctor, if needed.
- Provide a safe environment for sports.

For children:

- Be in proper condition to play the sport.
- Get a physical exam before you start playing sports.
- Follow the rules of the game.
- Wear gear that protects, fits well, and is right for the sport.
- Know how to use athletic gear.
- Don't play when you are very tired or in pain.
- Always warm up before you play.
- Always cool down after you play.

SOURCE: "Can I prevent them?" in *Health Topics: Sports Injuries*, US Department of Health and Human Services, National Institutes of Health, National Institute of Arthritis and Musculoskeletal and Skin Diseases, February 28, 2016, https://www.niams.nih.gov/health-topics/sports-injuries#tab-prevention (accessed February 13, 2018)

during adolescence, can result in diminished bone density and muscle flexibility, heightening the risk of overuse injuries during sports participation. Meanwhile, increased competition, combined with a trend toward athletic specialization, can also lead to overuse injuries, as young athletes feel pressure to overexert themselves to succeed. The prevalence of overuse injuries among young athletes varies by sport. DiFiori et al. indicate that nearly two-thirds (63%) of all swimming injuries among elite athletes between the ages of eight and 16 years are related to overuse. By comparison, one-third (33%) of all injuries suffered by elite gymnasts and tennis players in that age group are overuse injuries, and only 15% of soccer injuries are overuse-related. Among all youth sports, running (68%) has the highest prevalence of injuries caused by overuse, whereas handball and skiing (37%) have the lowest prevalence.

Skeletal injuries from sports are less common than soft-tissue injuries. Haggerty, Odle, and Frey indicate that fractures account for 5% to 6% of sports injuries, with arms and legs being the most common sites of a break. Repeated foot pounding that is associated with sports such as long-distance running, basketball, and volleyball, and the stress fractures that can result, sometimes cause an injury called shin splints. Shin splints, according to Haggerty, Odle, and Frey, "are characterized by soreness and slight swelling of the front, inside, and back of the lower leg, and by sharp pain that develops while exercising and gradually intensifies."

The most dangerous class of sports injuries are those to the brain. Although fractures of the skull or spine are rare in sports, concussions have become increasingly common. Concussions are caused by a violent jarring of the brain from a blow to the head. They often cause loss of consciousness and may also affect balance, coordination, hearing, memory, and vision.

The early 21st century has seen an increase in awareness of the damaging effects of concussions on professional athletes, notably football players. The *New York Times* reports in "Head Injuries in Football" (2015, https://www.nytimes.com/topic/subject/head-injuries-in-football) that a 2000 survey of more than 1,000 former National Football League (NFL) players revealed that over 60% had suffered at least one concussion during their professional career; another quarter (26%) had incurred three or more concussions. In 2009 the NFL commissioned the Institute for Social Research at the University of Michigan to research cases of Alzheimer's and other memory-related diseases in retired NFL players. The study found that former professional football players aged 30 to 49 years were nearly 20 times more likely to be diagnosed with brain diseases than men of the same age who had not played football.

Concussions have also been linked to other mental disorders in former football players, including degenerative brain diseases. This disturbing trend received national attention in February 2011, after the former Chicago Bears safety Dave Duerson (1960–2011) committed suicide by shooting himself in the chest. Alan Schwarz reports in "Duerson's Brain Trauma Diagnosed" (NYTimes.com, May 2, 2011) that a subsequent medical examination revealed that Duerson had suffered from chronic traumatic encephalopathy (CTE), an incurable degenerative brain disorder that is linked to dementia, memory loss, and depression. According to Schwarz, CTE can currently be detected only through a brain autopsy. In a suicide note to his family, Duerson wrote, "Please, see that my brain is given to the NFL's brain bank." In "What Will Happen to Former NFL Player's Brain?" (CNN.com, February 26, 2011), Stephanie Smith indicates that Duerson's brain was donated to the Boston

University School of Medicine Center for the Study of Traumatic Encephalopathy so that it could be studied.

In May 2012 the former All-Pro linebacker Junior Seau (1969–2012) also died from a self-inflicted gunshot wound to the chest; an autopsy of Seau's brain revealed that he had CTE. The article "Junior Seau's Family Sues NFL" (Associated Press, January 24, 2013) notes that in January 2013 Seau's family sued the NFL, accusing the league of willfully concealing the risk of head injuries from its players. The family said in a statement, "We know this lawsuit will not bring back Junior. But it will send a message that the NFL needs to care for its former players, acknowledge its decades of deception on the issue of head injuries and player safety, and make the game safer for future generations." Des Bieler notes in "Family of Junior Seau Talks about Why It Is Pursuing a Lawsuit against the NFL" (WashingtonPost.com, January 5, 2015) that Seau's family rejected a $4 million class action settlement offer from the NFL to pursue its own lawsuit against the league.

In April 2015 the NFL reached a settlement agreement in a lawsuit filed by 5,000 former players over the issue of football-related head injuries. In "NFL Concussion Awards on Hold amid Appeals through This Fall" (Associated Press, June 24, 2015), Maryclaire Dale reports that the settlement required the NFL to make more than $1 billion in payouts and covered 21,000 former players. Ninety former players rejected the terms of the agreement, which launched an appeals process. In December 2016 the US Supreme Court declined to hear appeals to the settlement proposal. As of April 2018, the former players who were party to the lawsuit had yet to receive any payments from the NFL.

The article "NFL Urging States to Pass Youth Football Concussion Laws" (Associated Press, February 23, 2011) notes that in response to the rise of head injuries among young players, in early 2011 the NFL began urging state legislatures to pass laws requiring more stringent safety measures in high school football. Joe Frollo explains in "See Where Your State Stands on Concussion Law" (April 21, 2013, https://web.usafootball.com/blogs/health-and-safety/post/4380/see-where-your-state-stands-on-concussion-law) that as of January 30, 2014, all 50 states and the District of Columbia had passed laws aimed at preventing athletes who have suffered a concussion from returning to the playing field before seeking proper medical treatment.

Furthermore, research shows that football players can incur long-term brain damage even without suffering concussions. In "Consequences of Repeated Blood-Brain Barrier Disruption in College Football" (PLoS One, vol. 8, no. 3, March 6, 2013), Nicola Marchi et al. investigate the effects of repeated physical contact on the brains of college football players. The researchers find

high levels of antibodies that are linked to brain trauma in players who absorbed repeated hard hits during play. They note, however, that these same antibodies can be present in athletes who have never actually been diagnosed with concussions. Marchi et al. conclude that these antibodies "may constitute a risk factor for premature neurodegeneration" for both types of players.

Since 2000 professional hockey has also witnessed a dramatic increase in the number of concussions that are suffered by players. In April 2011 researchers at the University of Calgary published a comprehensive study of concussions in the National Hockey League (NHL). According to the article "Study: Games Lost to Concussions Rises" (Associated Press, April 18, 2011), the researchers found that of the 559 concussions reported by the NHL between 1997 and 2004, 529 caused players to lose playing time. Of these, 31% resulted in a player losing 10 or more days on the ice.

In March 2011, after concussions forced high-profile players such as Sidney Crosby (1987–) and Marc Savard (1977–) to miss the remainder of the 2010–11 season, the NHL announced strict new rules concerning the treatment of head injuries. The article "NHL Announces Plan to Limit Concussions" (FoxSports.com, March 14, 2011) reports the new guidelines, which include improved in-game medical attention for players, as well as the implementation of higher safety standards at NHL hockey rinks. Stu Hackel notes in "Study Shows Where NHL Can Improve Concussion Prevention" (SI.com, July 19, 2013) that the new restriction, known as Rule 48, was originally aimed at banning blindside and lateral hits to the head. During the 2011–12 season the NHL modified the rule to include any hits that targeted the head as the main point of contact. Nevertheless, in "Bodychecking Rules and Concussion in Elite Hockey" (PLoS One, vol. 8, no. 7, July 17, 2013), Laura Donaldson, Mark Asbridge, and Michael D. Cusimano report that the rate of concussions in the NHL remained the same between the 2009–10 and 2011–12 seasons. According to the researchers, blindside hits to the head accounted for fewer than 5% of all concussions in the NHL; indeed, the majority (64.2%) of concussions were found to be caused by body checking.

Travis Waldron indicates in "Concussions Are at the Heart of a New Lawsuit against the NHL" (ThinkProgress.org, May 15, 2015) that by 2015 the NHL faced multiple lawsuits from former players and the families of former players who had suffered hockey-related head injuries during their career. One of the lawsuits was filed on behalf of the former defenseman Steve Montador (1979–2015), who died suddenly in February 2015 at age 35. Although the cause of death remained undetermined, an autopsy revealed that Montador suffered from CTE at the time of his death, prompting his family to sue the league. According to Kevin McSpadden, in "Judge Rejects Motion to Dismiss NHL Concussion Lawsuit" (Time.com, March 26, 2015), in March 2015 a federal judge denied the NHL's motion to dismiss another lawsuit filed by six former players. This ruling paved the way for the legal action to proceed. As of April 2018, the lawsuit against the NHL was still pending.

PHYSICAL INJURIES AMONG YOUNG ATHLETES. In March 2011 the child safety advocacy group Safe Kids USA surveyed parents of child athletes between the ages of five and 14 years. The organization reports in *A National Survey of Parents' Knowledge, Attitudes, and Self-Reported Behaviors Concerning Sports Safety* (April 2011, https://www.safekids.org/sites/default/files/documents/ResearchReports/sports-safety-report-2011.pdf) that the percentage of young athletes who suffered injuries while participating in sports rose from 31% in 2000 to 34% in 2011. The largest increase was among girls between the ages of 10 and 14 years. In 2000, 28% of girls in this age group had suffered a sports-related injury, compared with 44% of boys aged 10 to 14 years. By 2011 the percentage for girls had risen to 43%, whereas injuries among boys in the same age group rose only slightly during the same period, to 45%. The proportion of young athletes who had been injured more than once also rose, from 15% in 2000 to 21% in 2011. In 2011, 5% of young athletes suffered four or more sports-related injuries, compared with 3% in 2000. According to the child advocacy group Safe Kids Worldwide (2018, https://www.safekids.org/sports), more than 1.2 million youth athletes under the age of 19 years visited emergency rooms for sports-related injuries in 2013.

In its 2011 study, Safe Kids USA also evaluates parents' knowledge concerning child injuries. The organization reports that children are more likely than adults to suffer injuries while participating in sports; however, fewer than half (46%) of parents recognized this fact in 2011. Safe Kids USA also finds that although 71% of parents believed it is "very important" that their child's coach is knowledgeable about sports injuries, only 29% actually believed that coaches are "very knowledgeable and well trained" to deal with injuries. This so-called knowledge gap widens further when it comes to understanding concussions. An overwhelming percentage (94%) of parents said it is very important for youth coaches to be able to recognize concussion symptoms; however, only 29% were confident that their child's coach can actually detect signs of a concussion. Moreover, although nearly half (49%) of parents had children who played multiple sports in 2011, only 13% felt serious concern about the potential for injury through overuse or stress.

FACTORS AFFECTING INJURY RATES. Studies indicate that women are more likely than men to suffer certain kinds of injuries. Allison Aubrey states in "Training

May Curb Some Sports Injuries in Women" (NPR.org, September 4, 2008) that "women are more prone than their male counterparts to specific injuries—namely knee injuries like tears of the ACL, or anterior cruciate ligament." Aubrey explains that the muscles in women's legs develop unevenly because women mostly use their front quadriceps. "This means that women's bodies [unlike men's] don't fully activate the muscles on the back side, namely the hamstrings and the glutes," so the imbalance places increased stress on the knee. As a result, strength training techniques have been implemented for women athletes to help them avoid this painful anterior cruciate ligament tear, an injury that requires surgery and long rehabilitation. Young male athletes, for their part, are more likely than female athletes to suffer fractures while participating in sports. According to the article "Sports-Related Injuries Requiring Surgery on the Rise among High School Athletes" (Newswise.com, November 16, 2012), fractures account for 10% of all high school sports injuries. Nearly four out of five (79%) of these injuries are sustained by boys.

PSYCHOLOGICAL IMPACT OF YOUTH SPORTS PARTICIPATION. According to DiFiori et al., excessive training and an overemphasis on competition can also exert a negative psychological impact on young athletes. Burnout can occur when young athletes cease to enjoy participating in their favorite sports. DiFiori et al. note that the risk factors for burnout among young athletes are both environmental and individual. The environmental causes of burnout include the excessive time commitments involved with sports participation, a lack of positive feedback from coaches, and young athletes feeling that they have little to no control over their life. Young athletes' individual personality can also affect their athletic performance over the long term. Qualities such as low self-esteem and perfectionism can lead young athletes to put too much pressure on themselves to succeed at their sport, leaving them vulnerable to burnout.

SPORTS AND HEALTH: THE OUTLOOK

Are Americans heeding all the advice that is coming from their doctors and the government about the importance of physical activity? Tainya C. Clarke, Jeannine S. Schiller, and Tina Norris indicate in *Early Release of Selected Estimates Based on Data from the January–June 2017 National Health Interview Survey* (December 19, 2017, https://www.cdc.gov/nchs/data/nhis/earlyrelease/ealyrelease201712.pdf) that, in general, the answer seems to be "not really." Figure 8.1 shows that the percentage of adults who met the federal government's 2008 guidelines for aerobic activity through regular leisure-time physical activity between 1997 and 2017 hovered somewhere between 40% and 55%, in spite of the aggressive promotion of exercise by the federal government and

FIGURE 8.1

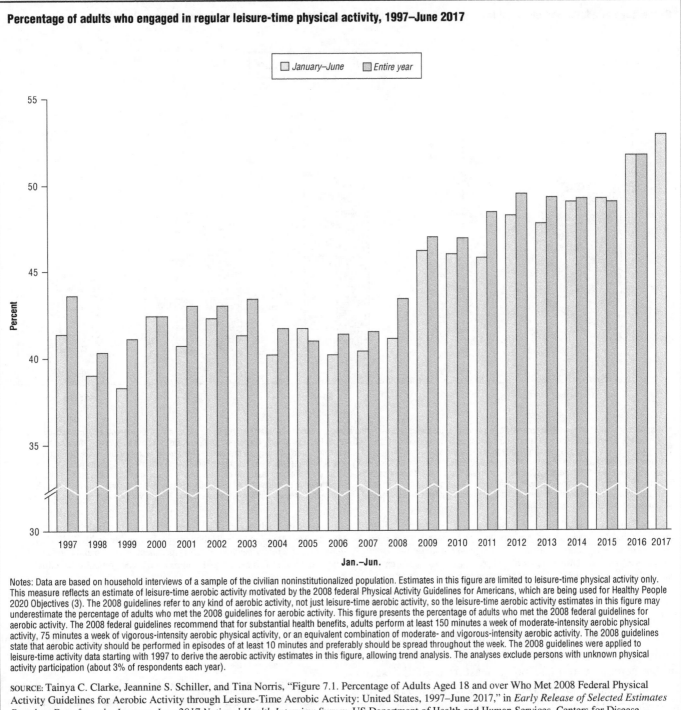

Percentage of adults who engaged in regular leisure-time physical activity, 1997–June 2017

☐ January–June ☐ Entire year

Percent

Jan.–Jun.

Notes: Data are based on household interviews of a sample of the civilian noninstitutionalized population. Estimates in this figure are limited to leisure-time physical activity only. This measure reflects an estimate of leisure-time aerobic activity motivated by the 2008 federal Physical Activity Guidelines for Americans, which are being used for Healthy People 2020 Objectives (3). The 2008 guidelines refer to any kind of aerobic activity, not just leisure-time aerobic activity, so the leisure-time aerobic activity estimates in this figure may underestimate the percentage of adults who met the 2008 guidelines for aerobic activity. This figure presents the percentage of adults who met the 2008 federal guidelines for aerobic activity. The 2008 federal guidelines recommend that for substantial health benefits, adults perform at least 150 minutes a week of moderate-intensity aerobic physical activity, 75 minutes a week of vigorous-intensity aerobic physical activity, or an equivalent combination of moderate- and vigorous-intensity aerobic activity. The 2008 guidelines state that aerobic activity should be performed in episodes of at least 10 minutes and preferably should be spread throughout the week. The 2008 guidelines were applied to leisure-time activity data starting with 1997 to derive the aerobic activity estimates in this figure, allowing trend analysis. The analyses exclude persons with unknown physical activity participation (about 3% of respondents each year).

SOURCE: Tainya C. Clarke, Jeannine S. Schiller, and Tina Norris, "Figure 7.1. Percentage of Adults Aged 18 and over Who Met 2008 Federal Physical Activity Guidelines for Aerobic Activity through Leisure-Time Aerobic Activity: United States, 1997–June 2017," in *Early Release of Selected Estimates Based on Data from the January–June 2017 National Health Interview Survey*, US Department of Health and Human Services, Centers for Disease Control and Prevention, National Center for Health Statistics, December 19, 2017, https://www.cdc.gov/nchs/data/nhis/earlyrelease/earlyrelease201712 .pdf (accessed February 13, 2018)

others. As shown in Figure 8.2, people tend to exercise less as they age, and this pattern holds true for both genders, with men more likely than women to be physically active in every age category. In 2017 non-Hispanic white adults (58.4%) were more likely to engage in regular leisure-time physical activity than either non-Hispanic African American (46.7%) or Hispanic (44.4%) adults. (See Figure 8.3.)

Vigorous physical activity among adolescents seems to be slightly higher. In *Vigorous Physical Activity by Youth* (March 2017, https://www.childtrends.org/wp-con tent/uploads/2017/03/16_Vigorous_Physical_Activity_ Youth.pdf), the nonprofit research agency Child Trends assesses vigorous physical activity trends among high school students. "Vigorous physical activity" is defined as physical activity for at least 60 minutes that made the

FIGURE 8.2

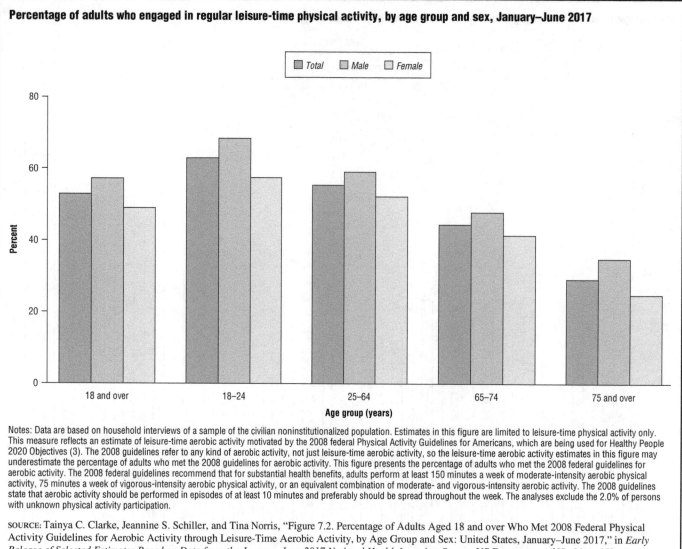

Percentage of adults who engaged in regular leisure-time physical activity, by age group and sex, January–June 2017

Notes: Data are based on household interviews of a sample of the civilian noninstitutionalized population. Estimates in this figure are limited to leisure-time physical activity only. This measure reflects an estimate of leisure-time aerobic activity motivated by the 2008 federal Physical Activity Guidelines for Americans, which are being used for Healthy People 2020 Objectives (3). The 2008 guidelines refer to any kind of aerobic activity, not just leisure-time aerobic activity, so the leisure-time aerobic activity estimates in this figure may underestimate the percentage of adults who met the 2008 guidelines for aerobic activity. This figure presents the percentage of adults who met the 2008 federal guidelines for aerobic activity. The 2008 federal guidelines recommend that for substantial health benefits, adults perform at least 150 minutes a week of moderate-intensity aerobic physical activity, 75 minutes a week of vigorous-intensity aerobic physical activity, or an equivalent combination of moderate- and vigorous-intensity aerobic activity. The 2008 guidelines state that aerobic activity should be performed in episodes of at least 10 minutes and preferably should be spread throughout the week. The analyses exclude the 2.0% of persons with unknown physical activity participation.

SOURCE: Tainya C. Clarke, Jeannine S. Schiller, and Tina Norris, "Figure 7.2. Percentage of Adults Aged 18 and over Who Met 2008 Federal Physical Activity Guidelines for Aerobic Activity through Leisure-Time Aerobic Activity, by Age Group and Sex: United States, January–June 2017," in *Early Release of Selected Estimates Based on Data from the January–June 2017 National Health Interview Survey*, US Department of Health and Human Services, Centers for Disease Control and Prevention, National Center for Health Statistics, December 19, 2017, https://www.cdc.gov/nchs/data/nhis/earlyrelease/earlyrelease201712.pdf (accessed February 13, 2018)

person sweat and breathe hard, such as basketball, soccer, running, swimming laps, fast bicycling, fast dancing, or similar aerobic activities, on at least five of the seven days preceding the interview. Figure 8.4 shows that in 2015 non-Hispanic white students (29%) were more likely than Hispanic (24.6%) and non-Hispanic African American (24.2%) students to have engaged in daily vigorous physical activity. As shown in Figure 8.5, 40.1% of ninth-grade boys reported engaging in daily vigorous physical activity in 2015, whereas 20.9% of ninth-grade girls reported such activity. These figures fell for both boys and girls as they progressed through high school. Among 12th graders, 32.6% of boys participated in regular vigorous physical activity, compared with 14.3% of girls. Table 8.5 shows the percentage of high school students who met physical activity recommendations for select years between 1993 and 2015, by sex, race

and ethnicity, and grade. In 2015 about one-quarter of students (27.1%) met physical activity recommendations.

In the face of an obesity epidemic in the United States, the federal government has taken an active role in promoting fitness among Americans. In 1996 the National Center for Chronic Disease Prevention and Health Promotion published *Physical Activity and Health: A Report of the Surgeon General* (https://www.cdc.gov/nccdphp/sgr/pdf/sgrfull.pdf), a blueprint for improving the physical condition of the US population. Among the report's major conclusions were that people of all ages and genders benefit from regular physical activity and that significant health benefits can be obtained by engaging in a moderate amount of physical activity, such as 45 minutes of volleyball, 30 minutes of brisk walking, or 15 minutes of running. The report noted that additional benefits can be gained through

FIGURE 8.3

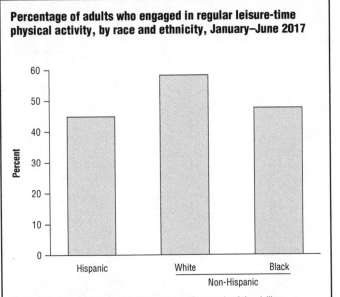

Percentage of adults who engaged in regular leisure-time physical activity, by race and ethnicity, January–June 2017

Notes: Data are based on household interviews of a sample of the civilian noninstitutionalized population. Estimates in this figure are limited to leisure-time physical activity only. This measure reflects an estimate of leisure-time aerobic activity motivated by the 2008 federal Physical Activity Guidelines for Americans, which are being used for Healthy People 2020 Objectives (3). The 2008 guidelines refer to any kind of aerobic activity, not just leisure-time aerobic activity, so the leisure-time aerobic activity estimates in this figure may underestimate the percentage of adults who met the 2008 guidelines for aerobic activity. This figure presents the percentage of adults who met the 2008 federal guidelines for aerobic activity. The 2008 federal guidelines recommend that for substantial health benefits, adults perform at least 150 minutes a week of moderate-intensity aerobic physical activity, 75 minutes a week of vigorous-intensity aerobic physical activity, or an equivalent combination of moderate- and vigorous-intensity aerobic activity. The 2008 guidelines state that aerobic activity should be performed in episodes of at least 10 minutes and preferably should be spread throughout the week. The analyses exclude the 2.0% of persons with unknown physical activity participation. Estimates are age-sex-adjusted using the projected 2000 US population as the standard population and five age groups: 18–24, 25–34, 35–44, 45–64, and 65 and over.

SOURCE: Tainya C. Clarke, Jeannine S. Schiller, and Tina Norris, "Figure 7.3. Age-Sex-Adjusted Percentage of Adults Aged 18 and over Who Met 2008 Federal Physical Activity Guidelines for Aerobic Activity through Leisure-Time Aerobic Activity, by Race and Ethnicity: United States, January–June 2017," in *Early Release of Selected Estimates Based on Data From the January–June 2017 National Health Interview Survey*, US Department of Health and Human Services, Centers for Disease Control and Prevention, National Center for Health Statistics, December 19, 2017, https://www.cdc.gov/nchs/data/nhis/earlyrelease/earlyrelease201712.pdf (accessed February 13, 2018)

FIGURE 8.4

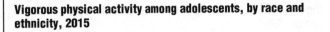
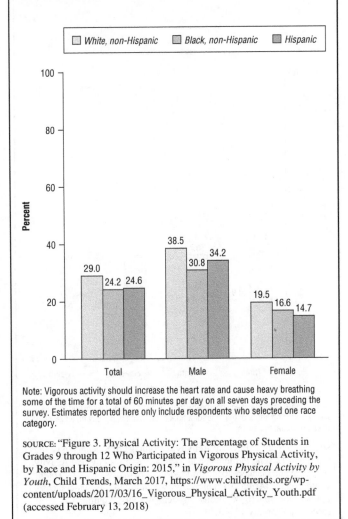

Vigorous physical activity among adolescents, by race and ethnicity, 2015

Note: Vigorous activity should increase the heart rate and cause heavy breathing some of the time for a total of 60 minutes per day on all seven days preceding the survey. Estimates reported here only include respondents who selected one race category.

SOURCE: "Figure 3. Physical Activity: The Percentage of Students in Grades 9 through 12 Who Participated in Vigorous Physical Activity, by Race and Hispanic Origin: 2015," in *Vigorous Physical Activity by Youth*, Child Trends, March 2017, https://www.childtrends.org/wp-content/uploads/2017/03/16_Vigorous_Physical_Activity_Youth.pdf (accessed February 13, 2018)

more vigorous and greater amounts of activity. Since then, the federal government has continued its efforts to promote physical fitness through a variety of programs and awards, including Healthy People 2020 and the President's Challenge, a fitness initiative of the President's Council on Sports, Fitness, & Nutrition (2018, https://www.hhs.gov/fitness/index.html). Other initiatives include the #0to60 Campaign (June 1, 2017, https://www.hhs.gov/fitness/programs-and-awards/zero-to-sixty-campaign/index.html), which encourages participants to kickstart their healthy living with a 60-day program to increase activity and improve nutrition, and I Can Do It, You Can Do It! (June 12, 2017, https://www.hhs.gov/fitness/programs-and-awards/i-can-do-it-you-can-do-it/index.html), a health promotion program designed to encourage physical activity among children and adults with a disability. The program, administered through school districts and other community-based organizations, encourages participants to set weekly goals for physical activity and healthful eating.

FIGURE 8.5

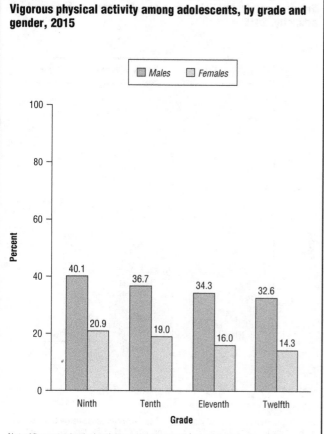

Vigorous physical activity among adolescents, by grade and gender, 2015

Note: Vigorous physical activity means that the heart rate increases and causes heavy breathing some of the time for a total of 60 minutes per day on all seven days preceding the survey.

SOURCE: "Figure 2. Physical Activity: Percentage of Students in Grades 9 through 12 Who Participated in Regular Vigorous Physical Activity, by Grade and Gender: 2015," in *Vigorous Physical Activity by Youth*, Child Trends, March 2017, https://www.childtrends.org/wp-content/uploads/2017/03/16_Vigorous_Physical_Activity_Youth.pdf (accessed February 13, 2018).

TABLE 8.5

Percentage of students who met current physical activity recommendations, by grade, gender, and race and ethnicity, selected years 1993–2015

	1993	1995	1997	1999	2001	2003	2005	2005[b]	2007[b]	2009[b]	2011[c]	2013[c]	2015[c]
All students	65.8	63.7	63.8	64.7	64.6	62.6	68.7	35.8	34.7	37.0	28.7	27.1	27.1
Race/Hispanic origin[a]													
Non-Hispanic white	67.7	67.0	66.8	67.4	66.5	65.2	70.2	38.7	37.0	39.9	30.4	28.2	29.0
Non-Hispanic black	60.0	53.2	53.9	55.6	59.7	54.8	62.0	29.5	31.1	32.6	26.0	26.3	24.2
Hispanic	59.4	57.3	60.4	60.5	60.5	59.3	69.4	32.9	30.2	33.1	26.5	25.5	24.6
Grade													
9	74.5	71.5	72.7	72.5	71.9	68.5	73.5	36.9	38.1	39.7	30.7	30.4	31.0
10	69.5	69.3	65.9	64.7	67.0	64.9	70.5	38.5	34.8	39.3	30.8	27.6	27.8
11	62.5	60.3	60.0	58.2	61.3	60.1	67.4	34.4	34.8	36.4	27.3	25.5	25.3
12	57.8	54.9	57.5	61.4	55.5	55.0	61.8	32.9	29.5	31.6	25.1	24.3	23.5
Male	74.7	74.4	72.3	72.3	72.6	70.0	75.8	43.8	43.7	45.6	38.3	36.6	36.0
Race/Hispanic origin[a]													
Non-Hispanic white	75.9	76.0	73.4	74.6	73.7	71.9	77.0	46.9	46.1	47.3	40.4	37.5	38.5
Non-Hispanic black	71.4	68.1	67.1	64.6	72.4	65.0	71.7	38.2	41.3	43.3	35.2	37.2	30.8
Hispanic	68.8	69.7	69.2	71.6	68.8	66.7	76.0	39.0	38.6	41.3	35.6	33.9	34.2
Grade													
9	81.2	79.9	78.7	77.0	77.1	73.1	78.4	42.8	44.4	47.5	38.8	40.5	40.1
10	77.2	78.6	74.3	73.3	74.0	71.5	77.8	46.8	45.1	47.4	42.6	34.6	36.7
11	71.4	72.3	68.9	67.1	72.2	70.4	74.2	43.8	45.2	46.2	36.2	37.0	34.3
12	69.8	67.2	68.4	70.7	66.1	63.7	71.9	41.9	38.7	40.4	34.9	33.5	32.6
Female	56.2	52.1	53.5	57.1	57.0	55.0	61.5	27.8	25.6	27.7	18.5	17.7	17.7
Race/Hispanic origin[a]													
Non-Hispanic white	58.8	56.7	58.4	59.7	59.8	58.1	63.3	30.2	27.9	31.3	19.7	18.7	19.5
Non-Hispanic black	48.8	41.3	41.3	47.2	47.8	44.9	53.1	21.3	21.0	21.9	16.9	16.0	16.6
Hispanic	50.0	45.2	49.9	49.5	52.4	51.8	62.6	26.5	21.9	24.9	16.9	17.4	14.7
Grade													
9	67.5	61.6	66.1	68.0	67.3	63.6	68.4	30.8	31.5	30.8	22.2	20.1	20.9
10	61.1	59.3	55.7	56.2	60.1	58.2	63.0	30.0	24.4	30.5	18.1	20.5	19.0
11	52.7	47.2	49.4	49.2	50.8	49.4	60.7	25.1	24.6	26.0	18.0	14.4	16.0
12	45.4	42.4	43.6	52.3	45.4	46.4	51.7	24.0	20.6	22.4	14.9	15.3	14.3

[a]Race/ethnicity estimates from 1999 and later are not directly comparable to earlier years, due to federal changes in race definitions. In surveys conducted in 1999 and later, respondents were allowed to select more than one race. Estimates presented include only respondents who selected one category.
[b]Recommendations for physical activity were revised in 2005 to encompass activities that increased heart rate and caused hard breathing some of the time for a total of 60 minutes a day on at least five or the seven days preceding the survey.
[c]Recommendations for physical activity were revised in 2008 to encompass activities that increased heart rate and caused hard breathing some of the time for a total of 60 minutes a day on all seven days preceding the survey.
Notes: Estimates do not include youth who dropped out of school and therefore may not reflect the total population in this age group. Students from Oregon, Washington, Minnesota were not included in the survey in any year. Additionally, students from Colorado, Georgia, Iowa, Kansas, Louisiana, New Jersey, Ohio, Texas, Utah, and Wisconsin were not included in the 2015 survey.
The recommendations for physical activity changed twice since 1993: 1993–2005 recommendations specified activities that caused sweating and hard breathing for at least 20 minutes on at least three of the seven days preceding the survey; 2005–2011 recommendations specified activities that increased heart rate and caused hard breathing some of the time for a total of 60 minutes/day on at least five of the seven days preceding the survey; 2011–2015 recommendations specified activities that increased heart rate and caused hard breathing some of the time for a total of 60 minutes/day on all seven days preceding the survey.

SOURCE: "Appendix 1. Percentage of Students in Grades 9 through 12 Who Met Current Recommendations for Physical Activity: Selected Years, 1993–2015," in *Vigorous Physical Activity by Youth*, Child Trends, March 2017, https://www.childtrends.org/wp-content/uploads/2017/03/16_Vigorous_Physical_Activity_Youth.pdf (accessed February 13, 2018)

CHAPTER 9
PERFORMANCE-ENHANCING DRUGS

The spirit of sport is the celebration of the human spirit, the body and the mind. Doping is contrary to the spirit of sport, erodes public confidence and jeopardizes the health and well-being of athletes.

—World Anti-Doping Agency, *Athlete Guide* (2005)

The word *doping* is often used to refer to any practice that involves prohibited substances or other methods to give an athlete an unfair advantage over other competitors. The article "Doping in Sports: Steroids and Supplements" (*World Almanac and Book of Facts*, 2007) notes that the word *dope* probably comes from the Dutch word *dop*, an alcoholic beverage made from grape skins that traditional Zulu warriors believed enhanced their fighting ability.

A BRIEF HISTORY OF DOPING

For as long as people have been engaging in athletic competition, they have been seeking ways to gain an edge on their opponents. There is evidence that doping took place during the ancient Olympics, whose competitions were held from 776 BC until AD 393. For example, Will Carroll notes in *The Juice: The Real Story of Baseball's Drug Problems* (2005) that Greece's Spartan coaches fed their athletes special herb and mushroom concoctions that were believed to render them oblivious to pain.

The first suspected case of an athlete dying as a result of doping occurred in 1896, when the Welsh cyclist Andrew Linton (1868–1896) died following a race from Bordeaux to Paris, France. The substance he ingested was thought to be trimethyl, an alcohol-based product that was used by distance racers to ease pain and increase stamina.

According to Carroll, the modern era of doping began with the development of injectable testosterone in 1935. Testosterone is a male hormone that is produced naturally by the body. Injecting additional testosterone into the system increases muscle mass and strength.

The father of anabolic steroids (chemical variants of testosterone) in the United States was John Benjamin Ziegler (1917–2000), a physician for the US weightlifting team during the mid-20th century. Ziegler learned from his Russian counterparts that the Soviet weightlifting team's success was in part attributable to its use of performance-enhancing drugs. Deciding that US athletes needed chemical assistance to remain competitive, Ziegler worked with the CIBA Pharmaceutical Company to develop an oral anabolic steroid. These efforts resulted in the creation of methandrostenolone, which became commercially available in the late 1950s. Drug testing was introduced at the Olympics in 1968; however, because no test had yet been invented that could distinguish between anabolic steroids and naturally occurring testosterone in the body, the testing was largely ineffective.

Steroids found their way into professional football during the late 1960s, as teams began hiring strength and conditioning coaches, who were charged with the task of growing a new breed of bigger players. Taking their cue from the weightlifting world, these coaches turned to steroids as the fastest way of accomplishing this goal.

By the 1970s the use of performance-enhancing drugs had reached epidemic proportions among elite athletes. One of the most high-profile incidences of doping occurred at the 1976 Olympics in Montreal, Canada, where the East German women's team dominated the swimming events. Years later, it emerged that the swimmers were the victims of a mandatory doping program overseen by East German Olympic officials, who injected the swimmers with steroids without their informed consent. Many of the athletes suffered serious long-term health consequences (ranging from liver damage to infertility) as a result of doping. East German swimmers of that era, Lillie Turlington writes in "American vs. East German: Women's Swimming, 1976" (August 9, 2016, https://www.theodysseyonline.com/american-vs-east-german-womens-swimming-1976), were given steroids beginning as young as age 13. The swimmers were told the pills and injections they were given were vitamins that would help them "regenerate and recuperate."

A breakthrough in drug testing took place in 1983, when a new technology for analyzing blood for banned substances was implemented at the Pan American Games in Caracas, Venezuela. The article "Inquiry Set on Pan Am" (Associated Press, September 14, 1983) reported at that time that 16 athletes from several countries were caught with performance-enhancing drugs in their system. Many other athletes, including 12 members of the US track and field team, withdrew from the event rather than risk the embarrassment of being caught. The first major Olympic disqualification due to steroids occurred in 1988, when the Canadian sprinter Ben Johnson (1961–) was stripped of both his gold medal and his world record in the 100-meter sprint after testing positive for the banned steroid stanozolol.

By the 21st century, testing athletes for performance-enhancing drugs had become an integral aspect of the Olympic Games. The article "Two Olympic Athletes Test Positive for Drugs" (ChicagoTribune.com, February 21, 2014) notes that the International Olympic Committee conducted a total of 2,453 drug tests at the 2014 winter games in Sochi, Russia. Lecia Bushak notes in "Undetectable Doping Agent, 'Full Size MGF,' Being Sold to Athletes at Sochi" (MedicalDaily.com, February 5, 2014) that this figure represented a 14% increase over testing at previous games. The UK-based Press Association reports in "WADA Reveals up to 50% of Drug Tests at 2016 Olympic Games Had to Be Aborted" (Guardian.com, October 27, 2016) that although more than 4,800 tests were conducted at the 2016 Summer Olympics in Rio de Janeiro, there were serious shortcomings in the coordination of tests, with "up to half of all planned drug tests aborted on some days because the athletes could not be found." The article further notes that 3,237 athletes were tested during the 2016 games, which represented just over a quarter (28.62%) of those competing.

As is detailed in Chapter 7, the Russian Olympic team was banned from participation in the 2018 Olympics in PyeongChang, South Korea, after an investigation revealed that the Russian Anti-Doping Agency (Rusada) systematically mishandled drug-testing results involving Russian athletes. In July 2016 the World Anti-Doping Agency (WADA) reported in "WADA Statement: Independent Investigation Confirms Russian State Manipulation of the Doping Control Process" (July 18, 2016, https://www.wada-ama.org/en/media/news/2016-07/wada-statement-independent-investigation-confirms-russian-state-manipulation-of) that Rusada officials had manipulated anti-doping procedures at major international competitions, including the 2014 Winter Olympics in Sochi, Russia. In the aftermath of the investigation, more than 100 Russian athletes, including all of the weightlifters and most of the track and field athletes, were barred from competing in the 2016 summer games in Rio de Janeiro. In December 2017 the IOC announced the ban for the winter games in PyeongChang. David Wharton reports in "IOC Clears 169 Russian Athletes to Compete at 2018 Olympic Games" (LATimes.com, January 27, 2018) that individual Russian athletes who complied with anti-doping rules were allowed to participate under the designation "Olympic Athlete from Russia (OAR)." These athletes, however, wore neutral uniforms and participated under the Olympic flag. They were not allowed to display the Russian flag at any time during the competition, and the Olympic hymn rather than the national anthem was played during medal ceremonies when Russian athletes won gold.

WHAT ARE PERFORMANCE-ENHANCING DRUGS?
Anabolic Steroids

In "Steroid Abuse in Today's Society" (March 2004, https://www.deadiversion.usdoj.gov/pubs/brochures/steroids/professionals/), the US Drug Enforcement Administration (DEA) defines anabolic steroids as "synthetically produced variants of the naturally occurring male hormone testosterone." The full name of this class of drugs is androgenic anabolic steroids. The word *androgenic* means the drugs promote masculine physical characteristics, and *anabolic* means tissue building.

The main users of anabolic steroids are athletes seeking to add bulk and strength to their bodies. Besides building lean body mass, another way steroids are purported to help athletes get stronger is by reducing the amount of recovery time that is needed between workouts, allowing them to train harder. Anabolic steroids are formally banned by most sports organizations both in the United States and worldwide.

Steroids are available in several forms, including tablets, liquids, gels, and creams. Typically, users ingest the drugs orally, inject them into muscle, or rub them on their skin. The doses taken by people who abuse steroids can be 10 to 100 times stronger than those recommended for medical conditions.

Steroid abuse has been linked to a wide range of health hazards, both physical and mental. Among the physical problems are liver and kidney tumors, high blood pressure, and elevated cholesterol levels. Some studies have associated steroid use with serious cardiovascular problems, including cardiomyopathies (inflammation of the heart muscle), irregular heart rhythm, embolisms (blockage of an artery by a clot or particle that is carried in the bloodstream), and heart failure. Men sometimes experience symptoms such as shrunken testicles, reduced sperm count, baldness, breast development, and increased risk of prostate cancer. Among women, growth of facial hair, male-pattern baldness, menstrual cycle disruptions, and deepening of the voice have been reported. Emotional/psychological problems stemming from abuse of steroids include extreme mood swings, depression, paranoid jealousy, irritability, delusions, and impaired judgment. Sometimes these steroid-induced mood swings lead to violent behavior, a condition popularly referred to as "'roid rage."

Other Substances and Supplements

There are numerous other performance-enhancing substances, some of which have, until recently, escaped the scrutiny of regulators. As a result, many of these substances, which are often billed as dietary supplements, have been readily available at nutrition and vitamin stores.

ERYTHROPOIETIN. Erythropoietin (EPO) is a hormone that is produced naturally by the kidneys. It plays a role in regulating the number of red blood cells in the blood stream. A synthetic version of EPO was developed during the 1980s, and it quickly became popular as a performance-enhancing drug, particularly among athletes who were involved in endurance sports such as cycling. Excessive doses of EPO can increase the number of red blood cells to such a degree that the blood becomes too thick to flow properly, potentially leading to heart attacks and strokes. Haroon Siddique reports in "Blood Doping: What Is It and Has Anyone Died as a Result of It?" (Guardian .com, August 2, 2015) that during the late 1980s, shortly after the appearance of synthetic EPO, more than two dozen top endurance athletes (mainly cyclists) in Belgium, the Netherlands, and Sweden died; the likely cause of their deaths was EPO. A variant of EPO known as continuous erythropoietin receptor activator (CERA) became available in 2008. Many of the athletes who were ejected from the 2008 Tour de France and the 2008 Beijing Olympics had tested positive for CERA.

CREATINE. One of the most popular supplements used by athletes at all levels is creatine. Creatine is available without a prescription and is reputed to improve performance in sports that require short bursts of power, such as weightlifting, wrestling, and sprinting. Although research has not yet established a connection between creatine and serious health problems, there is some evidence that heavy use may cause kidney, liver, and heart damage. Known side effects of creatine include muscle cramps, stomach pain, diarrhea, and nausea. In "Performance-Enhancing Drugs: Know the Risks" (October 15, 2015, https://www.mayoclinic.org/healthy-lifestyle/fitness/in-depth/performance-enhancing-drugs/art-20046134), the Mayo Clinic explains that creatine causes the muscles to draw water away from the rest of the body. As a result, increased body mass is most likely caused by excess water stored in the muscles.

ANDROSTENEDIONE. Androstenedione (or andro) enjoyed a huge burst of popularity during the late 1990s, after the Major League Baseball (MLB) player Mark McGwire (1963–) shattered the single-season home run record in 1998. McGwire admittedly used andro, which was perfectly legal and within the rules of the MLB at the time.

Andro is a direct precursor to testosterone (meaning it turns into testosterone in the body) and is found naturally in humans. It is also found naturally in Scotch pine trees, which is why manufacturers were allowed to sell it as a dietary supplement. Andro was discovered during the 1930s, but it was not until the 1950s that scientists learned that it is a precursor to testosterone. Andro is widely believed to boost testosterone production, which in turn increases muscle mass, energy, and strength. The Mayo Clinic disputes these claims, although proponents of andro cite research supporting andro's effectiveness as a performance enhancer. The Anabolic Steroid Control Act of 2004 reclassified andro as an anabolic steroid, making it illegal for use as a performance enhancer.

Heavy use of andro can produce side effects that are similar to those associated with other anabolic steroids. In men, andro can decrease testosterone production while increasing production of the female hormone estrogen. It can also cause acne, shrinking of the testicles, and reduced sperm count. In women side effects of andro can include acne as well as the onset of masculine characteristics such as deepening of the voice and male-pattern baldness.

EPHEDRA. Ephedra is an herb that has been used in Chinese medicine for thousands of years. An American version widely used by early settlers in the Southwest was called Mormon or Squaw tea. The main chemical constituent in ephedra is ephedrine, a powerful stimulant that is similar to amphetamines. It also contains a chemical called pseudoephedrine, long used as a nasal decongestant, although it has become tightly regulated because of its use in manufacturing illegal methamphetamine. Athletes primarily use ephedra as an energy booster.

Ephedra can cause elevated blood sugar levels and irregular heartbeats. It has also been linked to serious side effects such as strokes, seizures, and heart attacks. Many people have died as a direct result of its use. In February 2003 the Baltimore Orioles pitcher Steve Bechler (1979–2003) died of heatstroke after a spring training workout. Ephedra toxicity was identified as a contributing factor in his death. Bechler's death sparked renewed efforts by the US Food and Drug Administration (FDA) to take action against ephedra. In December 2003 the FDA banned ephedra from being sold over the counter as a dietary supplement. In April 2005, however, a federal judge overturned the FDA's ban on procedural grounds. The Combat Methamphetamine Epidemic Act of 2005, which was signed into law in March 2006, placed strict regulations on the sale of ephedrine-containing products.

THE BALCO SCANDAL

A major breakthrough in the effort to detect doping came in June 2003, when the track and field coach Trevor Graham (1963–) gave authorities a syringe containing what turned out to be tetrahydrogestrinone (THG), a previously unknown anabolic steroid. THG was considered to be a designer steroid, in that it was manufactured to be undetectable by the existing methods. Lab testing methods were quickly adjusted to detect THG. Investigators soon turned their attention to the Bay Area Laboratory Co-Operative (BALCO), the California-based distributor of the drug.

On September 3, 2003, agents of the Internal Revenue Service, the FDA, the San Mateo County Narcotics Task Force, and the US Anti-Doping Agency (USADA) raided BALCO facilities and seized containers of steroids, human growth hormone (HGH), and testosterone. Two days later officials searched the home of Greg Anderson (1966–), the personal weight trainer of the baseball star Barry Bonds (1964–), and seized more steroids, as well as documents and computer files thought to implicate a number of high-profile athletes. Over the next few months urine samples from the US Track and Field Championships were retested for THG, and several came up positive. One of those athletes was Kelli White (1977–), who had won both the 100- and 200-meter world championships in 2003. White was stripped of her titles and banned from competition for two years.

Victor Conte Jr. (1950–), the BALCO founder and owner; James Valente, a BALCO executive; Anderson; and the track coach Remi Korchemny (1932–) were indicted in February 2004 for distributing steroids. In March 2005 a congressional committee held hearings on the issue of steroids in baseball. A number of legislators mocked MLB officials for the sport's weak policy and feeble efforts to deal with the problem. Many current and former baseball players testified, including McGwire, José Canseco (1964–), Rafael Palmeiro (1964–), Curt Schilling (1966–), Sammy Sosa (1968–), and Frank Thomas (1968–).

In October 2005 Conte was sentenced to four months in prison and another four months of house arrest. Anderson received three months each of prison time and home confinement. Valente and Korchemny were given probation: Valente for three years and Korchemny for one year.

A year before he was convicted, Conte appeared on a December 2004 broadcast of the American Broadcasting Company's 20/20. During his interview, Conte revealed that he had provided performance-enhancing drugs to other elite athletes, including the sprinters Tim Montgomery (1975–) and Marion Jones (1975–). As the controversy unfolded, Jones repeatedly proclaimed her innocence and eventually sued Conte for defamation of character. She settled the suit out of court in 2006; later that year she was cleared after her alternate blood sample tested negative for banned substances.

The case, however, was not over. In October 2007, in the US District Court for the Southern District of New York, Jones admitted to having used illegal performance-enhancing drugs during the period surrounding the 2000 Olympics in Sydney, Australia, and lying about it to two grand juries. She pleaded guilty to lying to federal agents about her use of steroids and making false statements in a check fraud case. Under pressure from the US Olympic Committee, she surrendered her three gold and two bronze medals from the 2000 Olympics. She was suspended for two years from all track and field competitions and was retroactively disqualified from all events dating back to September 1, 2000. In January 2008 Judge Kenneth M. Karas (1964–) of the US District Court sentenced Jones to six months in prison, 200 hours of community service, and two years of probation. Several other high-profile track and field athletes received bans in the wake of the BALCO scandal, including the sprinters White, Montgomery, and Chryste Gaines (1970–).

STEROID USE AND YOUTH

Data from Lloyd D. Johnston et al. in *Monitoring the Future: National Survey Results on Drug Use, 1975–2017. Overview: Key Findings on Adolescent Drug Use* (January 2018, http://www.monitoringthefuture.org/pubs/monographs/mtf-overview2017.pdf), an ongoing study of behavior among secondary school students, college students, and young adults, suggest that steroid use among young people peaked during the early part of the 21st century and has been tapering off since then. (See Figure 9.1.) As steroid use has declined, Johnston et al. also note a decline in the percentage of high school students who claim the drug is "fairly easy" or "very easy" to obtain. (See Figure 9.2.) Meanwhile, as Figure 9.3 shows, the perception of risk that is associated with steroid use increased very slightly among high school students between 2000 and 2012, before declining between 2013 and 2017. Between 1989 and 2017 the proportion of high school students who disapproved of any form of steroid use remained at roughly 90%. (See Figure 9.4.)

FIGURE 9.1

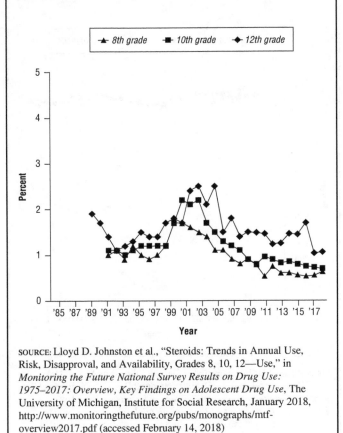

Steroid use trends among 8th-, 10th-, and 12th-graders, 1989–2017

[% who used in last 12 months]

SOURCE: Lloyd D. Johnston et al., "Steroids: Trends in Annual Use, Risk, Disapproval, and Availability, Grades 8, 10, 12—Use," in *Monitoring the Future National Survey Results on Drug Use: 1975–2017: Overview, Key Findings on Adolescent Drug Use*, The University of Michigan, Institute for Social Research, January 2018, http://www.monitoringthefuture.org/pubs/monographs/mtf-overview2017.pdf (accessed February 14, 2018)

FIGURE 9.2

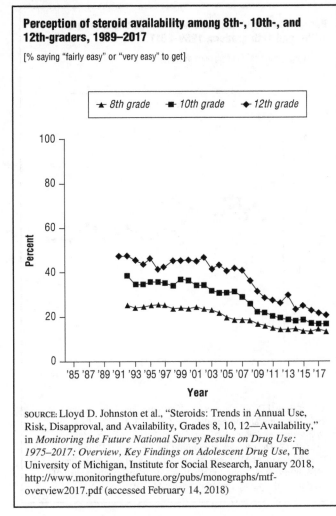

Perception of steroid availability among 8th-, 10th-, and 12th-graders, 1989–2017

[% saying "fairly easy" or "very easy" to get]

SOURCE: Lloyd D. Johnston et al., "Steroids: Trends in Annual Use, Risk, Disapproval, and Availability, Grades 8, 10, 12—Availability," in *Monitoring the Future National Survey Results on Drug Use: 1975–2017: Overview, Key Findings on Adolescent Drug Use*, The University of Michigan, Institute for Social Research, January 2018, http://www.monitoringthefuture.org/pubs/monographs/mtf-overview2017.pdf (accessed February 14, 2018)

PERFORMANCE-ENHANCING DRUGS IN COLLEGE SPORTS

In *NCAA National Study of Substance Use Habits of College Student-Athletes: Final Report July 2014* (August 2014, http://www.ncaa.org/sites/default/files/Substance%20Use%20Final%20Report_FINAL.pdf), Markie Rexroat of the National Collegiate Athletic Association (NCAA) tracks the use of performance-enhancing and other substances among student-athletes. As Table 9.1 shows, NCAA men's lacrosse players were the most likely athletes in Division I to have taken any category of performance-enhancing drugs in 2014. Among female athletes in Division I, lacrosse players (8.5%) were the most likely to have used amphetamines in 2014, whereas gymnasts were the most likely to have taken anabolic steroids (0.8%) and ephedrine (2.5%) that year. (See Table 9.2.)

As Table 9.3 shows, in 2014 more than a quarter (26.4%) of all NCAA athletes had been subject to drug testing by their college or university at some point during their athletic career, and nearly one out of five (18.4%) had been subject to drug testing by the NCAA. Among male athletes, football players were the most likely to

have experienced drug testing by either their college or university (35%) or the NCAA (30.2%). (See Table 9.4.) Female swimmers (43%) were the most likely to have been tested for drug use by their college or university, whereas female gymnasts (28.6%) were the most likely to have experienced drug testing by the NCAA. (See Table 9.5.) Among male student-athletes who indicated that a teammate had been tested by their school's drug testing program, NCAA football players (59.5%) and baseball players (58.1%) were the most likely to report a teammate being tested. (See Table 9.6.) As Table 9.7 shows, nearly three-quarters (74%) of NCAA women soccer players reported that their school had tested at least one of their teammates for banned substance use. In 2014 sizable majorities of student-athletes either agreed or strongly agreed that they should be subject to drug testing by their school (60.4%) or by the NCAA (60.3%). (See Table 9.8.)

STEROIDS IN PROFESSIONAL SPORTS

Every sport has its own way of testing for performance-enhancing drugs and its own policy for dealing with players who use them. The National Football League

FIGURE 9.3

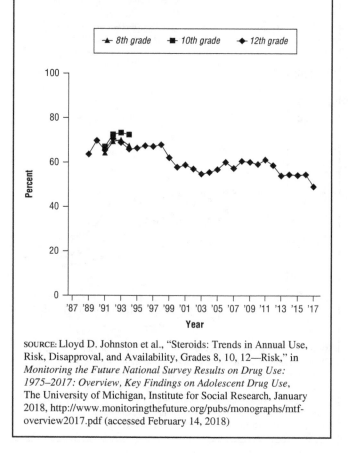

Perception of risk involved with steroid use among 8th-, 10th-, and 12th-graders, 1989–2017

[% seeing "great risk" in using once or twice]

SOURCE: Lloyd D. Johnston et al., "Steroids: Trends in Annual Use, Risk, Disapproval, and Availability, Grades 8, 10, 12—Risk," in *Monitoring the Future National Survey Results on Drug Use: 1975–2017: Overview, Key Findings on Adolescent Drug Use*, The University of Michigan, Institute for Social Research, January 2018, http://www.monitoringthefuture.org/pubs/monographs/mtf-overview2017.pdf (accessed February 14, 2018)

FIGURE 9.4

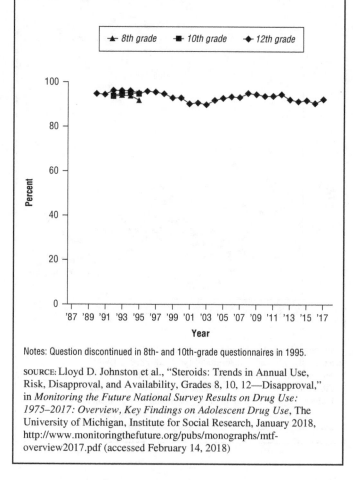

Disapproval of steroid use among 8th-, 10th-, and 12th-graders, 1989–2017

[% disapproving of using once or twice]

Notes: Question discontinued in 8th- and 10th-grade questionnaires in 1995.

SOURCE: Lloyd D. Johnston et al., "Steroids: Trends in Annual Use, Risk, Disapproval, and Availability, Grades 8, 10, 12—Disapproval," in *Monitoring the Future National Survey Results on Drug Use: 1975–2017: Overview, Key Findings on Adolescent Drug Use*, The University of Michigan, Institute for Social Research, January 2018, http://www.monitoringthefuture.org/pubs/monographs/mtf-overview2017.pdf (accessed February 14, 2018)

(NFL) requires its players to take year-round drug tests. The penalty for those caught using banned substances for the first time is a suspension that lasts four games, a loss of pay for missed games, and a prorated forfeiture of any signing bonuses. The second offense results in an eight-game suspension without pay, while a third infraction results in a suspension of at least a year, and potentially longer, without pay. The MLB, which has the most widely publicized steroid problem among the major sports, implemented a new, much harsher drug policy in 2014. Under the new policy, an athlete's first positive test results in an 80-game suspension without pay. A second failed test brings a 162-game suspension without pay. A player who tests positive three times is banned for life. In the National Basketball Association (NBA) first-time offenders are suspended for 20 games without pay, and second-time offenders are suspended for 45 games without pay. A third offense results in a lifetime ban. In the National Hockey League (NHL) a first positive drug test results in a 20-game suspension without pay, and a second offense carries a 60-game suspension without pay. A third offense results in a lifetime ban (although players can apply for reinstatement after two years).

Football

Although steroids have long been associated with the NFL, in recent years other performance-enhancing drugs, notably HGH, have become a major problem for the league. HGH is a protein-based hormone that occurs naturally in the body and helps promote tissue growth. Because HGH is believed to increase muscle mass, reduce body fat, and help accelerate the healing process for injuries, it has become a popular substance among professional athletes in the 21st century. Nevertheless, because HGH is detectable only through blood samples, testing for the banned substance has proven to be a challenge. The league introduced a comprehensive HGH testing program in 2014.

Baseball

In 2002, as part of the new collective bargaining agreement between MLB players and owners, a plan was put in place to hold survey testing for steroids during the 2003 season. If more than 5% of players came up positive in anonymous tests, a formal testing policy, with

TABLE 9.1

Performance-enhancing drug use among male National Collegiate Athletic Association Division I athletes, by sport, 2014

[Overall percentage of use within last 12 months]

Year	Baseball	Basketball	Football	Golf	Ice Hockey	Lacrosse	Soccer	Swimming	Tennis	Track	Wrestling
Amphetamines	8.8%	1.8%	3.9%	3.5%	6.8%	16.7%	3.4%	5.2%	4.9%	3.1%	11.9%
Anabolic steroids	0.7%	0.4%	0.7%	0.0%	0.5%	1.7%	0.0%	0.0%	0.0%	0.2%	0.6%
Ephedrine	0.1%	0.7%	0.4%	0.0%	1.0%	2.5%	0.5%	0.4%	0.0%	0.5%	0.0%

SOURCE: Markie Rexroat, "Division I Ergogenic Aid Use by Men's Sport," in *NCAA National Study of Substance Use Habits of College Student-Athletes: Final Report July 2014*, National Collegiate Athletic Association, August 2014, http://www.ncaa.org/sites/default/files/Substance%20Use%20Final%20Report_FINAL.pdf (accessed February 14, 2018)

TABLE 9.2

Performance-enhancing drug use among female National Collegiate Athletic Association Division I athletes, by sport, 2014

[Overall percentage of use within last 12 months]

Year	Basketball	Crew	Golf	Gymnastics	Lacrosse	Soccer	Softball	Swimming	Tennis	Track	Volleyball
Amphetamines	0.9%	0.9%	3.8%	4.9%	8.5%	3.5%	4.1%	2.3%	4.0%	0.8%	3.1%
Anabolic steroids	0.0%	0.0%	0.0%	0.8%	0.0%	0.0%	0.0%	0.0%	0.0%	0.3%	0.0%
Ephedrine	0.0%	0.0%	0.0%	2.5%	1.6%	0.0%	0.2%	0.7%	0.0%	0.3%	0.0%

SOURCE: Markie Rexroat, "Division I Ergogenic Aid Use by Women's Sport," in *NCAA National Study of Substance Use Habits of College Student-Athletes: Final Report July 2014*, National Collegiate Athletic Association, August 2014, http://www.ncaa.org/sites/default/files/Substance%20Use%20Final%20Report_FINAL.pdf (accessed February 14, 2018)

TABLE 9.3

National Collegiate Athletic Association student-athletes who have experienced drug testing, by athletic division, 2014

[Personal experience with drug testing]

		Division I	Division II	Division III	Overall
Have YOU ever been drug tested by your college's drug testing program	Yes	44.4%	23.6%	9.0%	26.4%
	No	55.6%	76.4%	91.0%	73.6%
Have YOU ever been drug tested by the NCAA	Yes	31.3%	17.3%	5.5%	18.4%
	No	68.7%	82.7%	94.5%	81.6%
Have YOU ever been drug tested by a national or international sports governing body	Yes	8.3%	5.0%	2.8%	5.4%
	No	91.7%	95.0%	97.2%	94.6%

SOURCE: Markie Rexroat, "Drug Testing Experiences—Personal by Division and Overall," in *NCAA National Study of Substance Use Habits of College Student-Athletes: Final Report July 2014*, National Collegiate Athletic Association, August 2014, http://www.ncaa.org/sites/default/files/Substance%20Use%20Final%20Report_FINAL.pdf (accessed February 14, 2018)

TABLE 9.4

Male National Collegiate Athletic Association student-athletes who have experienced drug testing, by sport, 2014

[Males reporting that they have been drug tested]

		Baseball	Basketball	Football	Golf	Ice hockey	Lacrosse	Soccer	Swimming	Tennis	Track	Wrestling
Have YOU ever been drug tested by your college's drug testing program	Yes	29.8%	26.9%	35.0%	20.6%	9.3%	16.1%	23.5%	25.7%	21.5%	21.4%	28.5%
	No	70.2%	73.1%	65.0%	79.4%	90.7%	83.9%	76.5%	74.3%	78.5%	78.6%	71.5%
Have YOU ever been drug tested by the NCAA	Yes	24.2%	19.9%	30.2%	14.0%	10.1%	5.3%	13.6%	12.4%	13.0%	14.4%	21.0%
	No	75.8%	80.1%	69.8%	86.0%	89.9%	94.7%	86.4%	87.6%	87.0%	85.6%	79.0%
Have YOU ever been tested by a national or international sports	Yes	7.0%	6.9%	8.0%	6.5%	7.5%	3.7%	5.1%	8.3%	6.0%	5.2%	7.2%
	No	93.0%	93.1%	92.0%	93.5%	92.5%	96.3%	94.6%	91.7%	94.0%	94.8%	92.8%

SOURCE: Markie Rexroat, "Drug Testing Experiences—Personal by Men's Sport," in *NCAA National Study of Substance Use Habits of College Student-Athletes: Final Report July 2014*, National Collegiate Athletic Association, August 2014, http://www.ncaa.org/sites/default/files/Substance%20Use%20Final%20Report_FINAL.pdf (accessed February 14, 2018)

TABLE 9.5

Female National Collegiate Athletic Association student-athletes who have experienced drug testing, by sport, 2014

[Females reporting that they have been drug tested]

		Basketball	Crew	Field hockey	Golf	Gymnastics	Ice hockey	Lacrosse	Soccer	Softball	Swimming	Tennis	Track	Volleyball
Have YOU ever been drug tested by your college's drug testing program	Yes	24.7%	6.7%	13.2%	31.3%	32.6%	4.2%	23.6%	30.2%	28.8%	43.0%	36.1%	21.6%	33.6%
	No	75.3%	93.3%	86.8%	68.7%	67.4%	95.8%	76.4%	69.8%	71.2%	57.0%	63.9%	78.4%	66.4%
Have YOU ever been drug tested by the NCAA	Yes	15.7%	1.5%	8.3%	19.5%	28.6%	8.3%	15.4%	16.6%	15.8%	17.9%	21.4%	16.1%	21.5%
	No	84.3%	98.5%	91.7%	80.5%	71.4%	91.7%	84.6%	83.4%	84.2%	82.1%	78.6%	83.9%	78.5%
Have YOU ever been drug tested by national or international sports governing body	Yes	3.0%	0.8%	1.5%	4.2%	3.6%	4.1%	2.3%	3.7%	3.7%	8.5%	4.6%	3.0%	2.1%
	No	97.0%	99.2%	98.5%	95.8%	96.4%	95.9%	97.7%	96.3%	96.3%	91.5%	95.4%	97.0%	97.9%

SOURCE: Markie Rexroat, "Drug Testing Experiences—Personal by Women's Sport," in *NCAA National Study of Substance Use Habits of College Student-Athletes: Final Report July 2014*, National Collegiate Athletic Association, August 2014, http://www.ncaa.org/sites/default/files/Substance%20Use%20Final%20Report_FINAL.pdf (accessed February 14, 2018)

TABLE 9.6

National Collegiate Athletic Association men's teams that have experienced drug testing, by sport, 2014

[Males reporting that their teammates have been drug tested]

		Baseball	Basketball	Football	Golf	Ice hockey	Lacrosse	Soccer	Swimming	Tennis	Track	Wrestling
To your knowledge, have other members of YOUR TEAM been drug tested by your college's drug testing program	Yes	58.1%	38.2%	59.5%	41.7%	27.1%	35.7%	50.8%	45.7%	37.9%	43.2%	49.1%
	No	41.9%	61.8%	40.5%	58.3%	72.9%	64.3%	49.2%	54.3%	62.1%	56.8%	50.9%
To your knowledge, have other members of YOUR TEAM been drug tested by the NCAA	Yes	61.0%	35.2%	61.2%	34.7%	39.7%	25.4%	44.7%	42.7%	29.2%	45.9%	50.4%
	No	39.0%	64.8%	38.8%	65.3%	60.3%	74.6%	55.3%	57.3%	70.8%	54.1%	49.6%
To your knowledge, have other members of YOUR TEAM been drug tested by a national or international sports governing body	Yes	18.5%	10.7%	22.8%	10.5%	15.8%	7.6%	11.6%	21.4%	9.6%	16.0%	18.8%
	No	81.5%	89.3%	77.2%	89.5%	84.2%	92.4%	88.4%	78.6%	90.4%	84.0%	81.2%

SOURCE: Markie Rexroat, "Drug Testing Experiences—Teammates by Men's Sports," in *NCAA National Study of Substance Use Habits of College Student-Athletes: Final Report July 2014*, National Collegiate Athletic Association, August 2014, http://www.ncaa.org/sites/default/files/Substance%20Use%20Final%20Report_FINAL.pdf (accessed February 14, 2018)

TABLE 9.7

National Collegiate Athletic Association women's teams that have experienced drug testing, by sport, 2014

[Females reporting that their teammates have been drug tested]

		Basketball	Crew	Field hockey	Golf	Gymnastics	Ice hockey	Lacrosse	Soccer	Softball	Swimming	Tennis	Track	Volleyball
To your knowledge, have other members of YOUR TEAM been drug tested by your college's drug testing program	Yes	41.0%	23.4%	31.3%	52.1%	70.8%	13.7%	58.3%	74.0%	56.9%	72.5%	61.2%	47.2%	56.1%
	No	59.0%	76.6%	68.7%	47.9%	29.2%	86.3%	41.7%	26.0%	43.1%	27.5%	38.8%	52.8%	43.9%
To your knowledge, have other members of YOUR TEAM been drug tested by the NCAA	Yes	32.8%	29.5%	32.3%	39.2%	60.0%	28.8%	47.8%	61.5%	52.3%	62.3%	44.4%	44.8%	50.2%
	No	67.2%	70.5%	67.7%	60.8%	40.0%	71.2%	52.2%	38.5%	47.7%	37.7%	55.6%	55.2%	49.8%
To your knowledge, have other members of YOUR TEAM been drug tested by a national or international sports governing body	Yes	5.6%	6.1%	5.1%	9.9%	9.1%	13.4%	7.5%	10.1%	11.5%	29.8%	7.9%	10.4%	6.5%
	No	94.4%	93.9%	94.9%	90.1%	90.9%	86.6%	92.5%	89.9%	88.5%	70.2%	92.1%	89.6%	93.5%

SOURCE: Markie Rexroat, "Drug Testing Experiences—Teammates by Women's Sports," in *NCAA National Study of Substance Use Habits of College Student-Athletes: Final Report July 2014*, National Collegiate Athletic Association, August 2014, http://www.ncaa.org/sites/default/files/Substance%20Use%20Final%20Report_FINAL.pdf (accessed February 14, 2018)

accompanying penalties, would be implemented. When the results of the survey showed a positive rate of between 5% and 7%, the league formally launched a testing program in 2004. Under the original policy, every player would be tested once per season. The first time a player tested positive, he was to be placed in treatment;

TABLE 9.8

Opinions on drug testing among National Collegiate Athletic Association athletes, 2014

[Drug testing opinions]

	Strongly agree	Agree	No opinion	Disagree	Strongly disagree
All professional athletes should be tested	47.0%	31.1%	12.6%	6.1%	3.2%
All Olympic athletes should be tested	58.5%	26.0%	10.3%	3.2%	2.1%
All college athletes should be tested by their school	30.8%	29.6%	16.0%	16.5%	7.1%
All college athletes should be tested by the NCAA	30.7%	29.6%	16.4%	16.1%	7.2%
Drug testing by individual colleges has deterred college athletes from using drugs	24.2%	32.2%	19.0%	32.2%	17.3%
Drug testing by the NCAA has deterred college athletes from using drugs	25.3%	33.1%	18.0%	16.5%	7.1%
Imposing team penalties would be fair and appropriate	30.8%	30.4%	15.9%	12.3%	10.6%

SOURCE: Markie Rexroat, "Drug Testing Opinions All Divisions," in *NCAA National Study of Substance Use Habits of College Student-Athletes: Final Report July 2014*, National Collegiate Athletic Association, August 2014, http://www.ncaa.org/sites/default/files/Substance%20Use%20Final%20Report_FINAL.pdf (accessed February 14, 2018)

a second positive test would result in a 15-day suspension. A fifth positive test could result in a suspension lasting up to a year.

Although no players were suspended under this new policy, it remained clear that performance-enhancing drugs were still being used on a large scale. In 2005 the league introduced a stricter policy in which steroids, steroid precursors (such as andro), designer steroids, masking agents, and diuretics were banned. All players would be subject to unannounced mandatory testing during the season. In addition, there would be testing of randomly selected players, with no maximum number, and random testing during the off-season. The penalties for a positive result were a 10-day suspension for the first offense, 30 days for the second, 60 days for the third, and one year for the fourth. All these suspensions were without pay. The following season, the penalties were increased to those noted earlier.

In 2006, in the wake of the congressional hearings of the previous year, the league commissioner Bud Selig (1934–) appointed the former US senator George J. Mitchell (1933–; D-ME) to head an independent investigation into steroid use in baseball in an effort to stave off further intervention by Congress. Released in December 2007, Mitchell's report (*Report to the Commissioner of Baseball of an Independent Investigation into the Illegal Use of Steroids and Other Performance Enhancing Substances by Players in Major League Baseball*, http://files.mlb.com/mitchrpt.pdf) documented the widespread use of steroids in baseball beginning in the 1980s, which involved players on every team. Mitchell noted that honest athletes were placed at a disadvantage in competing with those who were on steroids and that many records from the period could be invalid.

In the aftermath of Mitchell's findings, the link between steroids and professional baseball had become firmly entrenched in the public's mind. Indeed, it came as little surprise when, in 2009, it was revealed that 104 players had tested positive for performance-enhancing drugs in the league's 2003 drug testing survey, even though those tests were supposed to remain confidential. Among the elite players whose names appeared on the list were David Ortiz (1975–), Manny Ramirez (1972–), and Alex Rodriguez (1975–). Ramirez later tested positive under the new testing policy, once in 2009 and a second time in 2011. Rodriguez publicly admitted to having used banned drugs between 2001 and 2003, when he was playing for the Texas Rangers, but speculation arose—notably in the 2009 book *A-Rod: The Many Lives of Alex Rodriguez* by Selena Roberts—that he had used steroids as far back as high school, and as recently as 2004, when he began playing for the New York Yankees. Rodriguez came under more intense scrutiny in 2013 after his name was linked with a Florida health clinic, Biogenesis of America, which had provided banned substances to more than a dozen major and minor leaguers. Although it was technically his first offense, Rodriguez received a suspension of 211 games, both for using performance-enhancing drugs and for attempting to cover up his involvement with Biogenesis; it was the longest penalty yet under the MLB's drug-testing program. As of 2018, the MLB's testing policy included mandatory urine tests for all players during spring training, a random second urine test during the season, and 400 random blood tests among the players for HGH.

Basketball

NBA players are tested up to four times per season, in addition to being subject to two random tests during the off-season. Players who test positive for hard drugs such as cocaine or opiates are automatically kicked out of the league, although they may eventually apply for reinstatement. Players testing positive for marijuana are required to seek treatment for a first offense, seek treatment and pay a fine for a second offense, and serve a five-game suspension for a third offense. The league took steps to strengthen its drug policy in April 2015, when it announced that it would introduce HGH testing during the 2015–16 season. According to Jeff Zillgitt, in "NBA Will Test for HGH in 2015–16" (USAToday.com, April 16, 2015), the HGH testing protocol requires all players to be tested twice during the regular season and a third time during the off-season.

Hockey

In the wake of the drug scandals that dogged the other major leagues, the NHL unveiled its first anti-doping policy in September 2005 at a congressional hearing on drug use in professional sports. As of 2018, teams are subject to two random teamwide tests with no advance notice—one during training camp and one during the regular season. Individual players are also subject to random testing during the regular season and playoffs, although no tests are administered on game days. Up to 60 individual players will also be selected for random testing during the off season. A list of banned substances is maintained by the league and the NHL Players Association that follows those designated by WADA in its "Prohibited List" (January 2018, https://www.wada-ama.org/sites/default/files/prohibited_list_2018_en.pdf).

Cycling

Perhaps no other sport has been tainted by doping scandals more than professional bicycle racing, particularly the sport's most illustrious event, the Tour de France. The first major drug scandal in cycling took place in 1998, when the Festina cycling team was thrown out of the competition after the team masseur, Willy Voet (1945–), was caught in possession of several banned substances, including EPO, growth hormones, testosterone, and amphetamines. Doping allegations destroyed the career of the US cyclist Lance Armstrong (1971–), who won his seventh consecutive Tour de France in 2005. In 2002 Armstrong was linked to the sports physician Michele Ferrari (1953–), who was reputed to have developed a system for taking EPO without detection. In 2005 EPO was found in Armstrong's old blood and urine samples from the 1999 Tour de France. Armstrong vehemently denied ever using banned drugs. In 2006 investigators cleared him of all charges, while criticizing anti-doping authorities for mishandling evidence.

Armstrong's exoneration notwithstanding, the situation only became worse for the Tour de France. On the eve of the 2006 race, several top riders, including the contenders Jan Ullrich (1973–) and Ivan Basso (1977–), were banned from competing as a result of accusations made by Spanish police after a long investigation called Operacion Puerto. The 2006 Tour was won by the US cyclist Floyd Landis (1975–). Shortly after the conclusion of the race, however, it was revealed that Landis had failed a drug test at the 17th stage of the tour, with tests showing an abnormally high level of testosterone in his blood. Landis maintained his innocence, but he was nevertheless stripped of his title and fired from his racing team.

Meanwhile, a new investigation alleging Armstrong's involvement in an international doping ring surfaced in 2011. The following year the USADA released an exhaustive report that detailed Armstrong's extensive use of steroids and other banned substances throughout his cycling career. In October 2012 Armstrong was stripped of all seven of his Tour de France titles. Three months later, in January 2013, Armstrong publicly admitted to using performance-enhancing drugs. According to the article "Lance Armstrong: 'Impossible' to Win Tour de France without Doping" (USAToday.com, June 28, 2013), in June 2013 Armstrong told the French newspaper *Le Monde* that he believed the uniquely grueling demands of the Tour de France made the race "impossible" to win without performance-enhancing drugs, at least during the era when he was competing. Armstrong also insisted that he still considered his record seven tour victories to be legitimate.

STEROIDS AND THE LAW

Anabolic steroids are Schedule III–controlled substances in the United States. In October 2004 the federal Anabolic Steroid Control Act was signed into law. The act updated the Anabolic Steroid Control Act of 1990 in a number of ways. It amended the definition of anabolic steroids by adding THG, andro, and certain related chemicals to the list of substances that the law covered. The act also directed the US Sentencing Commission to review federal sentencing guidelines for offenses related to steroids and provided for increased penalties for committing these offenses. It authorized the US attorney general to exempt from regulation steroid-containing drugs that do not pose a drug abuse threat. Finally, the law directed the US secretary of health and human services to provide grants for the development of science-based educational programs for elementary and secondary schools on the hazards of anabolic steroid use. A number of states have passed their own laws that are aimed at curbing steroid use among youths.

In December 2014 President Barack Obama (1961–) signed into law the Designer Anabolic Steroid Control Act of 2014 (DASCA), an extension of the Controlled Substances Act. Josh Hodnik reports in "A Look at the Designer Anabolic Steroid Control Act of 2014" (Iron Magazine.com, May 13, 2015) that the new law added more than two dozen compounds to the list of Schedule III anabolic steroids. Hodnik notes, "Many of these substances were recently sold over-the-counter, but are now classified with steroids like trenbolone, oxandrolone, and boldenone." In addition, DASCA increased criminal penalties for illicit trafficking in controlled anabolic steroids.

Hodnik reports that the law targets a type of steroids sold in capsule form and known as "prohormones." He writes, "Many of the prohormones sold were weak anabolic substances themselves, but they would convert to stronger steroidal compounds after ingested. These products were popular among bodybuilders and athletes that wanted to add muscle and strength with the help of an anabolic agent, while still staying within the parameters of the law."

Anti-doping Agencies

By the end of the 20th century the global sports community recognized that it would take a coordinated international effort to bring the problem of performance-enhancing drugs under control. WADA was created in 1999 as a collaborative initiative between sports agencies and governments across the globe. WADA's role is to lead international efforts against doping in sports through public education, advocacy, research, and drug testing and to provide leadership for the efforts of agencies working against doping in individual countries. The USADA was launched in 2000 to lead this work at the national level. According to the USADA, in "Independence & History" (2018, https://www.usada.org/about/independence-history/), over the next decade the agency played a key role in several high-profile international doping scandals, including the BALCO case and the investigation of Armstrong and the US Postal Service cycling squad. By 2018 the USADA had conducted more than 100,000 tests to detect performance-enhancing drugs.

CHAPTER 10
SPORTS AND GAMBLING

People have been betting on the outcome of sporting events since ancient times. In ancient Rome the wealthy class wagered on chariot races, animal fights, and gladiator battles. The Romans spread their penchant for gambling across the breadth of their empire. During the 16th and 17th centuries people throughout Europe enjoyed betting on cockfights, wrestling, and footraces. In the 18th century horse racing and boxing rose to prominence as spectator sports on which the public enjoyed gambling. The 19th and 20th centuries brought a new emphasis on team sports, and Europeans began risking their wages on rugby, soccer, and cricket.

Most forms of gambling, including sports gambling, became illegal in the United States during the 19th century. Nevertheless, it remained legal to bet on horse racing, and other sports gambling continued to flourish underground. The state of Nevada legalized gambling in 1931, although it eventually became so tainted by organized crime and other scandals that during the 1950s it became the subject of government crackdowns. A new, tightly regulated version of sports betting returned to Nevada in 1975 and continues to thrive in the 21st century.

Modern sports gambling in the United States can be roughly divided into three categories: pari-mutuel gambling on horse and greyhound racing; legal sports betting through a licensed bookmaker; and illegal sports gambling. The third category makes up the biggest portion of sports gambling in the nation.

PARI-MUTUEL GAMBLING

Pari-mutuel betting was invented in late 19th-century France by Pierre Oller. *Pari-mutuel* is a French term that means "mutual stake." In this kind of betting, all the money bet on an event is combined into a single pool, which is then split among the winning bettors, with management taking some share, called a "takeout," off the top. The takeout rate, which in the United States is set by state law, is usually about 20% of the total betting pool. Unlike many other forms of sports wagering, an individual betting on a pari-mutuel event is betting against other gamblers rather than against the house. The house keeps the same percentage of the total bets regardless of the outcome of the event.

In pari-mutuel betting every bet that is placed on a particular horse or greyhound affects the odds. As a result, the more people who bet on a particular outcome, the lower the payout is for those who bet on that outcome. Betting on a long shot offers a lower likelihood of winning but a potentially larger payout.

The pari-mutuel system did not become widespread until the 1920s and 1930s, with the introduction of the totalizator (often shortened to "tote"), a special calculator that could automatically calculate the odds for each horse in a race based on the bets that had been placed. Before the 1930s most betting on horse races was done through bookmakers. In 1933 California, Michigan, New Hampshire, and Ohio legalized pari-mutuel gambling on horse racing. Many other states followed their lead over the next several years.

Historically, most pari-mutuel betting has taken place in person at the location where the event is happening. Nevertheless, bets can also be placed at off-track betting facilities, which were first approved by the New York legislature in 1970. Wagering via telephone or the internet is also available in some states. In the 21st century an increasing share of pari-mutuel wagering has been taking place at racinos. Racinos, a growing phenomenon in the gaming industry, are horse or greyhound racetracks that also offer on-site casino gaming.

Thoroughbred Horse Racing

People have been betting on horse races for thousands of years. Horse racing was a popular spectator sport among wealthy Greeks and Romans. Later, knights returning to western Europe from the Crusades brought with them speedy Arabian stallions, which were bred with English mares to create the line now called Thoroughbred. Thoroughbreds are fast, graceful runners and are identified by their height and long, slim legs. Thoroughbred racing quickly caught on among the British aristocracy, and it was soon dubbed the "Sport of Kings." The sport came to North America with the colonists; there are records of horse racing taking place in the New York area as early as 1665.

Thoroughbred racing remained popular in the United States throughout the 18th and 19th centuries. The sport was scaled back significantly during World War II (1939–1945), and after the war it remained in steep decline. Nevertheless, although attendance at horse races has decreased substantially, the money continues to flow and has increased since the 1990s. In "Pari-Mutuel Handle" (2018, http://www.jockeyclub.com/default.asp?section=FB&area=8), the Jockey Club reports that the annual handle (the total amount bet) for Thoroughbred racing in the United States climbed from $9.4 billion in 1990 to an all-time high of $15.2 billion in 2003, before falling to $10.9 billion by 2017.

The Daily Racing Form reports in "Racing Links: Race Tracks" (2018, http://www1.drf.com/racing_links/links_tracks.html) that there were 93 Thoroughbred racetracks in the United States and Canada in 2018. The Thoroughbred gambling business is dominated by a handful of companies, the largest being two publicly traded firms: Churchill Downs Inc. and Magna Entertainment Corporation. The three most prestigious Thoroughbred races together make up the Triple Crown of horse racing. These races, which take place over a five-week period between May and June each year, are the Kentucky Derby at Churchill Downs in Louisville, Kentucky; the Preakness Stakes at Pimlico in Baltimore, Maryland; and the Belmont Stakes at Belmont Park in Elmont, New York.

Non-Thoroughbred Horse Racing

Although Thoroughbreds dominate the horse racing scene in the United States, pari-mutuel gambling is available for other types of horses as well. Harness racing, in which horses trot or pace rather than gallop and pull the jockey in a two-wheeled cart called a sulky, uses a horse called a Standardbred, which is typically shorter and more muscular than a Thoroughbred. The US Trotting Association (USTA) reports in "Track Information" (2018, http://www.ustrotting.com/trackside/trackfacts/trackfacts.cfm) that in 2018 there were 33 pari-mutuel USTA tracks in the United States. Another type of horse commonly raced is the quarter horse, which gets its name from the fact that it excels at sprinting distances under a quarter of a mile. Finally, the Arabian Jockey Club (2018, https://www.arabianracing.org) is the governing body for races that feature Arabian horses, the only true purebred horses on the circuit, throughout the United States and Canada.

Greyhound Racing

Like horses, greyhounds have been raced for amusement and gambling purposes for centuries. Greyhound racing has been called the "Sport of Queens," probably because it was Queen Elizabeth I (1533–1603) of England who first standardized the rules for greyhound coursing (a sport in which greyhounds are used to hunt rabbits) during the 16th century. Greyhound racing was brought to the United States during the late 19th century, and the first circular greyhound track was opened in California in 1919. In "Racing in America" (http://www.gra-america.org/the_sport/tracks.php), the Greyhound Racing Association of America reports that in 2018 there were 40 greyhound tracks operating in 12 states, with gamblers betting more than $2 billion annually on races.

LEGAL SPORTS GAMBLING

As of May 2018, unlimited gambling on multiple sports was legal in only one state: Nevada. In Nevada legal sports gambling takes place through licensed establishments (books) that accept and pay out bets on sporting events. Sports books are legal only in Nevada. Betting on sports such as professional football, basketball, or baseball is prohibited elsewhere in the United States, although Delaware, Oregon, and Montana allow limited forms of sports gambling. These limitations were reinforced with the passage of the Professional and Amateur Sports Protection Act of 1992.

In May 2009 the Delaware legislature voted to legalize certain kinds of betting on various big-time sports. The four major professional sports leagues, as well as the National Collegiate Athletic Association (NCAA), filed a lawsuit against Delaware, claiming the state was in violation of the 1992 ban because it had not previously allowed that specific type of wagering. A federal court of appeals eventually ruled that sports betting in Delaware would be limited to parlay wagers (where the bettor must choose the winners of at least three separate games in one bet) on professional football games. In 2010 the New Jersey Senate approved a measure to amend the state constitution to legalize sports wagering. Although New Jersey voters overwhelmingly approved legalized sports betting in a November 2011 referendum, the NCAA and the four major professional sports leagues once again filed suit in federal court, where they succeeded in blocking the law's implementation under the 1992 law.

During this time, some high-ranking executives from the major professional sports leagues were beginning to reconsider prevailing attitudes toward sports betting. For example, in the op-ed "Legalize and Regulate Sports

Betting" (NYTimes.com, November 13, 2014), Adam Silver (1962–), the commissioner of the National Basketball Association (NBA), acknowledges that it might be time to adopt a more sensible and realistic approach to the issue. "There is an obvious appetite among sports fans for a safe and legal way to wager on professional sporting events," Silver asserts. He goes on to argue that subjecting sports betting to "strict regulatory requirements and technological safeguards" would enable lawmakers to exert far greater control over sports gambling and thereby bring it "out of the underground and into the sunlight where it can be appropriately monitored and regulated."

In October 2014 the New Jersey governor Chris Christie (1962–) signed into law Senate Bill 2460, which legalized sports wagering at the state's casinos and racinos. The following month, the US district judge Michael Shipp (1965–) delivered an injunction blocking the state from implementing the new law. The US Court of Appeals for the Third Circuit twice rejected New Jersey's appeal of Shipp's ruling, first in August 2015 and again after rehearing the case in February 2016. New Jersey subsequently appealed the verdict to the US Supreme Court, which agreed to consider the case. Travis Waldron writes in "Supreme Court Appears Ready to Legalize Sports Gambling" (HuffingtonPost.com, December 5, 2017) that the Supreme Court heard arguments in *Christie v. NCAA* (No. 16-476) in December 2017. (Note that in January 2018 the case became known as *Murphy v. NCAA* when Phil Murphy [1957–] succeeded Christie as governor of New Jersey.) According to Waldron, the case centered on the question of "how much control the federal government can exert over states." In May 2018 the Supreme Court ruled 6–3 that the Professional and Amateur Sports Protection Act was unconstitutional, thereby paving the way for the legalization of sports gambling at the state level.

Bookmaking

Bookmaking is the term used for determining gambling odds and handling bets and payouts. The person doing the bookmaking is called a bookmaker or bookie. Bookmakers make their money by charging a commission on each bet; the commission is usually between 4% and 5%.

Most sports bets are based on a point spread, which is set by the bookmaker. A point spread is how much a favored team must win a game by for those betting on that team to collect. For example, if Team A is a 10-point favorite to defeat Team B, the bettor is actually betting on whether Team A will beat Team B by at least this margin. If Team A wins by nine points, then those betting on Team B are the winners and those picking team A are the losers. In this example, Team B has lost the game but has "beat the spread." The point spread concept was introduced during the 1940s by the bookmaker Charles

K. McNeil (1903–1981) as a way of encouraging people to bet on the underdogs. Before the point spread system, bookmakers risked losing large sums on lopsided games in which everybody bet on the favorite to win.

Nevada: The Gambling Capital of the United States

Nevada legalized gambling in the 1930s as a way of generating revenue during the Great Depression (1929–1939). The state's legislature made off-track betting on horses legal during the 1940s. Betting on sports and horse racing was popular in Nevada's casinos throughout that decade. At the beginning of the 1950s, however, the Nevada gambling world came under the scrutiny of Congress for its ties to organized crime. The US. senator Estes Kefauver (1903–1963; D-TN) initiated hearings to investigate the matter. These nationally televised hearings drew attention to a culture of corruption and gangland activity that had settled in Las Vegas. The hearings resulted in the imposition of a 10% federal excise tax on sports betting. This tax effectively strangled casino-based sports bookmaking in Nevada.

In 1974 the federal excise tax on sports betting was reduced to 2%; by 1983 it had been reduced to 0.3%. The reduced tax appeared to have an immediate impact on the state's sports wagering business. Between 1984 and 1987, Nevada sports book betting increased by more than 100%. Although the total amount wagered on sports betting dropped slightly in 2008 and 2009, it grew substantially over the next eight years, topping $4.9 billion by 2017. (See Table 10.1.)

Football is the biggest betting draw among the major sports. As Table 10.2 shows, nearly $1.8 billion was wagered on football in 2017, and just under $1.5 billion was wagered on basketball. Overall, gamblers won $87.4 million on basketball games in 2017, compared with $76.9 million won on football. (See Table 10.3.) As Table 10.4 shows, basketball (39.9%) and football (35.1%) combined accounted for three-quarters (75%) of all sports gambling winnings in 2017. The Super Bowl is a gigantic gambling event. Super Bowl betting rose steadily between 2009, when gamblers bet $81.5 million on the Pittsburgh Steelers–Arizona Cardinals matchup, and 2018, when a total of $158.6 million was wagered on the title game between the New England Patriots and the Philadelphia Eagles. (See Table 10.5.)

ATTITUDES TOWARD SPORTS GAMBLING

On the whole, a relatively small percentage of the American public engages in sports betting. In *More Americans Bet on Legalized Sports Wagering Than Oppose It* (November 2, 2016, http://publicmind.fdu.edu/2016/161102/final.pdf), Fairleigh Dickinson University's PublicMind Poll found that 48% of adults surveyed approved of legalized sports betting in 2016. (See Table 10.6.) Support

TABLE 10.1

Amounts wagered and won on sports betting in Nevada, with win percentages, 1984–2017

[Dollar amounts in thousands]

	Units	Win amount	% Change	Win %	Drop	Total gaming win	% Total	Win/unit
1984	51	20,899	—	2.34%	894,564	3,092,980	0.68%	409.78
1985	56	21,485	2.80%	2.52%	851,786	3,309,372	0.65%	383.66
1986	59	34,921	62.54%	3.23%	1,081,161	3,492,474	1.00%	591.88
1987	67	29,054	−16.80%	1.55%	1,875,400	3,949,427	0.74%	433.64
1988	66	42,023	44.64%	3.19%	1,318,052	4,429,023	0.95%	636.71
1989	71	45,776	8.93%	3.35%	1,366,448	4,750,716	0.96%	644.73
1990	90	48,839	6.69%	2.92%	1,671,479	5,480,664	0.89%	542.66
1991	104	52,300	7.09%	2.80%	1,867,857	5,579,128	0.94%	502.88
1992	114	50,602	−3.25%	2.81%	1,800,783	5,864,228	0.86%	443.88
1993	112	75,035	48.28%	3.74%	2,006,283	6,247,508	1.20%	669.96
1994	112	122,450	63.19%	5.73%	2,136,998	7,007,586	1.75%	1,093.30
1995	119	79,415	−35.14%	3.27%	2,428,593	7,368,580	1.08%	667.35
1996	133	76,486	−3.69%	3.08%	2,483,312	7,426,192	1.03%	575.08
1997	136	89,718	17.30%	3.69%	2,431,382	7,801,920	1.15%	659.69
1998	146	77,375	−13.76%	3.41%	2,269,062	8,064,970	0.96%	529.97
1999	156	109,192	41.12%	4.42%	2,470,407	9,021,570	1.21%	699.95
2000	165	123,836	13.41%	5.33%	2,323,377	9,602,586	1.29%	750.52
2001	162	118,077	−4.65%	5.78%	2,042,855	9,468,559	1.25%	728.87
2002	149	110,383	−6.52%	5.70%	1,936,544	9,447,660	1.17%	740.83
2003	150	122,630	11.10%	6.58%	1,863,678	9,625,304	1.27%	817.53
2004	159	112,504	−8.26%	5.39%	2,087,273	10,562,247	1.07%	707.57
2005	164	126,176	12.15%	5.59%	2,257,174	11,649,040	1.08%	769.37
2006	168	191,538	51.80%	7.89%	2,427,605	12,622,044	1.52%	1,140.11
2007	169	168,363	−12.10%	6.49%	2,594,191	12,849,137	1.31%	996.23
2008	177	136,441	−18.96%	5.29%	2,579,225	11,599,124	1.18%	770.85
2009	185	136,380	−0.04%	5.31%	2,568,362	10,392,675	1.31%	737.19
2010	183	151,096	10.79%	5.47%	2,762,267	10,404,731	1.45%	825.66
2011	183	140,731	−6.86%	4.89%	2,877,935	10,700,994	1.32%	769.02
2012	182	170,062	20.84%	4.93%	3,449,533	10,860,715	1.57%	934.41
2013	186	202,838	19.27%	5.60%	3,622,107	11,142,915	1.82%	1,090.53
2014	190	227,045	11.93%	5.82%	3,901,117	11,018,688	2.06%	1,194.97
2015	196	231,787	2.09%	5.47%	4,237,422	11,114,081	2.09%	1,182.59
2016	192	219,174	−5.44%	4.86%	4,509,753	11,257,147	1.95%	1,141.53
2017	192	248,777	13.51%	5.11%	4,868,434	11,571,114	2.15%	1,295.71

Note: "Drop" is the estimated total amount bet by bettors during the calendar year, derived by dividing the Win by the Win Percentage.

SOURCE: David G. Schwartz, "Sports Betting Win, 1984–2017," in "Nevada Sports Betting Totals: 1984–2017," University of Nevada-Las Vegas, Center for Gaming Research, January 2018, http://gaming.unlv.edu/reports/NV_sportsbetting.pdf (accessed February 15, 2018)

was strongest among younger adults, with 60% of individuals aged 18 to 34 years voicing approval for legalized sports betting. (See Table 10.7.) Of the respondents who favored legalization, 45% approved of sports betting because people were already doing it; another 39% believed it would generate revenue for the state. (See Table 10.8.) As Table 10.9 shows, more than half (52%) of respondents between the ages of 55 and 64 years cited potential tax revenue as their primary reason for supporting legalized sports wagering, the highest proportion of any age group. Of those who oppose legalized sports betting, 55% did so because they believe it promotes gambling addiction. (See Table 10.10.) This sentiment was strongest among respondents aged 35 to 44 years, with 70% of individuals in that age group who oppose legalized sports betting doing so out of a concern that it promotes gambling addiction. (See Table 10.11.)

ILLEGAL SPORTS GAMBLING

Although legal sports betting is a multibillion dollar industry in the United States, the amount of money involved is dwarfed by the sums that are wagered illegally each year. The American Gaming Association reports in "New Report Says: End the Failing Ban on Sports Betting" (March 2, 2017, https://www.american gaming.org/newsroom/press-releasess/new-report-says-end-failing-ban-sports-betting) that an estimated $9.2 billion in illegal sports wagers were placed on the 2016 NCAA men's basketball tournament, compared with $262 million that was wagered legally in Nevada. Data concerning illegal sports wagering can vary widely. Will Hobson notes in "Sports Gambling in U.S.: Too Prevalent to Remain Illegal?" (WashingtonPost.com, February 27, 2015) that somewhere between an estimated $80 billion and $380 billion is placed in illegal sports wagers annually, compared with $4 billion in legal sports wagers placed in Nevada each year.

FIXING, SHAVING, AND TAMPERING: SPORTS GAMBLING SCANDALS

In the 21st century a large portion of illegal sports gambling is still believed to be controlled by organized

TABLE 10.2

Amounts wagered on sports betting in Nevada, by sport, 1992–2017

[In dollars; amounts in thousands]

	Football	Basketball	Baseball	Parlay	Other	Total
1992	735,799	509,608	433,333	57,584	64,434	1,800,783
1993	864,310	549,873	455,874	66,717	72,093	2,006,283
1994	1,016,112	604,702	373,000	67,800	74,317	2,136,998
1995	1,039,936	679,704	533,023	71,088	96,031	2,428,593
1996	999,964	680,739	608,373	78,324	114,385	2,483,312
1997	949,086	637,477	566,172	66,882	132,166	2,431,382
1998	915,937	557,723	600,513	68,280	134,433	2,269,062
1999	980,276	610,333	678,254	63,510	129,433	2,470,407
2000	914,212	638,993	567,537	65,301	137,822	2,323,377
2001	806,319	567,179	495,657	58,004	112,780	2,042,855
2002	860,000	513,503	386,783	66,431	109,444	1,936,544
2003	826,244	489,167	378,875	63,984	106,634	1,863,678
2004	969,129	543,661	426,479	59,943	86,813	2,087,273
2005	1,051,198	579,396	464,067	62,864	100,176	2,257,174
2006	1,136,397	635,365	457,541	68,265	131,147	2,427,605
2007	1,176,512	687,193	528,792	68,616	134,000	2,594,191
2008	1,122,229	738,268	522,013	64,614	131,486	2,579,225
2009	1,093,596	803,529	488,630	58,981	126,848	2,568,362
2010	1,185,462	830,422	528,668	56,707	158,563	2,762,267
2011	1,341,788	737,432	558,011	62,633	179,465	2,877,935
2012	1,566,499	975,153	693,687	58,178	157,692	3,449,533
2013	1,622,791	1,053,132	681,007	57,658	204,889	3,622,107
2014	1,749,723	1,109,182	721,831	57,782	266,990	3,901,117
2015	1,698,477	1,251,732	897,312	54,070	333,174	4,237,422
2016	1,692,820	1,402,779	1,045,584	60,255	307,216	4,509,753
2017	1,755,616	1,481,881	1,139,783	62,923	427,579	4,868,434

Note: This is the total amount bet in each sport.

SOURCE: David G. Schwartz, "Drop by Sport, 1992–2017," in *Nevada Sports Betting Totals: 1984–2017,* University of Nevada-Las Vegas, Center for Gaming Research, January 2018, http://gaming.unlv.edu/reports/NV_sportsbetting.pdf (accessed February 15, 2018).

crime. The history of sports is rife with tales of gamblers paying off athletes to "take a dive" or miss the crucial shot. Major professional sports leagues and the NCAA have taken measures to distance themselves from sports gambling, but their efforts have not prevented a long list of sports gambling scandals from taking place in the last several decades.

Perhaps the most notorious sports gambling scandal in history was the so-called Black Sox scandal of 1919, in which gamblers bribed several members of the Chicago White Sox to intentionally throw the World Series. A huge point-shaving scandal encompassing seven schools and 32 players rocked college basketball in 1951. Point shaving is a type of game fixing in which players accept bribes to avoid beating a published point spread. In 1978 associates of the Lucchese organized crime family orchestrated a point-shaving scheme with key members of the Boston College basketball team. Another point-shaving scheme involving college basketball was uncovered at Arizona State University in 1994.

Many high-profile professional athletes have gotten into trouble over the years for gambling on the sport in which they participate. Gambling by players inevitably creates suspicion about game fixing. In 1963 the National Football League (NFL) players Alex Karras (1935–2012) of the Detroit Lions and Paul Hornung (1935–) of the

Green Bay Packers were suspended for betting on their own teams' games. Denny McLain (1944–) of the Detroit Tigers, the last pitcher to win 30 or more games in a season, was suspended for most of the 1970 season for associating with gamblers. In 1989 the baseball player Pete Rose (1941–), who holds the record for the most career hits, was kicked out of baseball for gambling on Major League Baseball (MLB) games. He denied doing so at the time but has since admitted to betting on baseball games while serving as manager of the Cincinnati Reds. Rose's lifetime suspension has kept him out of the Baseball Hall of Fame.

The NBA was rocked during the summer of 2007 by revelations that the veteran referee Tim Donaghy (1967–) had been involved in gambling on NBA games, including games in which he had officiated. The NBA immediately took the position that Donaghy's activities represented an isolated case and that gambling among referees was extremely rare. In August 2007 Donaghy pleaded guilty to two felony charges that he had provided betting recommendations to gamblers based on inside information about games.

Since the 1990s college sports have been at the center of some of the most visible gambling scandals. During the 1994–95 season two Northwestern University basketball players were caught shaving points. Two years later,

TABLE 10.3

Amount won on sports betting in Nevada, by sport, 1989–2017

[In dollars; amounts in thousands]

	Football	Basketball	Baseball	Parlay	Other	Total
1984	—	—	—	—	—	20,899
1985	—	—	—	—	—	21,485
1986	—	—	—	—	—	34,921
1987	—	—	—	—	—	29,054
1988	—	—	—	—	—	42,023
1989	19,042	6,485	6,616	9,865	3,769	45,776
1990	16,905	6,611	10,281	11,694	3,339	48,839
1991	17,584	15,827	5,000	10,455	3,432	52,300
1992	19,793	10,396	7,800	9,939	2,674	50,602
1993	30,683	17,266	9,391	17,073	620	75,035
1994	63,507	19,290	10,071	25,554	4,028	122,450
1995	32,550	18,352	4,584	19,855	3,774	79,415
1996	27,599	19,333	10,099	21,594	−2,139	76,486
1997	32,174	14,152	14,494	19,924	6,833	89,718
1998	28,852	21,305	4,684	15,841	6,399	77,375
1999	49,700	27,526	4,273	19,739	7,300	109,192
2000	49,276	27,285	19,353	20,942	6,643	123,836
2001	46,444	29,550	17,348	18,689	6,045	118,077
2002	40,334	30,348	11,062	21,796	6,884	110,383
2003	48,831	34,046	12,124	21,070	6,558	122,630
2004	46,712	30,445	9,084	19,943	6,320	112,504
2005	40,366	38,356	26,127	15,628	5,700	126,176
2006	91,139	46,191	22,145	21,087	10,977	191,538
2007	73,532	37,452	25,382	20,283	11,792	168,363
2008	39,278	43,484	23,595	20,263	9,822	136,441
2009	48,665	38,248	21,402	19,210	8,854	136,380
2010	56,428	39,362	22,627	18,997	13,684	151,096
2011	44,279	48,818	19,642	17,600	10,391	140,731
2012	68,456	47,880	30,106	13,573	10,045	170,062
2013	80,815	59,186	29,079	19,967	13,789	202,838
2014	113,732	54,239	21,294	21,281	16,500	227,045
2015	82,546	72,976	39,392	15,983	20,890	231,787
2016	91,243	66,632	32,204	10,412	18,648	219,174
2017	76,896	87,431	36,815	15,177	32,325	248,777

SOURCE: David G. Schwartz, "Sports Betting Win by Sport (Total Amount), 1989–2017," in *Nevada Sports Betting Totals: 1984–2017*," University of Nevada-Las Vegas, Center for Gaming Research, January 2018, http://gaming.unlv.edu/reports/NV_sportsbetting.pdf (accessed February 15, 2018)

13 football players at Boston College were suspended for gambling on college football games. Other cases have involved the University of Florida basketball player Teddy Dupay (1979–), the Florida State University quarterback Adrian McPherson (1983–), and the University of Michigan basketball player Chris Webber (1973–).

GAMBLING IN COLLEGE SPORTS

Gambling on sports has become increasingly common among college athletes, even though it represents a direct violation of NCAA rules regarding sports wagering. Thomas Paskus and Jeffrey Derevensky report in *Trends in NCAA Student-Athlete Gambling Behaviors and Attitudes* (November 2017, https://www.ncaa.org/sites/default/files/2017RES_wagering_powerpoint_20171129.pdf) that 16.5% of Division I male athletes wagered on sporting events in 2016, compared with 18.7% who did so in 2012. The highest proportion of sports gambling in 2016 occurred at Division III schools, where nearly one-third (32.1%) of male athletes wagered on sports. By comparison, 2.8% of Division I female athletes bet on sports in 2016, as did 3.5% of female athletes at Division II schools, and 6.7% of Division III female athletes.

The NCAA has long supported a complete ban on college sports gambling. Since 2000 some members of Congress have also advocated banning college sports betting, but they have met with little success. Among the biggest proponents of banning all gambling on college sports has been the US senator John McCain (1936–; R-AZ), who first introduced the Amateur Sports Integrity Act in 2000. In the end, however, the proposed law made little progress in the face of heavy lobbying on the part of the gaming industry. McCain reintroduced the bill during the next two congressional sessions, but it met the same fate. In August 2009 the NCAA approved a new policy banning championship tournaments from taking place in the few states that allow betting on individual games.

ONLINE GAMBLING

The new frontier of sports gambling is the internet. Online gambling first became available during the late 1990s, and the Nevada sports books quickly sensed that it presented a serious challenge. Many authorities argued

TABLE 10.4

Sports betting win percentages in Nevada, by sport, 1989–2017

	Football	Basketball	Baseball	Parlay	Other
1989	41.60%	14.17%	14.45%	21.55%	8.23%
1990	34.61%	13.54%	21.05%	23.94%	6.84%
1991	33.62%	30.26%	9.56%	19.99%	6.56%
1992	39.12%	20.54%	15.41%	19.64%	5.28%
1993	40.89%	23.01%	12.52%	22.75%	0.83%
1994	51.86%	15.75%	8.22%	20.87%	3.29%
1995	40.99%	23.11%	5.77%	25.00%	4.75%
1996	36.08%	25.28%	13.20%	28.23%	−2.80%
1997	35.86%	15.77%	16.16%	22.21%	7.62%
1998	37.29%	27.53%	6.05%	20.47%	8.27%
1999	45.52%	25.21%	3.91%	18.08%	6.69%
2000	39.79%	22.03%	15.63%	16.91%	5.36%
2001	39.33%	25.03%	14.69%	15.83%	5.12%
2002	36.54%	27.49%	10.02%	19.75%	6.24%
2003	39.82%	27.76%	9.89%	17.18%	5.35%
2004	41.52%	27.06%	8.07%	17.73%	5.62%
2005	31.99%	30.40%	20.71%	12.39%	4.52%
2006	47.58%	24.12%	11.56%	11.01%	5.73%
2007	43.67%	22.24%	15.08%	12.05%	7.00%
2008	28.79%	31.87%	17.29%	14.85%	7.20%
2009	35.68%	28.05%	15.69%	14.09%	6.49%
2010	37.35%	26.05%	14.98%	12.57%	9.06%
2011	31.46%	34.69%	13.96%	12.51%	7.38%
2012	40.25%	28.15%	17.70%	7.98%	5.91%
2013	39.84%	29.18%	14.34%	9.84%	6.80%
2014	50.09%	23.89%	9.38%	9.37%	7.27%
2015	35.61%	31.48%	16.99%	6.90%	9.01%
2016	41.63%	30.40%	14.69%	4.75%	8.51%
2017	35.08%	39.89%	16.80%	6.92%	14.75%

Note: This is the percent of total sports betting win represented by each category.

SOURCE: David G. Schwartz, "Sports Betting Win by Sport (Percentage), 1989–2017," in *Nevada Sports Betting Totals: 1984–2017*," University of Nevada-Las Vegas, Center for Gaming Research, January 2018, http://gaming.unlv.edu/reports/NV_sportsbetting.pdf (accessed February 15, 2018)

TABLE 10.5

Super Bowl betting history, Nevada, 2009–18

Year	Wagers	Win/(loss)	Win %	Game results
2018	$158,586,934	$1,170,432	0.7%	Philadelphia 41, New England 33
2017	$138,480,136	$10,937,826	7.9%	New England 34, Atlanta 28
2016	$132,545,587	$13,314,539	10.1%	Denver 24, Carolina 10
2015	$115,986,086	$3,261,066	2.8%	New England 28, Seattle 24
2014	$119,400,822	$19,673,960	16.5%	Seattle 43, Denver 8
2013	$98,936,798	$7,206,460	7.3%	Baltimore 34, San Francisco 31
2012	$93,899,840	$5,064,470	5.4%	N.Y. Giants 21, New England 17
2011	$87,491,098	$724,176	0.8%	Green Bay 31, Pittsburgh 25
2010	$82,726,367	$6,857,101	8.3%	New Orleans 31, Indianapolis 17
2009	$81,514,748	$6,678,044	8.2%	Pittsburgh 27, Arizona 23

SOURCE: "Summary of Nevada Sport Book Performance for the Last Ten Super Bowls," State of Nevada Gaming Control Board, February 5, 2018, http://media.graytvinc.com/documents/2018+Super+Bowl.pdf (accessed February 15, 2018)

that, based on the federal Wire Act of 1961, which was originally enacted to get organized crime out of sports betting, online sports gambling is technically illegal in the United States; however, not everyone agreed with this analysis. Moreover, most internet gambling operations are based outside the United States, which complicates legal issues. The internet knows no geographic boundaries—an online gambling operation based in Antigua can be accessed as easily from Riyadh, Saudi Arabia, as it can from Dubuque, Iowa. The US government has attempted to take measures to curb online gambling, both

sports betting and other types, but because these businesses are not based in the United States, enforcement is problematic. After all, these businesses are legal in the countries in which they are based.

Nobody knows exactly how much money is bet online, and the legal status of some aspects of online gambling remains ambiguous. In 2006 Congress passed the Unlawful Internet Gambling Enforcement Act (UIGEA), a provision of the Security and Accountability for Every Port Act that prohibited the transfer of wagering

TABLE 10.6

Attitude toward legalizing sports betting nationwide, by political party affiliation, gender, and race, 2016

CURRENTLY, BETTING ON SPORTS—LIKE FOOTBALL AND BASKETBALL GAMES—IS LEGAL ONLY IN NEVADA, OREGON, DELAWARE, AND MONTANA. DO YOU FAVOR OR OPPOSE [ROTATE] CHANGING THE LAW TO ALLOW PEOPLE TO PLACE BETS ON SPORTS IN ALL STATES?

| | All | Gender | | Political ID | | | Race | | |
		Male	Female	Dem	Ind	Repub	White non-Hispanic	Black non-Hispanic	Hispanic
Support	48%	52	45	45	53	52	47	44	49
Oppose	39%	36	42	45	22	36	40	49	34
Don't know (vol)	10%	10	10	9	20	10	9	7	14
Refused (vol)	2%	2	3	2	5	2	3	0	3

SOURCE: "Currently, betting on sports—like football and basketball games—is legal only in Nevada, Oregon, Delaware, and Montana. Do you favor or oppose [rotate] changing the law to allow people to place bets on sports in all states?" in *More Americans Bet on Legalized Sports Wagering Than Oppose It*, Fairleigh Dickinson University's Public Mind Poll, November 2, 2016, http://publicmind.fdu.edu/2016/161102/final.pdf (accessed February 15, 2018)

TABLE 10.7

Attitude toward legalizing sports betting nationwide, by age and gambling history, 2016

CURRENTLY, BETTING ON SPORTS—LIKE FOOTBALL AND BASKETBALL GAMES—IS LEGAL ONLY IN NEVADA, OREGON, DELAWARE, AND MONTANA. DO YOU FAVOR OR OPPOSE [ROTATE] CHANGING THE LAW TO ALLOW PEOPLE TO PLACE BETS ON SPORTS IN ALL STATES?

| | Age | | | | | Been to a casino? | | Bet on sports? | |
	18–34	35–44	45–54	55–64	65+	Yes	No	Yes	No
Support	60%	48	52	36	37	40	54	79	44
Oppose	25%	43	37	53	47	49	36	15	42
Don't know (vol)	12%	6	11	6	14	8	9	5	11
Refused (vol)	2%	2		5	3	3	1	1	3

SOURCE: "Currently, betting on sports—like football and basketball games—is legal only in Nevada, Oregon, Delaware, and Montana. Do you favor or oppose changing the law to allow people to place bets on sports in all states?" in *More Americans Bet on Legalized Sports Wagering Than Oppose It*, Fairleigh Dickinson University's Public Mind Poll, November 2, 2016, http://publicmind.fdu.edu/2016/161102/final.pdf (accessed February 15, 2018)

TABLE 10.8

Reasons for supporting legalization of sports betting nationwide, by political party affiliation, gender, and race, 2016

WHICH OF THE FOLLOWING BEST EXPLAINS WHY YOU FAVOR MAKING SPORTS BETTING LEGAL IN ALL STATES? (READ LIST)

| | All | Gender | | Political ID | | | Race | | |
		Male	Female	Dem	Ind	Repub	White non-Hispanic	Black non-Hispanic	Hispanic
More tax revenue for states	39%	41	38	43	45	38	40	40	40
People are already doing it	45%	43	46	41	47	44	44	41	39
Will make sports more exciting	9%	10	8	12	7	7	6	16	16
Other (vol)	3%	3	2	2	0	7	4	2	1
Don't know (vol)	3%	2	5	1	1	3	4	1	4
Refused (vol)	1%	0	1	1	0	1	1	0	0

SOURCE: "Which of the following best explains why you FAVOR making sports betting legal in all states?" in *More Americans Bet on Legalized Sports Wagering Than Oppose It*, Fairleigh Dickinson University's Public Mind Poll, November 2, 2016, http://publicmind.fdu.edu/2016/161102/final.pdf (accessed February 15, 2018)

money over the internet. By 2017, however, as public attitudes in general shifted in favor of legalized sports betting, Congress began to reconsider the federal prohibition on internet sports wagering. Dave Purdum reports in "GAME Act Proposing Repeal of Federal Prohibition on Sports Betting Revealed" (ESPN.com, May 25, 2017) that in May 2017 a congressional committee released a draft of the Gaming Accountability and Modernization Enhancement (GAME) Act, aimed at repealing both the 1992 Professional and Amateur Sports Protection Act and UIGEA. Dustin Gouker writes in "NJ Congressman Introduces New Bill to Lift Sports Betting Ban, Update Gaming Laws" (LegalSportsReport.com, December 4, 2017) that the US representative Frank Pallone Jr. (1951–; D-NJ) introduced the bill in the US House of Representatives in December 2017, just as the US Supreme Court was hearing arguments in *Christie v. NCAA* (which was renamed *Murphy v. NCAA* in January 2018). As of May 2018,

TABLE 10.9

Reasons for supporting legalization of sports betting nationwide, by age and gambling history, 2016

WHICH OF THE FOLLOWING REASONS BEST EXPLAINS WHY YOU FAVOR MAKING SPORTS BETTING LEGAL IN ALL STATES? (READ LIST)

	Age					Been to a casino?		Bet on sports?	
	18–34	35–44	45–54	55–64	65+	Yes	No	Yes	No
More tax revenue for states	39%	33	37	52	41	37	40	44	38
People are already doing it	44%	52	49	37	36	47	43	38	46
Will make sports more exciting	11%	11	6	7	8	10	0	14	8
Other (vol)	3%	4	1	5	4	5	0	3	3
Don't know (vol)	2%	0	4	0	10	0	0	1	4
Refused (vol)	0%	0	3	0	0	1	17	0	1

SOURCE: "Which of the following best explains why you FAVOR making sports betting legal in all states?" in *More Americans Bet on Legalized Sports Wagering Than Oppose It*, Fairleigh Dickinson University's Public Mind Poll, November 2, 2016, http://publicmind.fdu.edu/2016/161102/final.pdf (accessed February 15, 2018)

TABLE 10.10

Reasons for opposing legalization of sports betting nationwide, by political party affiliation, gender, and race, 2016

WHICH OF THE FOLLOWING REASONS BEST EXPLAINS WHY YOU OPPOSE MAKING SPORTS BETTING LEGAL IN ALL STATES? (READ LIST)

		Gender		Political ID			Race		
	All	Male	Female	Dem	Ind	Repub	White non-Hispanic	Black non-Hispanic	Hispanic
Promotes gambling addiction	55%	53	56	56	70	52	57	47	58
Opens the door for organized crime	22%	25	19	21	0	25	20	26	24
Changes the expectation that the event or game is fair	16%	15	17	19	22	14	15	19	17
Other (vol)	4%	1	5	3	0	5	4	6	0
Don't know (vol)	3%	5	2	1	8	4	3	2	1
Refused (vol)	1%	0	0	0	0	0	0	0	0

SOURCE: "Which of the following reasons best explains why you OPPOSE making sports betting legal in all states?" in *More Americans Bet on Legalized Sports Wagering Than Oppose It*, Fairleigh Dickinson University's Public Mind Poll, November 2, 2016, http://publicmind.fdu.edu/2016/161102/final.pdf (accessed February 15, 2018)

TABLE 10.11

Reasons for opposing legalization of sports betting nationwide, by age and gambling history, 2016

WHICH OF THE FOLLOWING REASONS BEST EXPLAINS WHY YOU OPPOSE MAKING SPORTS BETTING LEGAL IN ALL STATES? (READ LIST)

	Age					Been to a casino?		Bet on sports?	
	18–34	35–44	45–54	55–64	65+	Yes	No	Yes	No
Promotes gambling addiction	65%	70	65	44	39	53	51	47	55
Opens the door for organized crime	9%	9	12	32	38	26	0	15	22
Changes the expectation that the event or game is fair	20%	18	13	14	17	11	32	32	15
Other (vol)	5%	1	3	5	3	8	18	3	4
Don't know (vol)	1%	2	7	4	2	1	0	3	3
Refused (vol)	0	1	0	0	0	1	0	0	1

SOURCE: "Which of the following reasons best explains why you OPPOSE making sports betting legal in all states?" in *More Americans Bet on Legalized Sports Wagering Than Oppose It*, Fairleigh Dickinson University's Public Mind Poll, November 2, 2016, http://publicmind.fdu.edu/2016/161102/final.pdf (accessed February 15, 2018)

lawmakers had yet to vote on the proposed bill. Meanwhile, in May 2018 the Supreme Court overturned the existing federal ban on sports wagering.

Fantasy Sports and Online Gambling Laws

Concerning the rapidly growing online fantasy sports industry, the relationship between athletic competition and online gambling also remained ambiguous. As is discussed in Chapter 2, fantasy sports leagues allow individuals to construct imaginary teams that consist of actual players from professional or college athletics. After setting their rosters, fantasy team owners accumulate points based on the weekly performances of their players; at the end of the season, the owner with the highest point total wins the league. Often, an owner who finishes first in a fantasy sports league also wins some sort of financial prize, typically derived from the entry fees collected from each player at the beginning of the season. Popular fantasy leagues have developed around all the major professional sports in the United States, notably the MLB and the NFL.

Despite the fact that fantasy sports participants are effectively wagering on athletes, their activities remained legal in 2018. Under the UIGEA, wagering on online fantasy sports does not constitute gambling, on the grounds that the ability to select winning combinations of players for athletic contests is based primarily on skill, rather than on chance. Ultimately, the UIGEA left the legality of online fantasy sports to the discretion of individual states. Ryan Rodenberg writes in "Daily Fantasy Sports State-by-State Tracker" (ESPN.com, July 26, 2017) that as of July 2017, 14 states had enacted laws allowing daily fantasy sports wagering, and five states had banned the practice outright. Meanwhile an entire industry had emerged to meet the rapidly increasing demand for online fantasy sports, with two fantasy sports sites—FanDuel and DraftKings—commanding the overwhelming bulk of the market.

Although fantasy sports participation did not technically constitute online gambling under the UIGEA, it gradually came under increased scrutiny, as lawmakers and prosecutors began investigating possible abuses associated with online fantasy sports betting. The industry garnered some unwelcome negative publicity in September 2015, when it emerged that a DraftKings employee won $350,000 playing on the rival site FanDuel. The news was accompanied by the revelation that the same employee had mistakenly released confidential information about which NFL players were popular lineup choices on DraftKings that week, raising questions about whether the employee had taken advantage of inside information in selecting his FanDuel roster. Although the employee was eventually cleared of any wrongdoing, both DraftKings and FanDuel decided to implement new policies that prohibited employees from participating in any form of online fantasy sports wagering.

Despite these measures, the industry soon found itself the target of intense criticism. One area of concern arose from the fact that a small pool of elite players dominated fantasy sports wagering. In "All the Reasons You (Probably) Won't Win Money Playing Daily Fantasy Sports" (WashingtonPost.com, October 12, 2015), Drew Harwell explains that during the first half of the

2015 MLB season the top 1% of fantasy players earned 91% of the total winnings. These players, known as "sharks," often have significant advantages over their competitors, whether by participating in high volumes to maximize their chances of winning or by using sophisticated software programs to receive and analyze up-to-the-minute data on specific players or game conditions. According the Harwell, these sharks rely heavily on the wagering habits of so-called big fish, the roughly 5% of daily fantasy sports participants who account for 30% of all entry fees and who consistently lose roughly one-third of their total investment.

In light of these circumstances, other states and jurisdictions began to question the legality of online fantasy sports. In October 2015 the Nevada Gaming Control Board concluded that online fantasy sports represented a form of gambling and immediately banned DraftKings, FanDuel, and other sites from accepting financial transactions in the state until they had obtained a proper gaming license. On November 10, 2015, Eric Schneiderman (1954–), the attorney general for New York State, issued a cease-and-desist order against DraftKings and FanDuel, prohibiting the sites from operating within the state. According to the press release "A.G. Schneiderman Issues Cease-and-Desist Letters to FanDuel and DraftKings, Demanding That Companies Stop Accepting Illegal Wagers in New York State" (November 11, 2015, https://ag.ny.gov/press-release/ag-schneiderman-issues-cease-and-desist-letters-fanduel-and-draftkings-demanding), Schneiderman's investigation "found that, unlike traditional fantasy sports, daily fantasy sports companies are engaged in illegal gambling under New York law, causing the same kinds of social and economic harms as other forms of illegal gambling, and misleading New York consumers." Schneiderman further asserted that "DraftKings and FanDuel are the leaders of a massive, multi-billion-dollar scheme intended to evade the law and fleece sports fans across the country."

Two days after receiving the cease-and-desist order, both DraftKings and FanDuel sued the attorney general. In their legal filings, executives from the two sites asserted that online fantasy sports relied heavily on skill and was therefore legal under the UIGEA. The case was effectively ended in August 2016, when the New York governor Andrew Cuomo (1957–) signed legislation that made daily fantasy sports betting legal in the state. The new law prompted an immediate appeal from gambling opponents who asserted that the legislation violated the state's constitution. As of May 2018, the appeal had not yet received a hearing.

IMPORTANT NAMES
AND ADDRESSES

Amateur Athletic Union
1910 Hotel Plaza Blvd.
Lake Buena Vista, FL 32830
(407) 934-7200
FAX: (407) 934-7242
URL: http://www.aausports.org/

American Gaming Association
799 Ninth St. NW, Ste. 700
Washington, DC 20001
(202) 552-2675
FAX: (202) 552-2676
URL: https://www.americangaming.org/

Association of Tennis Professionals Tour
201 ATP Tour Blvd.
Ponte Vedra Beach, FL 32082
(904) 285-8000
FAX: (904) 285-5966
URL: https://www.atpworldtour.com/

Bowling Proprietors' Association of America
621 Six Flags Dr.
Arlington, TX 76011
1-800-343-1329
URL: http://www.bpaa.com/

Center for Gaming Research
4505 Maryland Pkwy., Box 457010
Las Vegas, NV 89154-7010
(702) 895-2242
FAX: (702) 895-2253
URL: http://gaming.unlv.edu/

Indy Racing League
4551 W. 16th St.
Indianapolis, IN 46222
(317) 492-6526
Email: indycar@indycar.com
URL: https://www.indycar.com/

International Boxing Federation
899 Mountain Ave., Ste. 2C
Springfield, NJ 07081
(973) 564-8046

FAX: (973) 564-8751
URL: http://www.ibf-usba-boxing.com/

International Olympic Committee
Château de Vidy 1007
Lausanne, Switzerland
(011-41-21) 621-6111
FAX: (011-41-21) 621-6216
URL: https://www.olympic.org/

Ladies Professional Golf Association Tour
100 International Golf Dr.
Daytona Beach, FL 32124-1092
(386) 274-6200
FAX: (386) 274-1099
URL: http://www.lpga.com/

Major League Baseball
Office of the Commissioner
245 Park Ave., 31st Floor
New York, NY 10167
(212) 931-7800
FAX: (212) 949-5654
URL: https://www.mlb.com/

Major League Baseball Players Association
12 E. 49th St., 24th Floor
New York, NY 10017
(212) 826-0808
Email: feedback@mlbpa.org
URL: http://www.mlbplayers.com/

Major League Soccer
420 Fifth Ave., Seventh Floor
New York, NY 10018
(212) 450-1200
URL: https://www.mlssoccer.com/

National Alliance for Youth Sports
2050 Vista Pkwy.
West Palm Beach, FL 33411
(561) 684-1141
1-800-688-5437
FAX: (561) 684-2546
Email: nays@nays.org
URL: http://www.nays.org/

National Association for Stock Car Auto Racing
1801 W. International Speedway Blvd.
Daytona Beach, FL 32114
(386) 253-0611
URL: https://www.nascar.com/

National Basketball Association
Olympic Tower
645 Fifth Ave.
New York, NY 10022
(212) 407-8000
FAX: (212) 832-3861
URL: http://www.nba.com/

National Basketball Players Association
1133 Avenue of the Americas
New York, NY 10036
(212) 655-0880
1-800-955-6272
FAX: (212) 655-0881
Email: info@nbpa.com
URL: https://nbpa.com/

National Collegiate Athletic Association
700 W. Washington St.
PO Box 6222
Indianapolis, IN 46206-6222
(317) 917-6222
FAX: (317) 917-6888
URL: http://www.ncaa.org/

National Football League
345 Park Ave.
New York, NY 10065
(212) 450-2000
URL: https://www.nfl.com/

National Football League Players Association
1133 20th St. NW
Washington, DC 20036
1-800-372-2000
URL: https://www.nflpa.com/

National Hockey League
1185 Sixth Ave., 15th Floor
New York, NY 10036
(212) 789-2000
URL: https://www.nhl.com/

National Hockey League Players Association
10 Bay St., Ste. 1200
Toronto, ON M5J 2R8 Canada
URL: https://www.nhlpa.com/

National Sporting Goods Association
1601 Feehanville Dr., Ste. 300
Mt. Prospect, IL 60056
(847) 296-6742
FAX: (847) 391-9827
Email: info@nsga.org
URL: https://www.nsga.org/

National Thoroughbred Racing Association
401 West Main St., Ste. 222
Lexington, KY 40507
1-800-792-6872
URL: https://www.ntra.com/

Nevada Gaming Commission and State Gaming Control Board
1919 College Pkwy.
Carson City, NV 89706
(775) 684-7750
FAX: (775) 687-5817
URL: http://gaming.nv.gov/

Professional Bowlers Association
55 E. Jackson Blvd., Ste. 401
Chicago, IL 60604
(206) 332-9688
FAX: (312) 341-1469
URL: https://www.pba.com/

Professional Golfers' Association of America
100 Avenue of the Champions
Palm Beach Gardens, FL 33418
(561) 624-8400
URL: https://www.pga.com/

Special Olympics
1133 19th St. NW
Washington, DC 20036-3604
(202) 628-3630
1-800-700-8585
FAX: (202) 824-0200
URL: https://www.specialolympics.org/

Sports & Fitness Industry Association
962 Wayne Ave., Ste. 300
Silver Spring, MD 20910
(301) 495-6321
FAX: (301) 495-6322
Email: info@sfia.org
URL: https://www.sfia.org/

US Anti-Doping Agency
5555 Tech Center Dr., Ste. 200
Colorado Springs, CO 80919
(719) 785-2000
1-866-601-2632
Email: usada@usada.org
URL: https://www.usada.org/

US Bowling Congress
621 Six Flags Dr.
Arlington, TX 76011
1-800-514-2695
Email: bowlinfo@bowl.com
URL: https://www.bowl.com/

US Golf Association
Golf House, PO Box 708
Far Hills, NJ 07931
(908)234-2300
URL: http://www.usga.org/

US Olympic Committee
One Olympic Plaza
Colorado Springs, CO 80909
1-888-222-2313
URL: https://www.teamusa.org/

US Tennis Association
70 W. Red Oak Ln.
White Plains, NY 10604
(914) 696-7000
URL: https://www.usta.com/

Women's National Basketball Association
645 Fifth Ave.
New York, NY 10022
URL: http://www.wnba.com/

Women's Sports Foundation
247 W. 30th St., Fifth Floor
New York, NY 10001
(646) 845-0273
1-800-227-3988
FAX: (212) 967-2757
Email: info@WomensSports
Foundation.org
URL: https://www.womenssports
foundation.org/

Women's Tennis Association
100 Second Ave. South, Ste. 1100-S
St. Petersburg, FL 33701
(727) 895-5000
FAX: (727) 894-1982
URL: http://www.wtatennis.com/

World Boxing Association
Avenue Aquilino de la Guardia
and Calle 47 Ocean Business Plaza,
14th Floor, Office 14-05
Marbella, Panama, Panama 0816-01091
(507) 203-7680
URL: http://www.wbaboxing.com/

World Boxing Council
Riobamba #835, Col. Lindavista
Mexico City, D.F. 07300 Mexico
(011-52-55) 5119-5274
FAX: (011-52-55) 5119-5294
Email: contact@wbcboxing.com
URL: http://www.wbcboxing.com/

World Boxing Organization
1056 Muñoz Rivera Ave., Ste. 711-714
San Juan 00927 Puerto Rico
(407) 448-3778
URL: http://www.wboboxing.com/

RESOURCES

Much of the information in this volume that pertains to sports participation originated in surveys conducted by the Sports & Fitness Industry Association (SFIA), which is the trade association for sporting goods manufacturers. The SFIA releases the annual *Topline Participation Report*, as well as other reports on specific aspects of sports participation.

The *ProQuest Statistical Abstract of the United States, 2018* includes information on attendance at sporting events. ProQuest obtains these data from a variety of sources, including the major sports leagues and private market research companies.

Polling data provided by Harris Insights and Analytics were key in assembling information on the preferences of sports fans, including trends that are related to race, gender, age, and geography.

"Sports and Television" (2018) by the Museum of Broadcast Communications provided information on the history of sports on television. Another key source on this topic, as well as on other aspects of sports media, was *The Business of Sports* (2004), edited by Scott R. Rosner and Kenneth L. Shropshire. The *Business of Sports* provides comprehensive coverage of all economic aspects of the sports industry. Besides sports media, the book includes essential information on the financial structure of professional team sports, college sports, and the Olympics. Also, the *SportsBusiness Journal* provided valuable information on the way that Americans use social media to engage with sports.

Nonprofit advocacy and public education groups provided substantial information for this volume. Child Trends provided data on exercise and fitness trends among young people. The Women's Sports Foundation offered research on gender equity in sports. Another key source of information on gender equity was *Women in Intercollegiate Sport: A Longitudinal, National Study—Thirty-Seven Year Update, 1977–2014* (2014) by R. Vivian Acosta and Linda Jean Carpenter.

The National Collegiate Athletic Association (NCAA) provided a wealth of data on many aspects of college sports. Key NCAA publications that contributed information include *Revenues & Expenses: 2004–15 NCAA Division I Intercollegiate Athletics Program Report* (Daniel L. Fulks, July 2016), *Trends in NCAA Student-Athlete Gambling Behaviors and Attitudes* (Thomas Paskus and Jeffrey Derevensky, November 2017), *NCAA National Study of Substance Use Habits of College Student-Athletes: Final Report July 2014* (Markie Rexroat, August 2014), and *NCAA Sports Sponsorship and Participation Rates Report: Student-Athlete Participation 1981–82—2016–17* (Erin Irick, October 2017). Information on eligibility rules for college athletes was found in the NCAA's *2017–18 Guide for the College-Bound Student-Athlete* (2017).

The Nielsen Company offered a range of data on national sports viewing trends. Team-by-team revenue and valuation figures were provided by *Forbes*, and *SportsBusiness Journal* provided data on sports media contracts. Most of the information about the structure and workings of the major sports leagues came from the leagues themselves. Likewise, information about the PGA Tour, the Association of Tennis Professionals Tour, the National Association for Stock Car Auto Racing, the various boxing organizations, and other nonteam sports was obtained from the websites of these organizations. Revenues from Sports Venues, a company that specializes in directories and other publications about the sports venue industry, also provided helpful information.

The International Olympic Committee provided helpful information about the structure and workings of the Olympic movement. *Olympic Marketing Fact File: 2018 Edition* (2018) offers detailed information on revenues and expenses associated with the Olympic games.

The Healthy People 2020 website, which is managed by the US Department of Health and Human Services (HHS), provided valuable information about government-sponsored fitness and healthy living initiatives. The HHS publication *2008 Physical Activity Guidelines for Americans* (October 2008) offered insights into various health benefits that are associated with physical exercise, as did the agency's follow-up reports: *Physical Activity Guidelines for Americans Midcourse Report: Strategies to Increase Physical Activity among Youth* (December 2012) and *2018 Physical Activity Guidelines Advisory Committee Scientific Report* (February 2018).

The American Gaming Association, the Nevada Gaming Commission and State Gaming Control Board, and the Center for Gaming Research at the University of Nevada, Las Vegas, were useful sources of information on legal sports gambling. Fairleigh Dickinson University's Public-Mind Poll provided information about the prevalence of and attitudes toward gambling among the American public.

INDEX

men's/women's sports teams, average number of per college, 76(t6.8)

NASCAR drivers, top-10, by earnings, 59f

NASCAR teams, top-10, by value/revenue, 60f

NBA television contracts, 32t

NCAA athletes, opinions on drug testing among, 121t

NCAA men's sports, participation in by division, 71t

NCAA men's sports teams, by sport, 75t–76t

NCAA men's/women's championship sports, participation in, 72t

NCAA sports teams, athletic directors by gender, 80f

NCAA sports teams, athletic directors by gender/division, 81f

NCAA sports teams, head coaches of by gender, 79(f6.3)

NCAA women's sports, participation in by division, 70t

NCAA women's sports teams, by sport, 73t–74t

NFL television contracts, by network/sate, 8t

outdoor sports, participation in, 20t

participation in by generation, 3f

participation in selected sports activities, by sex/age group/income level, 14t–15t

participation, trends in, 2f

performance-enhancing drug use among female NCAA Division I athletes, by sport, 119(t9.2)

performance-enhancing drug use among male NCAA Division I athletes, by sport, 119(t9.1)

physical activity, adults who engaged in regular leisure-time, percentage of, 107f

physical activity, adults who engaged in regular leisure-time, percentage of, by age group/sex, 108f

physical activity, adults who engaged in regular leisure-time, percentage of, by race/ethnicity, 109(f8.3)

racquet sports, participation in, 19t

revenues/expenses, NCAA Division I—Football Bowl Subdivision, by sport, 82t

school sports, monies spent on by parents, 5(f1.4)

sources of revenue, NCAA Division I—Football Bowl Subdivision, 83t

sporting event attendance, adult, 25t–26t

sports betting, amounts wagered/won in Nevada, 128t

sports betting in Nevada, amounts wagered on by sport, 129t

steroid availability, perception of among 8th/10th/12th graders, 117(f9.2)

steroid use, disapproval of use among 8th/10th/12th graders, 118(f9.4)

steroid use, perception of risk involved with among 8th/10th/12th graders, 118(f9.3)

steroid use trends among 8th/10th/12th graders, 117(f9.1)

strength activities, participation in, 22(t2.9)

student-athletes, average number of per college, by gender/division, 77t

students who met current physical activity recommendations, by grade, gender, race/ethnicity, 111t

Super Bowl betting history, Nevada, 131(t10.5)

team sports participation among high school students by sex/grade/race/ethnicity, 89(t6.17)

team sports, participation in, 17t

telecasts, US most-watched, 7t

tennis players, top-10, by earnings, 57f

total amount won in Nevada by sport, 130t

vigorous physical activity among adolescents, by grade/gender, 110f

vigorous physical activity among adolescents, by race/ethnicity, 109(f8.4)

water sports, participation in, 21t

win percentages in Nevada, by sport, 131(t10.4)

"Statistics" (ESPN), 24

Staudohar, Paul D., 40

Steinberg, Leigh, 62

"Steroid Abuse in Today's Society" (DEA), 114

Steroids

availability, perception of among 8th/10th/12th graders, 117(f9.2)

baseball scandals involving, 37

creation of, 113

disapproval of use among 8th/10th/12th graders, 118(f9.4)

doping, use of in, 10

elite athletes, use of among, 113–114

harmful effects of, 10–11

legal restrictions on, 122–123

overview of, 114–116

perception of risk involved with among 8th/10th/12th graders, 118(f9.3)

roid rage, 115

use of in sports, overview of, 10

use trends among 8th/10th/12th graders, 117(f9.1)

youth and, 116

Stock car racing

description of, 7, 57

development of, 58

Strains, 103

Strength activities, 22(t2.9)

Stricker, Steve, 55

Strikes. See Labor disputes

Stringer, C. Vivian, 72

"Study: Games Lost to Concussions Rises" (AP), 105

"Study Shows Where NHL Can Improve Concussion Prevention" (Hackel), 105

"Subsidies Are the Name of the Game in D-1 College Sports" (Fear), 73

Summer Olympic Games

description of, 9, 91

locations of, 93(t7.5)

Sunday Night Football, 30

Super Bowl (NFL)

creation/popularity of, 42

media coverage of, 30

viewership of, 7–8

"Super Bowl XLIX Posts the Largest Audience in TV History" (Pallotta), 6

"Super Bowl Ads 2018: Latest Info on Cost of 2018 Super Bowl Commercials" (Gould), 30

Svitolina, Elina, 56

Symetra Tour (LPGA), 55

Syracuse University, 68

T

Tagliabue, Paul, 42

Tampering, game, 129

Taxes, 40

Team sports

collegiate, numbers of, 69–70

high school, participation among students by sex/grade/race/ethnicity, 89(t6.17)

numbers participating in, 1, 13

participation in, 17t

Teenagers. *See* Adolescents

Television

auto racing, viewership of, 32–33

baseball, viewership of, 29

basketball, viewership of, 31–32

football, viewership of, 29–31

history of sports on, 7

hockey, viewership of, 32

major sports on, 7–8

Mayweather-Pacquiao boxing match, viewership of, 62

NASCAR, viewership of, 57–58

NCAA broadcast contracts, first, 67

NFL television contracts, by network/satellite provider, 8t

NHL viewership, 51

Olympics, broadcast revenues of, 95–96

PGA Tour viewership, 54

sports on, history of, 27–28

sports viewing, gender and, 33

telecasts, most-watched in US, 7t

Tendinitis, 103

Tennis, professional

development of, 56

men's, 6

overview of, 55–56

top-10 players, by earnings, 57f

women's, 6–7

CPSIA information can be obtained
at www.ICGtesting.com
Printed in the USA
FFHW01n2259121018
48792253-52926FF